Edward Lucie-Smith

Movements in art since 1945

Issues and Concepts

263 illustrations, 78 in colour

Thames and Hudson

For Agatha Sadler

First published in Great Britain in 1969 by
Thames and Hudson Ltd, London
Revised edition 1975
New revised edition 1984
Third edition: revised and expanded 1995

Designed by Liz Rudderham

© 1969, 1975, 1984 and 1995 Thames and Hudson Ltd,
London

British Library Cataloguing-in-Publication Data
A catalogue record for this book is available
from the British Library

ISBN 0-500-20282-6

Printed and bound in
Singapore by C. S. Graphics Pte Ltd

Contents

CHAPTER ONE

Style into Content

When the first edition of this book was published in 1969 (it has been twice revised since then), *Movements in Art since 1945* seemed a perfectly adequate, indeed a conventional title. It had been the custom to think of artists and art movements as falling into primarily stylistic categories for many years, and, though much of my material was new, my actual method of arrangement was not. Now to many people such an arrangement seems not only inadequate but also morally wrong. The mere notion of arranging and discussing artists and their work in terms of style or allegiance to a particular movement or group, rather than in those of social relevance, context, and (above all) content, generates an inordinate amount of heat.

As we approach the end of the twentieth century, the world of contemporary art has gradually become aware of a drastic shift in attitudes concerning the purposes and development of the avant-garde, if this phrase still remains at all meaningful. People who make art, or exhibit it, or discuss it on a professional basis, are especially sceptical of the idea of hierarchy – which roughly speaking means the whole idea of saying that one thing is better than another, at least in stylistic terms. However, though they express this hostility to the notion of a hierarchy based on essentially aesthetic foundations, the idea of hierarchical arrangement cannot be suppressed completely. For the 'style' or 'manner' – essentially words that pay more attention to how an object looks or seems than to what message it conveys to the spectator – commentators substitute the idea of what the work of art contains. Essentially this means that they attempt to relate it to a quite different hierarchy, one based on their own necessarily subjective view of what constitutes a moral order. It is this, fundamentally, which governs relationships within the new system, which nevertheless remains, in its own fashion, just as dependent on an idea of hierarchy, of one thing being superior to, or inferior to, another, as the old arrangement that is now condemned.

It is perfectly true that contemporary art, and still more so the ways in which we perceive it, have both greatly changed since the beginning of the 1970s. Some of these changes were already latent in the art of the 1960s, but had not yet made themselves sufficiently visible to be accommodated in the earlier versions of this book. For example, we now tend to have a very different view about the universality of twentieth-century avant-garde art. In the 1960s, it was still possible to assume that the vital, experimental art of the century flowed essentially from a single source, the great creative explosion that took place in Europe during the first decade-and-a-half of the century. While influences from other cultures – the tribal art of black Africa, for example – were acknowledged, there was no perception that these might want to claim equal status. If these cultures showed the influence of Western art, and this included the influence of modernist ideas, it was assumed that this was a weakening and corrupting element, rather than a vivifying one. For early modernist commentators the situation was clear: Western art (a category that also came to include the art produced in the United States) was by its nature dynamic, and its virtues were allied to this dynamism. Non-Western art retained its true qualities only if it remained static. The west made a claim to universal hegemony in art, and at the same time mock-humbly acknowledged itself to be a corrupting influence.

The weaknesses of this position have now become clear. During the past three decades in particular, the rapid expansion of technology and the way in which all means of communication have been elaborated and at the same time speeded up, have between them led to a breakdown of any remaining barriers between cultures. Non-Western cultures, though fascinated by many aspects of contemporary European and North American art, have nevertheless wished to retain important aspects of their own inherited traditions. Artists in these countries have often sought for a bridge between the two – for a means of making art that was visibly modernist, but which would allow them to continue to speak their own cultural language. There has, at the same time, been an enormous expansion in the number of artists active throughout the world, all of them thinking of themselves as being in one manner or another 'modern' – in step with the characteristic developments of the late twentieth century.

The consequences are obvious. The rigid structures of modernist art history have started to break down, and this for at least two reasons. The first is that the whole business of cultural admixture produces conflicting value systems. A kind of art that seems valuable when viewed by one set of criteria will seem less so when looked at according to another. The second is the sheer quantity of information now available to the critic or historian of modernism. One can draw a parallel here with what has happened to systems of knowledge in general. Until perhaps the late eighteenth century an educated person could claim practical working acquaintanceship with all branches of knowledge – literature, the arts and the sciences. This was no longer true in the nineteenth century, but someone who described himself or herself as a scientist could probably still claim knowledge of all the major scientific specialities – from biology, through chemistry, to physics. We have now reached a stage where no one can claim to know even contemporary art thoroughly, in absolutely all of its current manifestations worldwide. The result is that the world of contemporary art can no longer be thought of as something rigidly organized, with an absolutely clear line of descent.

Yet there are also good reasons for challenging aspects of the new, supposedly non-hierarchical art criticism. The first has already been hinted at: that it does not abolish hierarchies but simply substitutes one system of value-judgments for another. Art criticism, at least in the west, has often tended to be intertwined with morality. This was so long before modernist artists spoke about truth to materials, or the influential American critic Clement Greenberg argued the case for formalist purity in painting free from disguise and illusion. In the eighteenth century Denis Diderot, the first major art critic, based his enthusiasm for Jean-Baptiste Greuze and his distaste for the work of François Boucher, whose technical merits he was more than willing to acknowledge, almost entirely on his perception of their respective moral status. This perception in turn was based on his dislike of the regime of Louis XV. Boucher was the king's official painter (*premier peintre du roi*) and a favourite of Louis XV's mistress, Mme de Pompadour, whose influence Diderot deplored. Diderot's nineteenth-century successors, chief among them John Ruskin, were equally moralistic in their approach, and it was only towards the very end of the period that the doctrine of 'art for art's sake' began to take hold, under the aegis of the French Symbolists. Symbolism was the parent of modernism, and the modernists took over important aspects of symbolist critical doctrine, in particular the emphasis on style as opposed to content. The main difference between them was the fact that the early modernists had a fierce impatience with what they saw as the effete and over-complex society of their time. Many of them, the Italian Futurists in particular, longed for some cataclysm to come

9

and reduce it to rubble. These hopes found their fulfilment with the outbreak of World War I, a disaster greater than anyone could have imagined. During and after the war the idea that art could exist in a state of detachment from social conditions was frequently under fire. In the Soviet Union, for instance, the suppression of the Constructivist avant-garde also brought with it the repression of what was then described as Formalist criticism.

Throughout the first half of its existence, however, modernism lived under the shadow of fiercely resented Victorian morality. Even near the mid-century, after World War II, one aspect of American Abstract Expressionism was opposition to the social concerns that had dominated American art during the 1930s. The neo-Puritanism of the 1990s seems to represent a point at which the cycle of opinion has reversed itself. The result is a violent swing back to an emphasis on moral values, and *ipso facto*, to an art where content is important and stylistic expression or group loyalty as defined through adherence to a particular style is of correspondingly little interest – irrelevant if not actually immoral. One fascinating aspect of the art of the past fifteen years has been the struggle to preserve avant-garde assumptions and fit them into a moral framework which was not present in the original Modern Movement.

There is, however, one very real difficulty here. The present critical climate is a revisionist one, in almost Soviet fashion. It will be remembered that the official Soviet *Encyclopaedia* was often subjected to radical changes as political figures came and went. The space once taken up by a biography of Bukharin, for instance, would be taken over by a greatly expanded article on buffalo. How far can one insist on describing, purely in terms of content, artists who did not perceive themselves in this fashion at the time?

It is clear, I think, if one looks at the early chapters in this book, that many of the artists discussed did see themselves in largely stylistic terms, just as their predecessors had done in the years before World War II. To omit the stylistic dimension would be a serious distortion of what they did. In this sense they remained the heirs of Cubism, which many art historians see as the seminal modernist initiative in art. Cubism deliberately reduced content to a minimum, to facilitate the exploration of a newly invented visual language – if we are looking for a definition of the term 'style' in art then 'a particular visual language, distinguishable from other forms of visual language' is perhaps as good as any. A number of post-World War II art initiatives, certainly until the early 1960s, have the character of conscious stylistic initiatives, closely engaged in oppositional dialectic with what had happened previously. Even those which sometimes claimed to be a-stylistic, like Pop's predecessor Abstract Expressionism, have the character of coherent artistic movements – a coming together of personalities closely linked both by friendship and by their attitudes towards aesthetic possibilities – and are always described in this way by their chroniclers.[1]

Pop, now widely regarded by commentators as constituting the historic moment at which the Modern Movement changed character and became something quite different from what had preceded it, is a particularly interesting case in point. The major Pop artists in New York, no matter what their personal differences, did see themselves as a guerrilla group, ready to bring down the Abstract Expressionists who were the ruling power at that time. It was their insolence in questioning established authority that roused so much indignation amongst the critical establishment of the time. But Pop went much further than Abstract Expressionism in its insistence on the importance of stylistic signals and indicators. Pop artists' interest in the new mass culture was directed towards its glittering surface, its methods of presentation, far more than towards any social, political, or even moral concepts which could be deduced from these.

It is thus for good historical reasons that the earlier chapters of this book have been allowed to stand virtually as they were originally written. Current hostility to stylistic categorization and description cannot be applied *post hoc* to situations where these were not only widely accepted, but part of the actual dynamic of the development of contemporary art.

In the mid-1960s, the situation began to change, and it is to take this change into account that this book has now been completely recast, from the beginning of Chapter Six onwards. It is also worth trying to summarize what I see as the nature of the change, here in my introductory chapter. In the United States, the destined successors of Pop were Minimalism, with its offshoot Land art, and Conceptual art. At first sight, these developments had some of the essential characteristics of the styles that had immediately preceded them, in the sense that their preoccupations were largely aesthetic. Minimal art, in particular, seemed to invite the spectator to concentrate on art alone, to the exclusion of everything that could be categorized as 'not art'. Its proposal was that art and the world existed in parallel but separate universes. This greatly added to the power of the museum, since museums now, by implication, became worlds in their own right, which the unqualified spectator could only successfully navigate with the aid of professional guides and interpreters. On the other hand, Minimal art also had one novel quality. In its determination to strip away all quirks and complications of form, it stripped away the very things through which a particular style in art generally made itself recognized, Conceptual art carried this process still further. The proposition, here, was that art could be reduced to documentation or a series of written statements and/or diagrams, and that physical embodiment, even of the reductive kind found in Minimalism, was therefore essentially superfluous. Contrary to what was intended, however, this allowed non-aesthetic content in through the back door, since the propositions put forward in the name of Conceptual art soon began to stray from the realm of pure aesthetics.

These developments, which were essentially identified with the United States, found a parallel, but one of a slightly unexpected kind, in Europe. In 1962 the first Fluxus concerts took place. Fluxus and its activities have always been difficult to describe coherently, chiefly because the participants were only loosely linked and, in addition, deliberately cultivated a kind of incoherence. Some of its roots were in the original Dada movement, and Dada survivors, such as Raoul Hausmann, associated themselves with it – this in contrast to the disapproval expressed by veteran Dadaists concerning Pop art in its American guise.[2] There were, nevertheless, connections between the origins of Fluxus and the Pop art activities of the early 1960s. There are, for example, the close similarities between Fluxus 'events' and the Pop art 'Happenings' devised by Claes Oldenburg and Jim Dine, though Fluxus incursions into live performance 'actions' often had more overtly intellectual, political or philosophical overtones than their Pop counterparts.

Much of the impetus for Fluxus came from outside the strict limits of the art world – for example, from the work and philosophy of the composer John Cage, who had been close to the original American Neo-Dadaists such as Rauschenberg, but who was much less so to leading practitioners of Pop such as Warhol and Lichtenstein. There was also an element of social criticism and provocation that had almost vanished from American art. Pop, when it provoked, did so lightheartedly. Within Fluxus, as within the later offshoots of Dada, which flourished in Germany in the years immediately following World War I, there was a determination to make changes in society itself. One lasting achievement of Fluxus was to provide a platform for the early activities of Joseph Beuys. However, Beuys soon outgrew the movement that had sheltered him, and became a power in his own right.

I BARBARA HEPWORTH
Two Figures 1947–8

One of the best ways of describing and quantifying the change which Beuys caused in the world of contemporary art is to compare him with some of the modernist artists who were already solidly established when he first appeared on the scene. Beuys always described himself as a sculptor, and he had certainly trained as such under the artist Edwin Mataré. Who were the most celebrated modernist sculptors of the epoch immediately before his own? They certainly included such artists as Constantin Brancusi, Hans Arp, Alberto Giacometti, Marion Marini, Henry Moore and Barbara Hepworth. All of these – even Arp and Hepworth, the most abstract of them – were essentially humanist. Their theme was humankind and its fate, and they expressed their concern with this by creating objects that were visual metaphors – see, for example, Hepworth's *Two Figures* and Moore's *Locking-piece* – set apart from the rest of the surrounding environment, generally by the simple device of placing them on pedestals.

2 HENRY MOORE *Locking-piece* 1963–4

3 JOSEPH BEUYS *Action in 7 Exhibitions* 1972

Beuys, as his career progressed, had less and less to do with objects of this type. He increasingly tended to see himself as a modern shaman, who affected the world about him through enacting rituals – the difference between his version of shamanism and the traditional one being twofold: first that he operated within a modern industrial society; second that the rituals were self-invented, not traditional, as in *Action in 7 Exhibitions*. It is true that he sometimes created an embodiment for his ideas by making objects, but these could scarcely be said to possess formal qualities, in any accepted sense. Their power lay, not in shapes or relationships of shapes, nor in their metaphoric relationship to forms found in nature, but in the fact that they were ritual collocations, often involving materials which Beuys thought had magical or therapeutic power – felt, fat, gold leaf and honey were some of those he employed. Compared with him, sculptors like Giacometti and Moore belong to a different and much more traditional world.

It is also possible to make an instructive comparison between Beuys and the most celebrated artist of the first generation of modernists: Picasso. Picasso's relationship to the idea of artistic style was an extremely intimate one. His progress can be charted only by plotting

15

a series of points on a line, each point or node marking a new stylistic departure. Despite these constant changes of style, the range of subjects in his work remained both relatively stable and relatively traditional. For example, he explored the possibilities of the traditional still life throughout his career, using inanimate objects in symbolic fashion just as artists had done since the invention of the genre in the late fifteenth century.

Towards the end of Picasso's astonishing career, the importance of stylistic criteria in his work increased rather than diminished. He engaged in a series of dialogues with the great artists of the past, making successive versions, for example, of Delacroix's *The Women of Algiers*. These versions were always more of a challenge than a tribute to the painter on whose work they were based. But Picasso never challenges the actual content – that he regards as a given. What he remakes is the style of the original, which he impatiently transforms so that it corresponds to his own artistic handwriting.

One cannot imagine Beuys undertaking an enterprise of this kind. Indeed, as his career progressed, Beuys more and more tended to separate himself from the art-making process, as this had been understood. Museums became arenas where shamanistic rituals could be staged, or, more simply, platforms from which Beuys could project a political programme. Politics itself he defined as 'social sculpture'. Where he continued to use objects this was in an entirely personal way. For example, in *Dernier espace avec introspecteur*, an installation of 1982, the kernel is the wing mirror of a car in which the artist suffered a near-fatal car crash. This functions like a relic within an elaborately constructed reliquary. The remaining products of Beuys's process of self-mythologization seem, now that he is dead, more like miraculous tokens – a thorn from the Crown of Thorns, a hair from the Prophet's board – than like works of art in any conventionally definable sense.

It was Beuys who pre-eminently opened the doors to a new perception of the way in which art functioned – or might function – within contemporary society. Art was now defined in two ways – through its relationship to the personality of the artist, of which it was simply a visible manifestation, and through its content. In other words, it offered a definition, one which continually changed as the artist himself or herself developed, of the artist's relationship to the world. It showed the deformations which occur when the subjective impinges on the objective, and vice versa.

One may argue that this essentially is what visual art has always done, and that the result of the conflict, willed or otherwise, is the thing we

16

6 GERHARD RICHTER *Three Candles* 1982

call artistic style. One may also argue, in a completely opposite sense, that many artists insist that their point of view is the only possible point of view, and that 'deformation', therefore, does not enter into it. What these contradictory arguments fail to take into account is the fact that content and expression are, in the art of the 1970s, 1980s and 1990s, inextricably intertwined. An artist may therefore express himself or herself in many different ways, in different media, using different strategies. It is this that explains the hybrid, heterogeneous, essentially a-stylistic art of the period, which has led to the frequent use of the label 'pluralism'. This pluralism can take two forms. First, it leads to contrasts which are often extreme between artists working in the same artistic milieu and pursuing what are apparently the same ends. Secondly, it releases artists from the pressure of stylistic expectation – either that of critics and curators or that of a more general audience. A case in point is the German artist Gerhard Richter (b. 1932), who is one of the quintessential figures in one version of postmodernism (it is indicative that this coupling of words has found several different and

<5 SIGMAR POLKE *Liebespaar II* 1965

somewhat self-contradictory definitions, when used by different commentators). Rather than proceeding in a series of stylistic leaps, as Picasso did, Richter has pursued several different ways of working, often simultaneously. Thus he has made 'photo-paintings' based on found photographs, e.g. *Three Candles*; 'Colour Chart' paintings featuring groups of flat colour samples; 'Colour Streaks', which are near Minimalist abstractions; and even paintings which are analyses of the work of the Old Masters, such as the *Annunciation after Titian* series (1972), in which a celebrated Titian altarpiece is progressively dissolved into pure abstraction.

Another German artist, once a collaborator of Richter, whose work shows the same hostility to the idea of fixed style is Sigmar Polke (b. 1941). His work shows the influence of American Pop art, then that of Francis Picabia (1879–1955), whose late work is one of the sources of Pop, as, for example, in *Liebespaar II*. He has also, however, done work which has appeared in exhibitions devoted to German Neo-Expressionism, though it remains uncertain whether or not these are intended as parodies of other artists linked to this tendency, such as Anselm Kiefer (b. 1945).

One factor which has tended to release artists from stylistic bonds is the popularity of environments and installations and also of Performance art. An artist such as the American Cady Noland (b. 1956) brings together various objects so as to create an image of contemporary American society, as illustrated in this installation view. The matrix which holds the objects together is not visual resemblance, but their relationship to a central idea, so that the issue of style becomes irrelevant. The same can be said about the installations of Christian Boltanski (b. 1944) and the Russian perestroika artist Ilya Kabakov (b. 1933). Boltanski and Kabakov both make use of memorabilia of various kinds so as to recreate the traces of lives lived out in a particular situation: Kabakov recreates a shabby corridor in a Soviet apartment block (see Chapter 10), Boltanski a bourgeois living room. Both make use of photographs, not for their aesthetic content but for their power to evoke a particular situation. Boltanski often uses likenesses of people whom the spectators know to be dead, half obscured by lamps which blot out the faces rather than making them more visible.

Many contemporary artworks, from the early 1970s onwards, are quantifiable chiefly as social gestures or indicators. An early example was *Seedbed* (1972) by Vito Acconci (b. 1940), in which the artist lay under the floor of the gallery, loudly describing his sexual fantasies

7 CADY NOLAND, installation view, 14 September–21 October 1989

while masturbating. A more recent one was Andres Serrano's briefly notorious *Piss Christ* (1987): a cheap crucifix, purchased ready-made, plunged into a twelve-by-eighteen-inch plexiglass tank filled with three gallons of urine. It existed only as a photograph documenting what had been done. One thing which *Seedbed* and *Piss Christ* had in common, apart from the wish to outrage certain sections of the bourgeois audience, was the fact that the audience, whether hostile or approving, had to take certain elements on trust. Since Acconci remained invisible there was no proof, beyond his own commentary, that he was in fact masturbating. Three gallons of urine, in purely photographic terms, are identical with three gallons of fizzy lemonade.

8

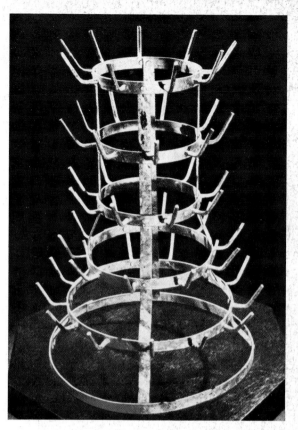

9 MARCEL DUCHAMP
Bottle Rack 1914

Few people, however, seemed willing to argue that either of these works lay outside the boundaries of what could now be defined as 'art'. And those who did pursue such an argument were not the professionals in the field of contemporary art. The consensus that activities and social gestures of this sort were indeed art lends additional strength to the notion that stylistic criteria are no longer sufficient. Art, despite all Platonic arguments to the contrary, is increasingly what a given society decrees it to be, and it is in this sense that Duchamp, who is the originator of so many of the ideas which are now common currency in the world of contemporary artistic activity, justifies himself. The ready-made, for example his *Bottle Rack* of 1914, becomes an authentic art object immediately on its acceptance as such. It is obvious that in a world where the notion of the ready-made becomes a given, stylistic criteria are immediately called into question.

23

<8 ANDRES SERRANO *Piss Christ* 1987

There are other anti-stylistic forces to be taken into account as well. The most important of these is the proliferation of modernist ideas, and also of centres of modernist activity already mentioned, which makes it impossible for any single individual to get a complete view of what is happening. Since so much of the newest art is concerned with issues, especially those to do with identity (cultural, national, racial or sexual), it is often easier for the viewer or critic unfamiliar with a particular situation to approach the artwork through easily identifiable content rather than through nuances of style.

In addition, this approach more easily satisfies the demand for a 'democratic', non-patriarchal, non-hierarchical approach to art, since it tends to assume that explanation is more or less the same thing as evaluation. The critic is largely released from the necessity to make pejorative judgments.

I myself do not believe that it is possible to write a fully meaningful criticism while at the same time abandoning all traditional tools – contrasting one work of art with another, for instance, with the implication that one may be better or more successful than another. Nevertheless the later chapters of this book do now take into account the considerable change in critical climate that has taken place since it was first written, and I hope in this sense they come closer to giving an evaluation of the artists they discuss in terms that those artists would recognize as being valid and true to their intentions.

CHAPTER TWO

Abstract Expressionism

Abstract Expressionism, the first of the great post-war art movements, had its roots in Surrealism, the most important movement of the period immediately before the war. Surrealism had routed Dada in Paris in the early 1920s. It is perhaps most satisfactorily defined by its leading figure, André Breton, in the First Surrealist Manifesto of 1924.

> SURREALISM, n. Pure psychic automatism, by which an attempt is made to express, either verbally or in writing, or in any other manner, the true functioning of thought. . . . Surrealism rests on the belief in the higher reality of certain neglected forms of association, in the omnipotence of dream, in the disinterested play of thought. It tends to destroy the other psychic mechanisms and to substitute itself for them in the solution of life's principal problems.[1]

Since 1924 its history, under the leadership of the volcanic Breton, had been one of schisms and scandals. In particular, the Surrealists had become increasingly preoccupied with their relationship with Communism. The question was: could artistic radicalism be reconciled with the political variety? So much time and energy was wasted in controversy, that, by the time the war came, the movement was visibly in decline. Maurice Nadeau, in his authoritative history of the movement, remarks: 'The adherence to the political revolution required the adherence of all the surrealist forces, and consequently the abandonment of the particular philosophy which had constituted the movement's very being at its origin.'[2]

By the time the war came, it looked as if this, the most vigorous and important of the art movements of the period between the wars, had exhausted its impetus. But the 'particular philosophy' of which Nadeau speaks was still very much alive when the Surrealist movement arrived, almost *en bloc*, in New York shortly after the outbreak of war. The exiles included not only Breton himself but also some of the most famous Surrealist painters: Max Ernst (1891–1976), Roberto Matta (b. 1912), Salvador Dali (1904–89), and André Masson (1896–1987).

Peggy Guggenheim, then married to Ernst, supplied the group with a centre for their activities by opening the Art of This Century Gallery in 1942. Many of the most important American painters of the 1940s were later to show there.

The situation of the Surrealist exiles was governed by several factors. For example, in the midst of the conflict, the old, rending political arguments were no longer relevant. New York provided a fresh and challenging territory for their activities, and they began to make converts among American artists.

As previously said, the United States had long been hospitable to the *avant-garde* art of Europeans. New York had a tradition of intermittent avant-gardism which stretched back to the Armory Show of 1913, and, beyond that, to the pre-World War I activities of Alfred Stieglitz, who presented a series of exhibitions by artists such as Rodin, Matisse, Picasso, Brancusi, Henri Rousseau, and Picabia in a small gallery at 291 Fifth Avenue. During World War I there had been an active group of Dadaists in the city, among them Marcel Duchamp (1887–1968), Picabia, and Man Ray (1890–1976). But the Depression years of the 1930s turned American art in upon itself. American critics, such as Barbara Rose in her classic book *American Art since 1900*, stress the fact that this period of introspection and withdrawal was crucial for American artists. They point to the effect, in particular, of the Federal Art Project (or W.P.A.), the measure by which the American government sought to give relief to artists suffering from the prevailing economic conditions. Rose contends that 'by making no formal distinction between abstract and representational art',[3] the Project helped to make abstract art respectable, and that the *esprit de corps* which the scheme created among artists carried over into the 1940s. Nevertheless, in 1939 American art counted for little where the European *avant-garde* was concerned, though a few distinguished *émigrés*, such as Josef Albers (1888–1976) and Hans Hofmann (1880–1966), were already preparing the ground through their teaching for the change that was to come. Albers taught at Black Mountain College in North Carolina, Hofmann at the Art Students' League in New York and at his own schools on 8th Street and in Provincetown, Mass.

Yet it was not these, but the more-recently arrived Surrealists who provided the decisive stimulus. Without their presence in New York, Abstract Expressionism would probably never have been born.

The transitional figure, the most important link between European Surrealism and what was to follow, was Arshile Gorky (1904–48).

26

10 RENÉ MAGRITTE *Exhibition of Painting* 1965

Gorky was born in Armenia in 1904, and did not arrive in America until 1920. His early work (undertaken in conditions of the bitterest poverty) shows a steady progression through the basic modernist styles, typical of an artist in a provincial environment who is conscious of his own isolation. He absorbed the lesson of Cézanne, then of Cubism. In the 1930s, under the spell of Picasso, he was already veering towards Surrealism. Then came the war, and he started to explore more boldly. Basically, the Surrealist tradition seemed to offer the convert two choices. One was the meticulously detailed style of Magritte (1898–1967), whose *Exhibition of Painting* is but one example, or Salvador Dali, as in his dazzling perspectival depiction of *Christ of St John of the Cross*. Even in those of Dali's pictures where the distortions are most violent, objects to some extent retain their identity. The other choice was the biomorphic style of artists such as Miró (1893–1983)

16

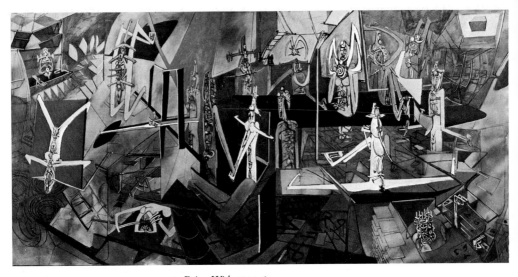

11 ROBERTO MATTA *Being With* 1945–6

or Tanguy (1900–55), where the forms merely hint at a resemblance
to real objects, usually parts of the human body – breasts, buttocks, the
17 sexual organs, as Tanguy's *The Rapidity of Sleep* demonstrates. Gorky
adopted this method, and used it with increasing boldness. Harold
Rosenberg speaks of the characteristic imagery of Gorky's developed
styles as

> . . . overgrown with metaphor and association. Amid strange, soft
> organisms and insidious slits and smudges, petals hint of claws in a
> jungle of limp bodily parts, intestinal fists, pudenda, multiple limb
> folds.[4]

The painter himself, in a statement written in 1942, declared:

> I like the heat the tenderness the edible the lusciousness the song of
> a single person the bathtub full of water to bathe myself beneath the
> water. . . . I like the wheatfields the plough the apricots those flirts
> of the sun. But bread above all.[5]

Gorky was especially influenced by the Chilean-born painter Roberto
11 Matta, which can be seen by comparing his *Being With* with the
12 former's *The Betrothal II*, and his work is often close to that which was

28

12 ARSHILE GORKY *The Betrothal II* 1947

13 ANDRÉ MASSON
*Landscape with
Precipices* 1948

being done by the veteran French Surrealist André Masson, as in
Landscape with Precipices, during the years the latter spent in America.
He did not finally come into contact with Breton until 1944, and this
completed his liberation as an artist. By 1947 he had begun to outstrip
his masters, and the way in which he outstripped them was through
the freedom with which he used his materials. The boldness of his
technique can be seen in the second version of *The Betrothal*, which
dates from 1947. The philosophy of art which Gorky put forward in
an interview with a journalist the same year had important implica-
tions for the future of American painting:

> When something is finished, that means it's dead, doesn't it? I
> believe in everlastingness. I never finish a painting – I just stop
> working on it for a while. I like painting because it's something I
> never come to the end of. Sometimes I paint a picture, then I paint
> it all out. Sometimes I'm working on fifteen or twenty pictures at
> the same time. I do that because I want to – because I like to change
> my mind so often. The thing to do is always to keep starting to
> paint, never finishing panting.[6]

This idea of a 'continuous dynamic' was to play an important part in
Abstract Expressionism, and especially in the work of Jackson Pollock

(1912–56). Gorky himself was unable to press it further. After a long series of misfortunes, he committed suicide in 1948. He was perhaps the most distinguished Surrealist that America has produced.

Far less 'European' was the work of Jackson Pollock, though it was Pollock who became the star of the Art of This Century Gallery. Like Gorky, Pollock developed very slowly. He spent his youth in the West, in Arizona, northern California, and (later) southern California. In 1929 Pollock left Los Angeles and came to New York to study painting under Thomas Benton, a 'regionalist' painter. During the 1930s, like many American artists of his generation, he fell under the influence of the contemporary Mexicans. Diego Rivera's enthusiasm for a public art 'belonging to the populace' may well have helped to develop Pollock's sense of scale. Later he fell under the influence of the Surrealists, just as Gorky had done, and Miss Guggenheim put him under contract for her gallery. By 1947, Pollock had broken through to the style for which he is now best known: free, informal abstraction, based on a technique of dripping and smearing paint on to the canvas, a spectacular example of which is his *Number 2*. 15

14 JACKSON POLLOCK
at work

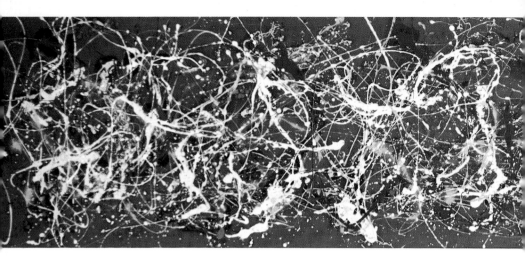

Here is Pollock's own description of what took place when he worked on such pictures:

My painting does not come from the easel. I hardly ever stretch my canvas before painting. I prefer to tack the unstretched canvas on the hard wall or floor. I need the resistance of a hard surface. On the floor I feel more at ease. I feel nearer, more part of the painting, since this way I can walk around it, work from the four sides and literally be *in* the painting. This is akin to the Indian sand painters of the West.

I continue to get further away from the usual painter's tools such as easel, palette, brushes, etc. I prefer sticks, trowels, knives and dripping fluid paint or a heavy impasto with sand, broken glass or other foreign matter added.

When I am *in* the painting I'm not aware of what I'm doing. It is only after a sort of 'get acquainted' period that I see what I have been about. I have no fears about making changes, destroying the image, etc., because the painting has a life of its own. I try to let it come through. It is only when I lose contact with the painting that the result is a mess. Otherwise there is pure harmony, an easy give and take, and the painting comes out well.[7]

Compare this to Breton's instructions as to how to produce a Surrealist text, as given in the manifesto of 1924:

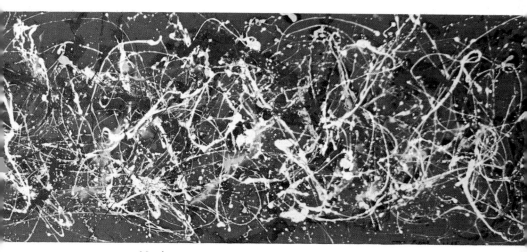

15 JACKSON POLLOCK *Number 2* 1949

> Have someone bring you writing materials after getting settled in a place as favourable as possible to your mind's concentration on itself. Put yourself in the most passive, or receptive, state you can. Forget about your genius, your talents, and those of everyone else. Tell yourself that literature is the saddest path that leads to everything. Write quickly, without a preconceived subject, fast enough not to remember and not to be tempted to read over what you have written.[8]

I think it is clear that in many ways Pollock's and Breton's attitudes correspond. It is important, for example, to remember that even in so-called 'gestural' or 'action' painting there is a large element of passivity.

One of the more radical consequences of Pollock's method of working, so far as the spectator was concerned, was the fact that it completely changed the treatment of space. Pollock does not ignore spatial problems; his paintings are not flat. Instead, he creates a space which is ambiguous. We are aware of the surface of the picture, but also of the fact that most of the calligraphy seems to hover a little way behind this surface, in space which has been deliberately compressed and robbed of perspective. Pollock is thus linked not only to the Surrealists, but to Cézanne. Indeed, when we think of the illusionist perspective used by Dali in *Christ of St John of the Cross* and even by Tanguy in *The Rapidity of Sleep*, it will be clear that this is one of the

16
17

33

points where Pollock differs most strikingly from his mentors. The shuttling rhythms which Pollock uses tend to suggest a spatial progression across the canvas, rather than directly into it, but this movement is always checked, and in the end returns towards the centre, where the main weight of the picture lies. As will be seen from his own description, these characteristics reflect Pollock's method of work. The fact that the image was created before the actual boundary of the canvas was settled (it was trimmed afterwards, to fit what had been produced) tended to focus attention on lateral motion. This rather primitive method of organization was to have important consequences.

Both by temperament and by virtue of the theories he professed – themselves largely the product of his temperament – Pollock was an intensely subjective artist. For him, inner reality was the only reality. Harold Rosenberg, the chief theorist of Abstract Expressionism, describes the style as a 'conversion phenomenon'. He goes so far as to call it 'essentially a religious movement'.[9] But it was a religious movement without commandments, as appears from Rosenberg's remark that 'the gesture on the canvas' was 'a gesture of liberation from Value

16 SALVADOR DALI
Christ of St John of the Cross
1951

17 YVES TANGUY
The Rapidity of
Sleep 1945

– political, aesthetic, moral'.[10] One might add that in Pollock's case as in some others, it also seems to have been a gesture of estrangement from society and its demands. Frank O'Hara describes the artist as being 'tortured with self-doubt and tormented by anxiety'.[11]

Pollock would not, however, have made the impact he did, first in America and subsequently in Europe, if he had been completely isolated as a painter. The real father-figure of the New York school of painting during the post-war years was probably the veteran Hans Hofmann, who exercised great influence as a teacher, and whose late style, as in *Rising Moon*, shows how keen was his sympathy with what the younger men were doing. Hofmann was typical of the things which go to make up the American amalgam. He had lived in Paris from 1904 to 1914, and had been in contact with Matisse, Braque, Picasso, and Gris. It was Matisse's work that he particularly admired, and it is this which can be thought of as underlying the more decorative side of Abstract Expressionist painting. That the new painters were not without roots in the past is something that can be judged from

19

Hofmann's own career. He had begun to teach in the United States in 1932, and had founded the Provincetown Art School in 1934. His last phase, upon which he embarked when he was over sixty, was both logical in the artistic climate of the time, and in human terms wonderfully unexpected: an example of a talent at last unfolding to its full extent when the right atmosphere was provided for it. Some of these late pictures are at least as bold as the work of younger men.

The 'organizer' of the Abstract Expressionist movement, in so far as it had one, was neither Pollock nor Hofmann, but Robert Motherwell (1915–91). Motherwell was an artist whose intellect and energies ranged wide. As a painter, he too began his career under the influence of the Surrealists, and, in particular, under that of Matta, with whom he made a trip to Mexico. He had his first one-man exhibition at the Art of This Century Gallery in 1944. As the Abstract Expressionist movement got under way, the range of Motherwell's activities continued to expand. He was co-editor of the influential but short-lived magazine *Possibilities* in 1947–8, and in 1948 founded an art school with three other important painters, William Baziotes (1912–63),

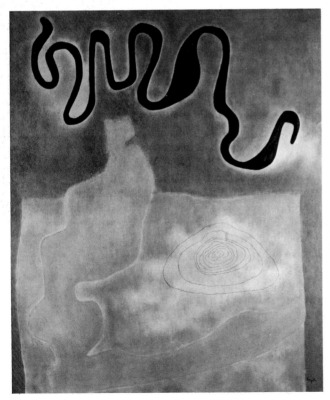

18 WILLIAM BAZIOTES
Congo 1954

19 HANS HOFMANN *Rising Moon* 1964

Barnett Newman (1905–70), and Mark Rothko (1903–70). In 1951 he published an anthology of the work of the Dada painters and poets which was one of the earliest signs of the arrival of 'Neo-Dada'.

The variety of these activities did not prevent Motherwell from having a large output as a painter. His best-known works are the long series of canvases known collectively as the *Elegies to the Spanish Republic, No. LV* from which is reproduced below. These pictures serve to correct some erroneous ideas about Abstract Expressionism. It is significant, for instance, that Motherwell's theme is one drawn from the recent history of Europe: recent, but not absolutely contemporary. Motherwell was in his early twenties when the Spanish Civil War broke out, and is looking back with nostalgia on his own youth. His choice of subject suggests that the 'subjective' painting which flourished in America during the late 1940s and early 1950s was by no means incapable of dealing with historical or social issues, but that these issues had to be approached in personal terms, and obliquely. The *Elegies* are certainly far more oblique than Picasso's *Guernica*. The

20 ROBERT MOTHERWELL *Elegy to the Spanish Republic No. LV* 1955–60

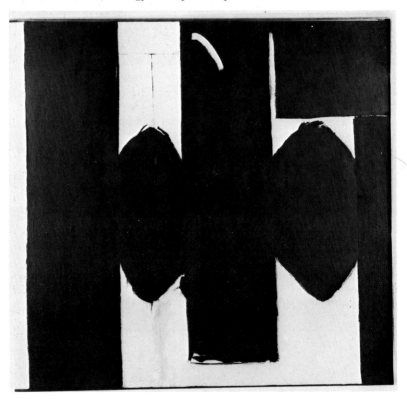

nostalgic rhetoric of Motherwell's paintings, sustained in painting after painting, is reminiscent of the tone to be found in a good deal of post-war American poetry: in that of poets as different from one another as Allen Ginsberg and Robert Duncan, for example. It is a mood which has few equivalents in the painting of post-war Europe, and which acts as a reminder both of the essentially American character of the style and of the fact that it was not necessarily the 'instantaneous' art which European painters at times mistook it for.

Essentially, there are two sorts of Abstract Expressionist painting, rather than one. The first kind, typified by Pollock, Franz Kline (1910–62) and Willem de Kooning (b. 1904), is energetic and gestural. Pollock and de Kooning are much involved with figuration. The other kind, typified by Mark Rothko, is more purely abstract and more tranquil. Rothko's work, in particular, serves to justify Harold Rosenberg's use of the adjective 'mystic', when describing the school. Rothko, like several other leading American artists of the post-war period – Gorky, de Kooning, Hofmann – was born abroad; he came to America from Russia in 1913, when he was ten. He began as an Expressionist, felt the influence of Matta and Masson, and followed the standard pattern by having an exhibition at the Art of This Century Gallery in 1948. Gradually his work grew simpler, and by 1950 he had reached the point where the figurative element had been discarded. In *Orange,* 22 *Yellow, Orange* of 1969, a few rectangles of space are placed on a coloured ground. Their edges are not defined, and their spatial position is therefore ambiguous. They float towards us, or away, in a shallow space of the kind that we also find in Pollock – it derives, ultimately, from the spatial experiments of the Cubists. In Rothko's paintings the colour relationships, as they interact within the rectangle and within this space, set up a gentle rhythmic pulsation. The painting becomes both a focus for the spectator's meditations and a screen before a mystery. The weakness of Rothko's work (just as the subtlety of colour is its strength) is to be found in the relative rigidity and monotony of the compositional formula. The bold central image became one of the trademarks of the new American painting – one of the things that differentiated it from European art. Rothko was an artist of real brilliance imprisoned in a straitjacket; he exemplifies the narrowness of focus which many modern artists imposed upon themselves.

The lesson is reinforced by the work of an artist who in many ways resembles Rothko, Adolph Gottlieb (1903–74) who, in paintings such as *The Frozen Sounds Number 1,* also evokes, like Rothko, or even 21

39

21 ADOLPH GOTTLIEB *The Frozen Sounds Number 1* 1951

depicts, a generalized landscape. He is also linked to Motherwell, in
that he is a rhetorician – by 'rhetoric' in painting, I mean the deliberate use of vague, expansive, generalized forms. An interest in Freud led
Gottlieb towards an art which he deliberately filled with cosmic
symbolism. The likeness between Gottlieb's most characteristic style
and the paintings done by Joan Miró in the late 1930s is something
that bears investigation. Miró, too, is fond of cosmic symbols, but
paints them more lightly and crisply, without too much stress on their
deeper meanings. Gottlieb's work makes me feel that I am being asked
to take a weighty significance on trust. This significance is not inher-
ent in the colour or the brushwork; one has to recognize the symbol
and make the historical connection.

The limitations I find in the work of Rothko and Gottlieb seem to
me to be shared by the earlier work of Philip Guston, and by that of

22 MARK ROTHKO *Orange Yellow Orange* 1969

23 PHILIP GUSTON
The Clock 1956–7

Franz Kline. Guston (1913–80) typified the boneless aspects of Abstract
Expressionism, when too often his pictures were no more than a riot
of lush paint and sweet colour, until he reversed direction at the end
of his life and started painting in a gritty 'cartoon' style which makes
a bridge between Pop art and Neo-Expressionism. *The Clock* (1956–7)
is an example of this earlier softly lyrical phase in Guston's work. Kline,
like Rothko, is an artist who runs to rather sterile extremes, and he is
speeded on his way to them by Abstract Expressionist doctrine. Unlike
Rothko's, his work is gestural, and his technical affiliations are with
Pollock. What he most frequently did was to create on the canvas
something which looked like a Chinese character, or part of one,
enormously magnified, as, for instance, in *Chief*. These strong, harsh
ideograms relied for their effect on the stark contrast of black strokes
on a white ground. Paint seems to be used only for reasons of breadth
and scale: there is little in most of the paintings that could not have
been said with Indian ink and paper. When, in the last years of Kline's
life (he died in 1962), colour began to play a part in his work, the

42

24 FRANZ KLINE *Chief* 1950>

results were not usually happy because we are never made to feel that colour is essential to the statement. Its purposes are cosmetic.

Kline was always very wary about admitting to any sort of Oriental influence in his work, yet influences of this kind have undoubtedly been important in American painting since World War II. Not only is there an element of passivity which grows increasingly powerful with each successive stylistic revolution – Rothko invites the spectator to contemplation, Morris Louis collaborates almost passively with the demands of his materials, Andy Warhol accepts the image and refuses to edit it – but the techniques of Oriental artists, as well as their philosophies, have made an important impact.

It is interesting to compare Kline's big gestural symbols with the work of an artist who had a very different sense of scale, Mark Tobey (1890–1976). Although not, strictly speaking, an Abstract Expressionist painter, Tobey pursued a parallel development, modified by different experiences and a different context. His career was centred not on New York but on Seattle – that is, until a final move to Switzerland. He visited the Near East and Mexico, besides making several visits to China and Japan. In Japan he stayed for a while in a

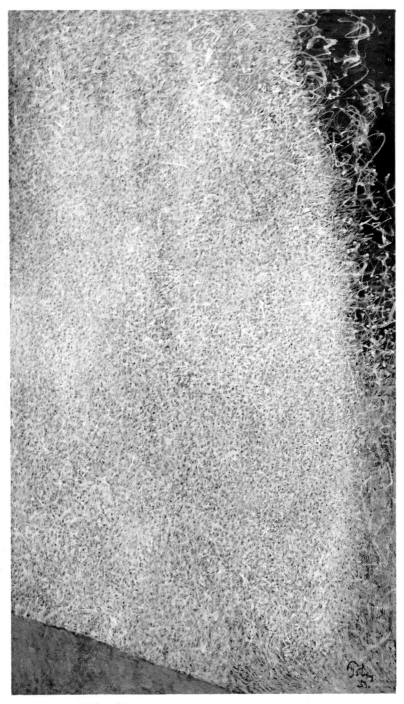

25 MARK TOBEY *Edge of August* 1953

26 WILLEM DE KOONING *Woman and Bicycle* 1952–3

Zen monastery, and became a convert to Buddhism (thus anticipating a similar conversion on the part of one of the most important of the American Beat poets, Gary Snyder). Tobey's journeys to the Orient were made with the specific purpose of studying Chinese calligraphy, and they had an avowed and decisive effect on his painting. He adopted a technique which he labelled 'white writing' – an excellent example of which is *Edge of August*, in the Museum of Modern Art, New York – a way of covering the picture surface with an intricate network of signs which are like Kline's hieroglyphs writ small. In many ways Tobey's work is a critique of Kline's, and of Abstract Expressionism as a whole. The thing which is impressive about Tobey's paintings, however tenuous his formal devices may sometimes appear, is the fact that what he produces is always complete in its own terms. Tobey's discoveries reinforced those of Pollock: in his later work, the canvas, or 'field', is articulated from end to end by the rhythmic marks of the brush. But he, more than the true Abstract Expressionists, gives the spectator a feeling of possibility. The marks, one feels, might at any moment rearrange themselves, but would retain a sense of ordered harmony. This is not an art straining against its own limitations, but one which is exploring a newly discovered and infinitely flexible means of expression.

Yet it would be a mistake to assume that Abstract Expressionism itself was entirely inflexible. The school was at any rate flexible enough to incorporate the art of Willem de Kooning, an artist who, in his best pictures, stands next to Pollock in force and originality of talent. De Kooning was born in Holland, and did not arrive in America until he was already an adult. His style tends to emphasize the Expressionist component of Abstract Expressionism, at the price of abstraction. He deals with imagery which seems to rise up out of the texture of the paint, and then to relapse again into the chaos which momentarily gave it form. What marks him off from contemporary European Expressionists is the characteristically American boldness – one might even say rawness – and sense of scale that appear in his pictures. When de Kooning bases himself on imagery taken from landscape, the work is so broad that it seems as if he has discovered a way of using oil-paint as the boldest Chinese and Japanese scholar-painters used ink: yet his grip on the original source of the image is never quite broken. When he paints in a more directly figurative way, as in the series of *Women*, such as *Woman and Bicycle*, the whole force of the sexual impulse is there in the painting. These Kali-like figures correspond to the kind of work which Jean Dubuffet (1901–85) did in his earliest period, and

46

again in his *Corps de Dame* series of 1950. De Kooning's work is an 66 important point of contact, therefore, between European and American art. In addition to this, it predicts certain aspects of Pop art. De Kooning's *Women* are the forerunners of Warhol's *Marilyns*.

The enormous success scored by Abstract Expressionism was to have important consequences for the arts on both sides of the Atlantic. Pollock's legend grew with tremendous rapidity in the years between the first European showing of his work in 1948 and his death in a car crash in 1956. Some of the effects of this success were all too predictable. An attempt was made to set up Abstract Expressionism as the only conceivable kind of art. A rapid succession of yet newer and more radical adventures seemed to disprove this claim almost immediately. Ironically enough, there was something in it. Abstract Expressionism looked both forward and back. Despite the huge scale on which they worked, Pollock and Kline seem to have had perfect faith in canvas and paint as a viable means of communicating something. That faith has since been questioned, and one reason for the questioning is the degree to which the Abstract Expressionist painters strained traditional categories of art; nothing further evolved from what they did. If one compares the work of a painter such as Clyfford Still (1904–80) in, for instance, *1957-D No. 1*, to the superficially very similar work of Sam 29 Francis (1923–94), one gets some idea of the extent to which Abstract Expressionism was at home only in America. Francis, as a Paris-domiciled American, introduces the European element of 'taste', in paintings such as *Blue on a Point* which immediately compromises the rigour 27 of the style. And again, if one compares the work of one of the few good Abstract Expressionists of the second generation, Helen Frankenthaler (b. 1928), in her painting *Mountains and Sea*, of 1952, 78 reproduced in Chapter 4, with that of the pioneers, one sees how difficult it was to build on what those pioneers had achieved. This least academic of styles made an astonishingly rapid descent into academicism. The art boom of the middle and late 1950s created a spate of bubble-reputations.

The effect of the new American art on Europe was not altogether happy. One reason for this was that Europeans misunderstood it, and tried to make use of criteria which had been suddenly outgrown. In England, for example, one still encounters a certain bitterness among early supporters of Abstract Expressionism. The British painter-critic Patrick Heron (b. 1920), who welcomed his American colleagues very 28 generously when they first appeared, has complained of their ingratitude.[12] He too suggests that the monotony of the central, heraldic

27 SAM FRANCIS *Blue on a Point* 1958

image to be found in much Abstract Expressionist painting could be remedied by a resort to more sophisticated European methods of composing the picture space. This shows that his initial enthusiasm was based on a misapprehension, as such methods of composition were just what the Americans had been most concerned to reject from the very beginning, even at the price of losing their freedom to develop and manœuvre.

The importance of Abstract Expressionism was arguably more to culture as a whole than to painting in particular. The success made by the new painting, and its attendant publicity, drew the attention of writers and musicians who were discontented with their own disciplines. Earle Brown, one of the most radical of the new composers, claimed to have found new inspiration for his own work in that of Pollock. At first, it was the gesture of liberation which counted, rather than any specific resemblance between the disciplines of the various arts. The so-called 'mixed media' and 'intermedia' were to come later, partly as a result of experiments with assemblage and collage.

48

28 PATRICK HERON *Manganese in Deep Violet: January 1967>*

29 CLYFFORD STILL *1957–D No. 1* 1957>

CHAPTER THREE

The European Scene

The course of events in France, and on the Continent as a whole, was very different to that in America. Paris was naturally the place towards which Europeans looked as soon as peace was restored. Equally naturally, it was the artists of the 'great generation' who began by attracting the most attention. Indeed, the six-year gap had served to establish these artists more, rather than less, firmly in the public mind. They were no longer outsiders; they had come to seem like representatives of the civilization which the Allies had been fighting for; and the Nazi condemnation of 'decadent art' was now of some considerable service to their reputations. Picasso became as much an object of pilgrimage to American GI's in liberated Paris as their own compatriot, Gertrude Stein.

On the other hand, there was a sense in which these senior artists found themselves cut off from their roots by what had happened. A feeling of change was in the air, and they, who had been the instigators of so many changes, were not the promoters but the victims of this one. The new eminence they were accorded often brought a certain aridity to their work.

This verdict seemed to apply particularly to Picasso (1881–1973). Immediately after the war he was awarded his final status as a mortal god: the most universally acclaimed and celebrated artist since Michelangelo. It says something for Picasso's furious creativity that, even when he had been placed in this uneasy situation, it showed no sign of slackening. His production after 1945 was prodigious, and new aspects of it were almost constantly revealed to the public. In 1966, for example, his extensive but previously almost unknown production as a sculptor was shown in exhibitions in London, Paris and New York. Despite his immense celebrity, however, Picasso's work gradually fell from favour with the leaders of taste in modern art. They were encouraged to downgrade him both by his Arcadian visions of nymphs and fauns, which seemed not only frivolous, but curiously 'thirties' in style – part of the repertoire of Art Deco (then still very much out of

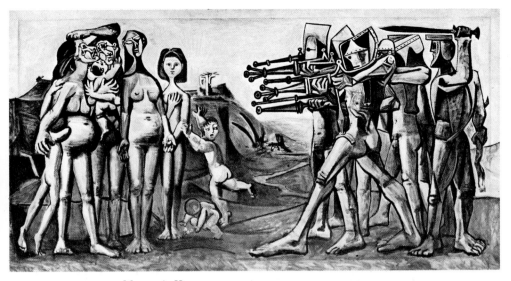

30 PABLO PICASSO *Massacre in Korea* 1951

favour) – and by the occasional propaganda pictures which expressed the painter's Communist sympathies. One such was his *Massacre in Korea*, painted at the time of the Korean war. Most people saw it as a rather barren paraphrase of Goya's *Dos de Mayo*.

Paraphrase was a habit which increasingly grew on the artist. Among the most characteristic works of the 'late' – but not the latest – period of his production were the series of variations on famous paintings by the great masters of the past, such as the *Las Meninas* of Velázquez, or the *Women of Algiers* by Delacroix. Picasso applied to these Monet's habit of working in series, conducting a kind of unpacking process, taking from the original work various ideas and qualities, and holding these up for our inspection, adding at the same time comments of his own. Often the spectator is conscious of a sort of hostility towards the achievements of the past; some of the versions might almost be described as rapes or dismemberments.

Picasso turned the same baleful eye on the effects of the ageing process as it applied to himself, and some of his most personal late works are a series of prints on this theme, often including self-portraits showing the artist as an aged voyeur or else as a monkey. They were produced in a great burst of creative energy between 16 March and 5 October 1968. Even more extraordinary are the very late paintings, done in the final years before the artist's death in April 1973. Painted with tremendous boldness, and even with a certain crudity, they met with incomprehension when they were first shown, but have since been hailed as the most important precursors of the new Expressionist figuration. Certainly there is a wild sense of risk about them which makes them exciting. Images are radically simplified, yet retain legibility thanks to Picasso's unsurpassed skill as a draughtsman.

Several other painters of the great generation continue to seem isolated from the main current of post-war events, though the work they did was often impressive. Georges Braque (1882–1963), for example, painted some undoubted masterpieces in his old age, such as the series of pictures devoted to the theme of the studio, such as *Studio IX*. These tranquil, monumental paintings sum up all the lessons of the painter's long lifetime. Yet it is surely significant that they are inward-turned without being truly introspective. They look, not at the world outside, nor at the psyche, but at the familiar paraphernalia of the artist's work-

31 FERNAND LÉGER
The Constructors 1950

32 GEORGES BRAQUE>
Studio IX 1952–6

shop. Their greatness comes, not from new invention, but from refinement of invention. Braque is giving a final polish to ideas which he
first began to use in the days of Cubism, and he deploys these ideas less
radically in the late than in the early work.

More willing to get to grips with the world around him was another
veteran, Fernand Léger (1881–1955). In a picture such as *The
Constructors*, painted in 1950, we see an attempt to bring a   31
Poussinesque classicism to terms with properly modern and Marxist

subject-matter. The results have been duly admired by Marxist critics. Nevertheless, a reversion to Poussin seems curiously eccentric and wilful even in the wilful world of post-war art.

Even the two acknowledged masters whose work seems most relevant to the post-war scene seem to have achieved this relationship almost by accident. The most conspicuous triumph was that of Matisse (1869–1954), who became in his old age almost as radical an artist as he had been at the time of the Fauves. Between the wars Matisse had specialized in a fluent hedonism which made increasingly few demands on his talent. In 1941 he underwent a series of operations, and emerged from them a permanent invalid. In some ways this ordeal and even the war itself seem to have sharpened his perceptions. In the late 1940s he painted a series of splendid interiors, flooded with light and colour, which form a parallel to the *Studios* of Braque. But he was to go beyond this. By 1950, the patches of colour in his pictures (for example, the *Zulma* in Copenhagen) had begun to enjoy an autonomy of their own. It was at about this time that, because of his increasing feebleness, Matisse began to use the *papier découpé* technique which was the chief creative resource of his last years. Pieces of paper were coloured to the artist's specification, and these were then cut and used to form designs. Thus the old man could create works of considerable size without too much strain. The method encouraged extreme simplification, and helped to discipline Matisse's decorative gift. *The* 35 *Snail* is one of the most abstract of all the designs of this period, severer even than the work which Matisse did around 1910. The activation of colour which Matisse achieved in these works was to mean something important to painters much younger than himself.

The other painter who had something to contribute was Miró. His great simple canvases of the Fifties were certainly close to the Abstract Expressionists, whom he influenced, and, in the 1960s, even to some 37 of the 'colour painters' whom I have yet to discuss, as in *Blue II* which plays on his characteristic ambiguity between representation and abstraction, but owes its greatest appeal to its wonderful use of colour. His sculpture, too, has links with Dubuffet. But Miró remains strangely elusive as an artistic personality: an artist who kept so many options open is difficult to interpret satisfactorily.

Other major artists, such as Max Ernst, continued their careers, but producing work which seemed at the time increasingly remote from 36 the current scene. His *Cry of the Seagull*, like Miró's *Blue II*, is evocative and lyrical, both abstract and representational in its effect and by now quite remote from Ernst's earlier Surrealist work. Some important painters acknowledged this dilemma quite openly. One seems to find a confession of this ambiguity between modernist Surrealism and Realism in the powerful portraits which the British painter Graham Sutherland (1903–80) produced after the war, numbering Sir Winston Churchill and Somerset Maugham among his sitters. These seem a surprising development of style for an artist who certainly began in the Surrealist tradition, and who continued, in other paintings, to produce work which was reminiscent of Surrealism.

'Realism' itself is not, however, an irrelevant issue, where the post-war painting of Europe is concerned. In fact, the sombre mood of

33 GRAHAM SUTHERLAND
Somerset Maugham 1949

34 HENRI MATISSE
Zulma 1950

35 HENRI MATISSE *The Snail* 1953

36 MAX ERNST *Cry of the Seagull* 1953>

37 JOAN MIRÓ *Blue II* 1961>

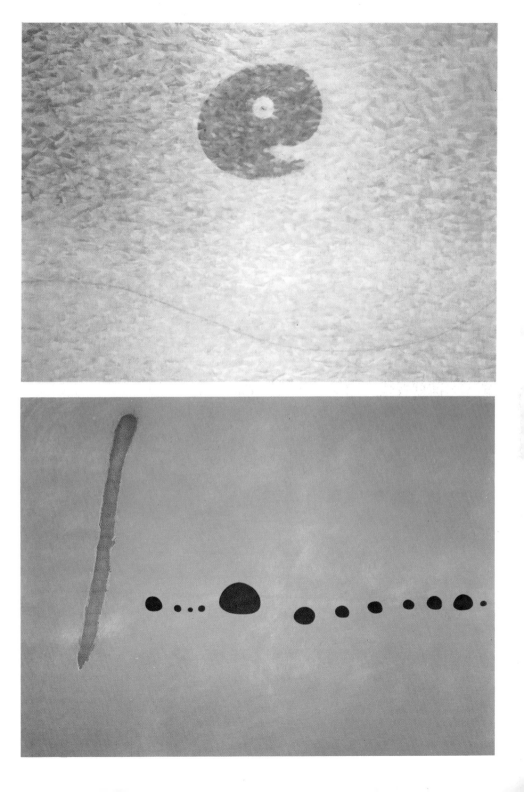

38 DAVID BOMBERG
*Monastery of Ay
Chrisostomos, Cyprus* 1948

39 FRANK AUERBACH>
Head of Helen Gillespie III
1962–4

40 LEON KOSSOFF>
Profile of Rachel 1965

immediately post-war Europe did seem to produce at least a theoretical leaning towards Realist art. There was a feeling that artists should now face up to their responsibilities, that they should participate in building a new and better world, and, in particular, that they should fall into line with film-makers and authors, both of whom were attracted towards a documentary style. In Italy, for example, Rossellini's early Neo-Realist films, *Città Aperta* and *Paisa*, were important – infinitely more so than the *Manifesto del Realismo* issued by leading Italian artists in 1945.

On the whole, Social Realism took root only in those countries which could be counted as markedly provincial. In England, for example, the so-called 'Kitchen Sink' painters enjoyed a considerable vogue. Their leader, David Bomberg (1890–1957), had begun his career as a pioneer modernist, under the influence of Vorticism, but later developed in a way which showed that his true masters were the German Expressionists, as is evident in landscapes such as *Monastery of Ay Chrisostomos, Cyprus*. Bomberg tried to create a balance: he wanted the spectator to be able to enter into his work, both in its role as a representation and in its role simply as paint. His followers tended to emphasize one of the terms of this occasion at the expense of the

other. The work of Frank Auerbach (b. 1931), e.g. *Head of Helen Gillespie III*, and of Leon Kossoff (b. 1926), e.g. *Profile of Rachel*, is concerned with a reality that is achieved literally: by means of the solidity of paint, which is piled up on the canvas in ropes and mounds. Though the approach is different, the final result has something in common with the French 'matter painters' whom I shall discuss in a moment.

The realism of the other 'Kitchen Sink' painters (those to whom the term more properly applies) was more descriptive, and their allegiance to it proved more fragile. The early work of artists such as Jack Smith, Edward Middleditch (b. 1923), and John Bratby (1928–92) dates only 41,43 from the middle 1950s, and is the equivalent of the kind of Realism which was then dominant in English literature and on the London stage: Kingsley Amis's novel *Lucky Jim*, John Osborne's play *Look Back in Anger*. However, none of these English painters produced work of the strength of that done by the Italian Realist Renato Guttuso (1912–87), who discovered a kind of neo-baroque idiom in which to describe the lives of 'ordinary people', as in his painting *The Discussion*, 44 a typical café scene of workers engaged in political debate. Where Léger, in his late years, looked back towards the Baroque of Poussin,

41 EDWARD MIDDLEDITCH
Dead Chicken in a Stream 1955

in trying to create an 'art of the people', Guttuso based himself on the more tactile art of the Carracci, and of Caravaggio.

There is, however, one British figurative painter who ranks among the most distinguished European contemporary artists: Francis Bacon (1909–92). Bacon and the Frenchman Balthus (b. 1908) seem to me, in fact, to be the only two artists who have managed to make figuration work in a contemporary European context. Both are so strange and individual that it is worth considering them side by side.

42,46   Bacon seems to me to represent the degree to which the demands of traditional figurative painting can be forced into a compromise with those of modernism. By the standards of many of the artists whose work is described in this book, he was an extremely traditional figure. He worked with the old materials, oil-paint on canvas, and he accepted the discipline of the old formats. In other ways he was far from orthodox. This is the way in which he described his method of work in a television interview with David Sylvester:

60

42 FRANCIS BACON *Study after Velázquez: Pope Innocent X* 1953

43 JOHN BRATBY
*Window, Self-Portrait,
Jean and Hands* 1957

44 RENATO GUTTUSO *The Discussion* 1959–60

I think that you can make, very much as in abstract painting, involuntary marks on the canvas which may suggest much deeper ways by which you can trap the facts you are obsessed by. If anything ever does work in my case it works from that moment when consciously I didn't know what I was doing. . . . It's really a question in my case of being able to set a trap with which one would be able to catch the fact at its most living point.[1]

This leaves open at least two questions: the precise one of the 'facts' the painter feels attracted towards, and the more general one of the future of figurative art. In Bacon's case the facts seem to be mostly those of terror, isolation, and anguish. A visit to any large retrospective exhibition of Bacon's work is an oppressive experience. Bacon went through a number of stylistic changes: the screaming popes and businessmen that made him famous were to give way to harder, clearer, and in a way more disturbing images. Distorted figures cower in glaringly lit rooms, which suggest both the luxury apartment and the execution chamber. These figures are not merely isolated, they are abject: man stripped of his few remaining pretensions.

Bacon's consistent, narrow art represents at least one of the positions that it is possible to take up, *vis-à-vis* mid-twentieth-century experience. But, though the unease of his work impressed both the ordinary spectator and his fellow artists, there is no such thing as a 'school of Bacon', even in England. The attitudes he took up precluded membership of any group of movement.

45 BALTHUS *The Bedroom* 1954

Easier to assimilate psychologically, but still isolated from the main current, is the work of Balthus. He differs from Bacon in being more naturalistic, in eschewing improvisation, in being influenced by artists such as Courbet and Piero della Francesca who could never be described as Bacon's masters (Bacon's debts were mostly to Velázquez). But they still have much in common. Like Bacon, Balthus broods on private obsessions; like Bacon, he often uses the symbolism of figures in a room which claustrophobically contains and shuts them in. If Bacon occasionally seemed to depict the aftermath of rape, Balthus gives its foretaste. Nude, adolescent girls sprawl in abandoned poses, inviting sexual violence, as in *The Bedroom*. Light gilds their contours, with a hand which is secretive and loving.

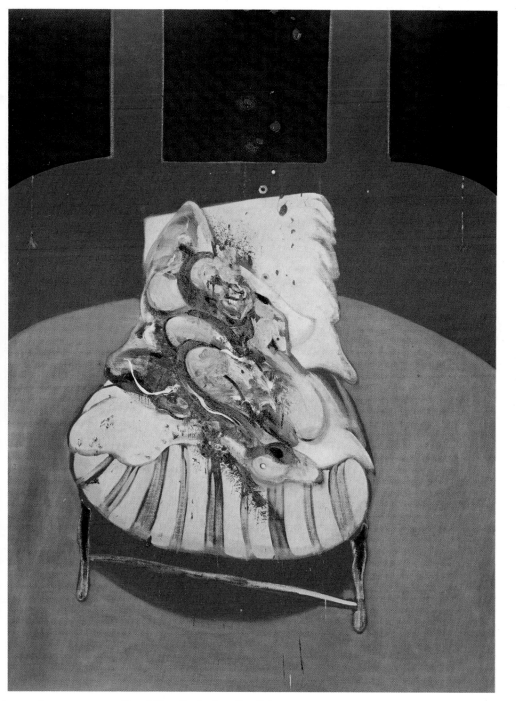

46 FRANCIS BACON *One of Three Studies for a Crucifixion* 1962

47 EDOUARD PIGNON
The Miner 1949

48 MAURICE ESTÈVE *Composition 166* 1957

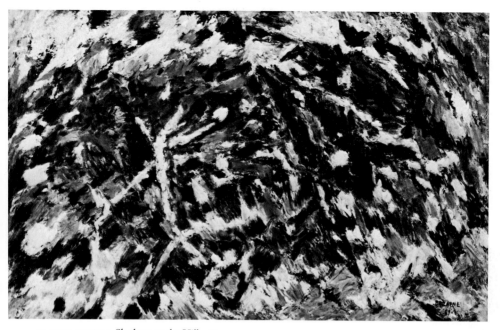

49 JEAN BAZAINE *Shadows on the Hill* 1961

Bacon and Balthus stand out among their contemporaries because each is endowed with a very special temperament, one which overrides all considerations of style. Few artists possess the perhaps burdensome qualities which these two seem to have, and the development of European painting was to go a very different way.

I have spoken of the sudden attention which was devoted to the great names of the Ecole de Paris immediately following the war. For younger artists in France, the process of growing up under the shadow of these giant reputations was bound to be a difficult one. Those artists most spoken of as 'promising' in Paris at this time were the so-called 'middle generation', which consisted of Jean Fautrier (1897–1964), Maurice Estève (b. 1904), Edouard Pignon (1905–93), and Jean Bazaine (1904–75) among others. These men were expected to do several entirely contradictory things at the same time. It was their duty to maintain the impetus of the modernist revolution; it was equally their duty to maintain the prestige of Paris, and the whole apparatus of dealers and critics that went with Paris as a centre. Naturally they found themselves in two minds. Their development was not made any easier by the vigorous promotion they received.

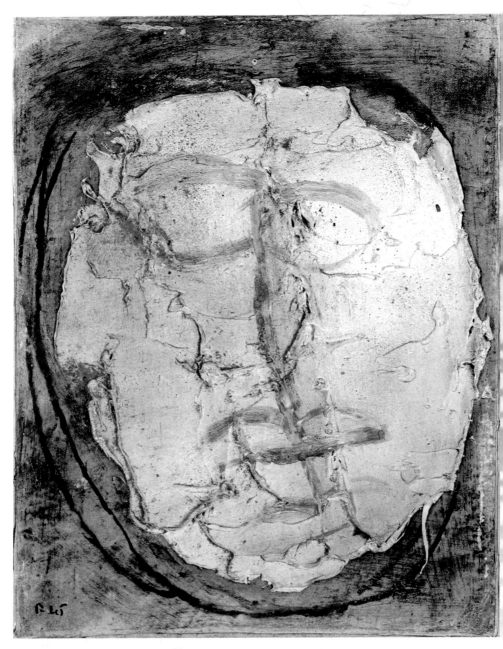

50 JEAN FAUTRIER *Hostage* 1945

51 WOLS *The Blue Pomegranate* 1946>

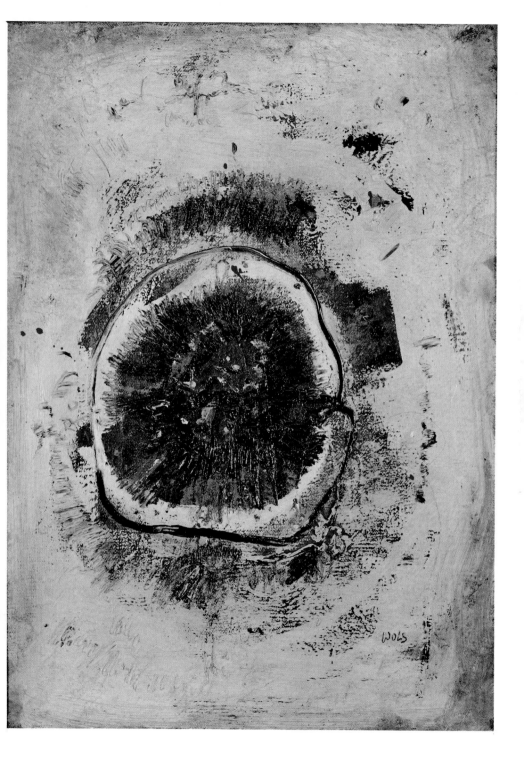

Of the painters whom I have just mentioned, Fautrier is without question the most original and important, as well as being the oldest. He was born in 1897, the other three in the middle of the next decade. Fautrier's first post-war show, at the Galerie Drouin in 1945, which consisted of the series of pictures called *Hostages* – one of which is reproduced on p. 68 – did have a significance for the future. The ostensible subject of *Hostages* was the mass deportations during the war, but the paintings put great stress upon the tactility of the painter's materials, the evocative quality of the surface itself, as is evident in the example reproduced. There is a narcissism in this which tells us something about the waning vitality of French painting, but it was also a genuine innovation. One sees in these pictures the first steps being taken towards *art informel* – art 'without form' – the style which was to dominate the next decade; and it is interesting to note that the step was made before the influence of the American Abstract Expressionists had reached France. Bazaine, Estève, and Pignon are lesser figures. In their work, such as Pignon's *The Miner*, Estève's *Composition 166* – both on p. 66 – and Bazaine's *Shadows on the Hill* – on p. 67, Fauvism, Cubism, and Expressionism jostled together to make an amalgam that had little that was new in it, save the fact of the mixture.

There were, however, better artists than these at work in the Paris of the late 1940s and the 1950s: men who did something, if not enough, to justify the critic Michel Tapié's claim, in his book *Un Art autre*, that there was now a kind of painting which started from premisses wholly different from the traditional ones. Most of the painters whom Tapié supported were working in a direction which paralleled that being taken by the Abstract Expressionists in America. The pioneer, almost the Arshile Gorky of this group, was the short-lived German artist Wols. Wols (1913–51) began by training as a violinist, then went to study at the Bauhaus in Berlin under Moholy-Nagy and Mies van der Rohe. In the early 1930s he moved to Paris, and formed links with the Surrealists. The rest of the decade was divided between France and Spain: at this period Wols worked mostly as a photographer. In 1939–40 he was interned, and began to achieve his mature style in a series of drawings. These were successfully shown at the Galerie Drouin in 1945, and Wols began to exercise a real influence over his contemporaries. The paintings he made in the few years that remained to him (he died in 1951), as in the characteristic *The Blue Pomegranate*, seem to blend the graphic sensibility of Klee with the new and more freely abstract way of seeing things. Wols's fascination with the actual substance of which the picture is made, as is evident even in

52 HANS HARTUNG
Painting T 54–16 1954

reproduction, the thick impasto which can be scratched and carved, prompts a comparison with Fautrier – see pp. 68–69.

Hans Hartung (1904–89) was a compatriot of Wols. During the art boom of the mid-1950s, he was to score a resounding success, thanks to a rather limited formula for picture-making which is correspondingly easy to recognize. Like Wols, Hartung left Germany in the 1930s, and settled in Paris, where he was encouraged by the sculptor Julio González. What he had to show now, in the years immediately following the war, was a vigorous calligraphy of bundled sheaves of lines. No picture of Hartung's is wholly without energy, but, once one has seen a group of them, it is certainly possible to wonder why a given mark, a given brushstroke, as in *Painting T 54–16*, above, appears in one canvas and not in another.

Another very fashionable painter in the 1950s was the French-Canadian Jean-Paul Riopelle (b. 1923). Riopelle, too, has an effective

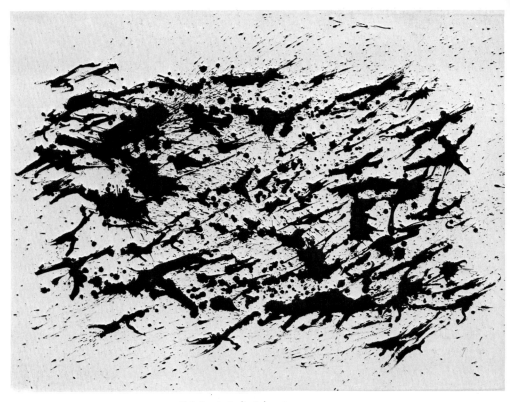

53 HENRI MICHAUX *Painting in India Ink* 1960–7

but limited formula. His work is an attempt to marry the spontaneity of 'informal' abstract painting to the rich texture and colour which are to be obtained from a heavy impasto, seen, for instance, in *Encounter*, on p. 73. Here, as in Hartung's paintings, there is vigour of rather an obvious sort. The bright colour emphasizes the mechanical roughness of the surface, but the two elements – colour and texture – do not quite coalesce. Furthermore, the use of a title, like *Encounter*, suggests meaning which is not visually supported.

A stronger artist, whose work is akin to informal abstraction, but stands somewhat apart from it, was the poet-draughtsman Henri Michaux (1899–1984). Michaux seems to have turned to making drawings as a means of conveying meanings which it was impossible to catch in writing (he had been a prominent literary figure since the

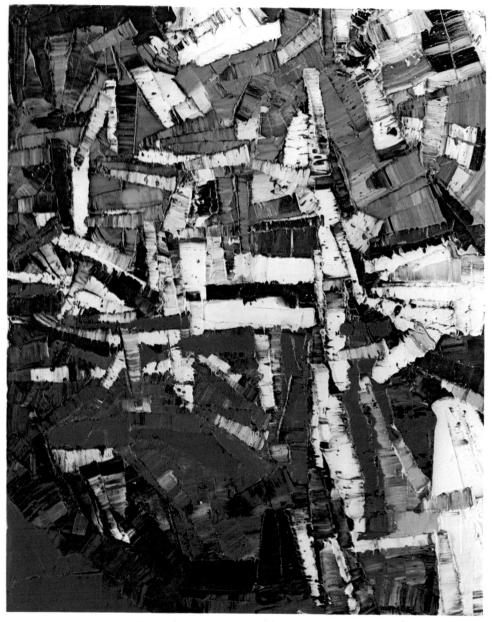

54 JEAN-PAUL RIOPELLE *Encounter* 1956

1930s). Many of these meanings were connected with the altered states of consciousness induced by hallucinogenic drugs. Michaux's drawings, like *Painting in India Ink*, are so alike that, when they are seen in bulk, the effect becomes monotonous; but the best of them come surprisingly close to the look of some of Pollock's work, at least in terms of surface similarity, but lack his toughness. *Painting in India Ink* may be suggestive and elegant, but compared to a Pollock drip painting, it looks more illustrational. The marks are on the verge of resolving themselves into shorthand representations of human figures.

The new abstraction scored an enormous success not only in Paris, but in the rest of Europe. Painters such as Antoni Tàpies (b. 1923) in Spain, and Alberto Burri (b. 1915) in Italy are recognizably part of the same impulse. Both are interesting because of the way in which they relate an international tendency to a national situation. Tàpies, who is self-taught, began to paint in 1946, and had his first one-man show in Barcelona in 1951. His work shows a fascination with surfaces, textures, and substances which links him closely to the French 'matter painters', such as Fautrier (see p. 68), who directly influenced him. Tàpies brings the spectator face to face with one of the paradoxes of the radical art of the post-war epoch. He is in politics a liberal, and it is not without significance that he comes from Barcelona, traditionally the centre of left-wing sentiment in Spain. Yet his work was by its nature and concepts too ambiguous to give much uneasiness to the Franco government. With its 'hand-made' textures, it tended to align itself with the products of the Spanish luxury crafts, such as fine leatherwork, as can be seen in *Black with Two Lozenges* on p. 76. This may give us the reason why Tàpies, and other Spanish artists whose work in a general way resembles his, such as Manolo Millares (1926–72) in, for instance, *No. 165*, enjoyed a certain degree of favour in the eyes of the authorities in Franco's day. What they created became a form of prestige export, better known abroad than in its country of origin.

Burri is a rather similar case. He was a doctor during the war, and first began to paint in 1944, in a prison camp in Texas. When he was set free, he gave up his practice in order to continue painting. His first exhibition was held in 1947. Burri is best known for works made of sacking and old rags, e.g. *Sacco*: his reason for using these materials was that they reminded him of the blood-soaked bandages he had seen in wartime. He has also made use of charred wood, of plastic foil burned and melted with a blow-lamp, and of battered plates of tin. The programme put forward to justify these works is the existentialist one of

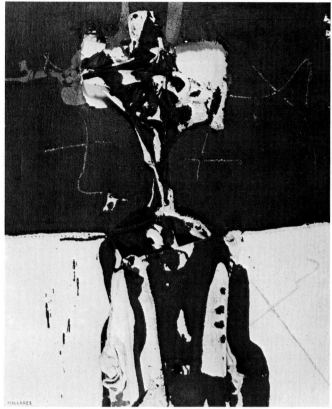

55 MANOLO MILLARES
No. 165 1961

metaphysical anguish, but what strikes one instead is their good taste, their easy sensuousness.

Indeed, it is possible to feel that nearly all the European free abstractionists of the late 1940s and early 1950s suffer from a thinness of emotion and a restriction of technical means. At the same time, one must sympathize with their predicament. As can be seen from the work of Wols and Fautrier, in *Hostage* and *The Blue Pomegranate*, on pp. 68 and 69, they were exploring a kind of painting which had also attracted the leading Americans. The European experiments were, however, less radical and less sure of their direction than those being made in New York. The long-standing European (and especially French) tradition of *belle peinture* – of the painting as a beautiful and luxurious object, a bed of delight for the senses – stood in the way of radicalism. The American worship of 'rawness' is to be found,

56 ANTONI TÀPIES *Black with Two Lozenges* 1963

57 ALBERTO BURRI *Sacco 4* 1954

although in another form, in Picasso's *Demoiselles d'Avignon*, but it is not visible in the art which was being produced in France some forty years later. When the new Americans began to be exhibited in Europe, as when Peggy Guggenheim's collection made a tour of European cities in 1948, the effect was overwhelming. One reason that the Americans triumphed so easily was to be found in the fact that their European colleagues were already partly converted – enough so to understand what they were being offered – but had not yet achieved so spectacularly radical a stance. Yet European artists found it difficult to use Abstract Expressionism as a starting-point, because the American statement had a completeness of its own.

The dilemma is clearly shown in the work of Pierre Soulages (b. 1919), and in that of Georges Mathieu (b. 1922). Soulages can, on occasion, look like a sweeter and less committed version of Franz Kline, but his broad strokes of the brush, e.g. *Painting*, do not have the energy or the constructional quality which one finds in the American

58

artist. Mathieu is a more interesting figure than Soulages. His work has certain affinities with that of Pollock, though he started painting in a freely calligraphic way so early (1937) that there can be no question of direct derivation. Rather, his has been an independent development along similar lines: which does not amount to a claim that Mathieu is an artist of the same stature as Pollock. For instance, his pictures, such as *Battle of Bouvines*, even the very large ones, are always far less complex than those painted by the American. Image and background have separate identities, which is not the case with Pollock; and there is in Mathieu's work little real feeling for space, even for the shallow, flattened version of it that Pollock uses. Mathieu writes on the canvas in a series of bravura scribbles. These scribbles do not blend with the ground; they dominate it. Rhythmical as they are, they express little beyond a delight in their own ease and dash. Mathieu seems very much the virtuoso, satisfied with his own tricks.

Nevertheless, he has an importance which is unconnected with the flashy triviality of so many of his pictures. He has been an efficient and

58 PIERRE SOULAGES *Painting* 1956

59 GEORGES MATHIEU *Battle of Bouvines* 1954

intelligent publicist and organizer: it was he who arranged the exhibition in which the new French and American painters were shown
together for the first time. More, he has been in all senses a forerunner,
a man keenly attuned to the seminal ideas of the time. When, in 1956,
Mathieu painted a twelve-foot canvas in the presence of a large audience at the Théâtre Sarah Bernhardt, he anticipated the 'Happenings'
which American artists were to make fashionable a few years later, as
well as recalling some of the antics of the Dadaists and Surrealists.
Modern art has produced a crop of dazzling showmen, and Mathieu,
like Salvador Dali, has been one of these.

Art informel, though the best publicized of the European developments after the war, was by no means the only new beginning. Even
more significant, in many ways, was the short-lived Cobra Group of
1948–50. The name is taken from the names of the cities which the
various participants hailed from: Copenhagen, Brussels, Amsterdam.
Among its members were the Dane Asger Jorn (1914–73), the
Dutchman Karel Appel (b. 1921), and the Belgians Corneille (b. 1922)
and Pierre Alechinsky (b. 1927). Like the Abstract Expressionists, the
artists of the Cobra Group were interested in giving direct expression
to subconscious fantasy, with no censorship from the intellect, as for
instance, in Alechinsky's *The Green Being Born*. But they did not rule   63
out figuration – as the aerial view *Souvenir of Amsterdam* by Corneille   64
shows: in this they resembled Fautrier and Wols, rather than Hartung,
Soulages, and Mathieu. Expressionism had struck deep roots both in

79

60 ASGER JORN *You Never Know* 1966
61 ALAN DAVIE *The Martyrdom of St Catherine* 1956

62 KAREL APPEL *Women and Birds* 1958

Scandinavia (with Munch) and in Holland and Belgium. The Dutch–American de Kooning shows its impress just as clearly as Karel Appel, a Dutchman who has remained a 'European' – see, for example, his *Women and Birds* on p. 81. In one sense, therefore, the Cobra Group revives and continues an old tradition, rather than making a completely fresh start. This led to a greater complexity of reference than we usually find in the art of the immediately post-war period. Jorn, for example, veered from the cheerful to the sinister. His pictures, such as *You Never Know*, on p. 80, incorporated a wide range of references; thanks to his interest in myths and magic, Jorn had access to a great range of signs and symbols. He was also a notably bold

62

60

63 PIERRE ALECHINSKY *The Green Being Born* 1960

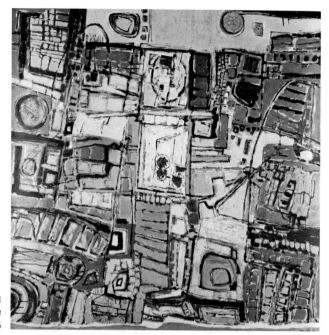

64 CORNEILLE
Souvenir of Amsterdam
1956

colourist. Yet he and his colleagues had less impact than one might have predicted. The same is true of an English artist whose work in some respects resembles theirs: Alan Davie (b. 1920) formed one of the few real bridges between English and Continental art at this period, and was exhibited in European exhibitions where English painters were seldom seen. 61

More loosely linked to the Cobra group than Davie, yet working in a parallel style, is the Austrian Hundertwasser (b. 1928). In his work such as *The Hokkaido Steamer*, on p. 84, Expressionism becomes formal and decorative, under the influence of Art Nouveau. 65

Yet there was one European artist of crucial importance who was related to the Cobra Group painters, as well as to Wols and to Fautrier. Jean Dubuffet was one of the few really major artists to have appeared in France since the war, though 'since the war' is perhaps the wrong phrase, for Dubuffet was at work as a painter long before 1945. But his first one-man show was held in 1945, a few months after the Liberation.

His painting *Corps de Dame* contains the clues to many of Dubuffet's preoccupations. He was interested in child art, in the art of madmen, in graffiti on walls and pavements, and in the accidental markings and 66

83

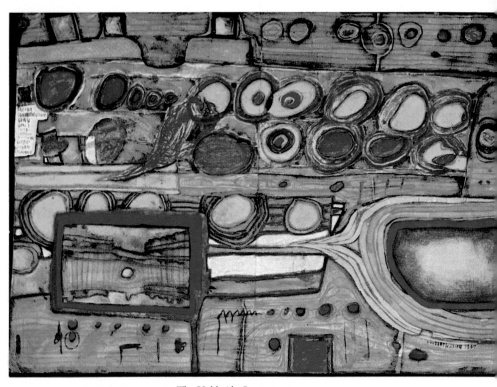

65 HUNDERTWASSER *The Hokkaido Steamer* 1961

maculations to be found on these surfaces. Dubuffet was the most persistent explorer of the possibilities offered by materials and surfaces to have appeared during the post-war period. He wrote:

> In all my works . . . I have always had recourse to one never-varying method. It consists in making the delineation of the objects represented heavily dependent on a system of necessities which itself looks strange. These necessities are sometimes due to the inappropriate and awkward character of the material used, sometimes to the inappropriate manipulation of the tools, sometimes to some strange obsessive notion (frequently changed for another). In a word, it is always a matter of giving the person who is looking at the picture the startling impression that a weird logic has directed the painting of it, a logic to which the delineation of every object

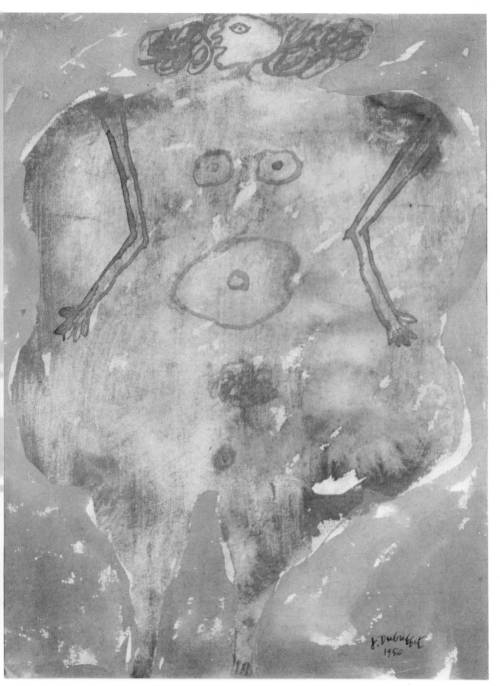

66 JEAN DUBUFFET *Corps de Dame* 1950

is subjected, is even sacrificed, in such a peremptory way that, curiously enough, it forces the most unexpected solutions, and, in spite of the obstacles it creates, brings out the desired figuration.[2]

The artist here proclaims himself the ally of certain important creators in the other arts. There seems to be a real affinity, for example, between Dubuffet's methods and those adopted by the dramatist Eugène Ionesco. Dubuffet and Ionesco alike are heavily permeated with the idea of 'the absurd', perhaps more thoroughly so than Sartre, with whom it originated. Dubuffet appears in his statements about art as a man of culture who is sophisticatedly obsessed with the anti-cultural. His work shows how hard it is for the modern artist to break out of the prison of 'taste'. His remarks about the *Corps de Dame* series, which I have already mentioned in connection with de Kooning, show just how such considerations crept into his work, more or less by the back door:

> It pleased me (and I think this predilection is more or less constant in all my paintings) to juxtapose brutally, in these feminine bodies, the extremely general and the extremely particular, the metaphysical and the grotesquely trivial. In my view, the one is considerably reinforced by the presence of the other.[3]

Dubuffet spent his life, not so much in breaking new ground, as in trying to see what could be done with the existing heritage of the Ecole de Paris, by misusing it as well as using it. He made sculpture out of clinker, foil, and papiermâché, and pictures from leaves and butterfly-wings. The result is an *œuvre* in which the individual works are nearly always fascinating, either in their grossness or their intricacy, or some intermingling of these two qualities. Dubuffet's creative limits are to be found in his selfconsciousness, and the degree to which his work is an exegesis rather than a truly original contribution to modernism. It comments both wittily and pertinently, but we are aware that, to savour these comments fully, we must have at least some knowledge of modern art, its theories and its controversies.

Nevertheless, Dubuffet seems to me to sum up many of the leading tendencies to be found in the visual arts in the period immediately following the war. The priority given to the inner world of the artist, and the rejection of the traditional claims of art to be more coherent, more organized, and more homogeneous than 'non-art', or 'reality', were pointers to the future.

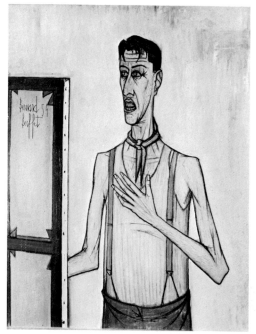

67 BERNARD BUFFET
Self-portrait 1954

The difficulties of a more traditional approach can be judged from the work of two other painters who made their reputations at about the same period. One of them need not detain us long, however. Dubuffet's near-namesake Bernard Buffet had a spectacular success in the 1940s and 1950s with schematic figurative paintings, e.g. *Self-por-trait*, which were literal interpretations of the gloomier and more superficial aspects of Sartre's existentialist philosophy. Buffet's interest really lies in the fact that quite a large section of the public received him so eagerly as an acceptable representative of modern art.

Another, equally popular and far more gifted painter was the tragic Nicolas de Staël (1914–55). In terms of natural endowments for paint-ing de Staël is the only French painter of the immediately post–war generation with serious claims to rival Dubuffet. The two artists pursued opposite courses. Instead of accepting absurdity and frag-mentation, and exploiting them, as Dubuffet did, de Staël looked for a synthesis, and in particular for a synthesis between the claims of modernism and those of the past. He began as an abstract painter, with certain affinities to Riopelle. Abstraction dissatisfied him, and gradu-ally he came closer and closer to figuration, first through a series of

68 NICOLAS DE STAËL *Agrigente* 1954

Football players, and then in the late landscapes and still-lifes for which
he is best known. These extremely simplified paintings, such as
Agrigente, can be seen both in abstract terms and as representations. A
skilful, delicate balancing-act is going on in them; the various planes
must be made to advance and recede in such a way that the 'abstract'
paint surface is never broken; so that we never feel that the representation is being forced on us, but rather, that it has come about naturally
as the result of the play of form against form and colour-area against
colour-area. In his best pictures, like the one reproduced opposite, de
Staël achieves his aim: the paint surface is placidly, creamily delicious;
the colours have a sonority that reminds us of the painter's Russian
ancestry.

88

But is this an art which lives up to the great claims that have been made for it since the painter's suicide in 1955? De Staël has been compared to Poussin (that high compliment of the academic art critic), has been called the greatest of post-war painters, and so forth. True, with his piquant combination of the traditional and the original, he appeals to many spectators: to find a Poussin-like scheme of forms under an apparently abstract and arbitrary surface is strangely reassuring. The question is if the power to reassure is enough to make a genius. De Staël's compromise between figuration and abstraction pales beside the obsessive force of Bacon or Balthus. The abrasive style of Bacon makes an especially interesting contrast, because Bacon, too, owes something to the arbitrary procedures of abstraction but tries to yoke them to a figurative vision. While it would be foolish to deny the calm beauty of de Staël's best work, it seems obsessed with a perfectionism which in the end becomes sterile. As a painter, he succeeds rather as Whistler did before him, not through the invention of new forms, but through tact and taste in the manipulation of pre-existing ones.

The path of tact and taste was certainly not the one which the post-war arts were to pursue. Abstract Expressionism and *art informel* were to be followed by a rapid succession of other initiatives, none of them owing much to traditional ideas about *belle peinture*.

CHAPTER FOUR

Post-painterly Abstraction

As it turned out, however, there was one style which held its own in the wake of Abstract Expressionism, and which, while owing something to the Abstract Expressionist example, had deep roots in the European art of the 1920s and 1930s. 'Hard edge' abstraction never completely died out, even in the palmiest days of Pollock and Kline. By 'hard edge' I mean the kind of abstract painting where the forms have definite, clean boundaries, instead of the fuzzy ones favoured, for example, by Mark Rothko. Characteristically, in this kind of painting, the hues themselves are flat and undifferentiated, so it is perhaps better to talk of colour-areas and not forms.

One of the progenitors of this kind of painting in America was Josef Albers, who has already been referred to because of his importance as a teacher. Albers had been closely connected with the Bauhaus during the 1920s: in fact, as student and teacher, he worked there continuously from 1920 to 1933, when it was closed, a longer period of service than any other *Bauhäusler*. During the 1930s, when he was already living in America, Alberts took part in the annual shows mounted by the Abstraction-Création group in Paris. He was thus thoroughly cosmopolitan. Albers's cast of mind is very typical of the Bauhaus atmosphere: systematic and orderly, but also experimental. He was, for instance, very much interested in Gestalt psychology, and this led him towards an exploration of the effects of optical illusion. Later he was drawn towards a study of the ways in which colours act upon one another. The pictures and prints of the *Homage to the Square* series – e.g. *Homage to the Square 'Curious'*, reproduced on p. 93 – Albers's best-known works, are planned experiments with colour.

Albers is interesting not only in himself, but because he seems to stand at the point where several attitudes towards painting converged. The systematic element in his work relates it to that of two Swiss artists, Max Bill (b. 1908) and Richard Lohse (b. 1902): Bill was also a Bauhaus alumnus, and, in his subsequent career, he became a sort of universal genius, at once artist, architect, and sculptor. The serial

69 MAX BILL *Concentration to Brightness* 1964

development of colour has been one of his interests throughout his career and *Concentration to Brightness* is but one characteristic example of austere, formal composition that makes use of optical data. Bill and Lohse are usually spoken of as exponents of 'Concrete art', and Albers is lumped in as a third member of the triumvirate. On the other hand, Albers's interest in optical illusion relates him to the so-called Op artists, while his particular treatment of form brings him into relationship with what critics labelled Post-painterly abstraction.

If one looks for a difference between Albers and his two Swiss colleagues, it seems to lie in the treatment of form. Albers's squares are free, passive, unanchored, floating, and it is this passivity which has come to seem particularly typical of a great deal of post-Abstract Expressionist painting in America. The difference between 'hard edge' and Post-painterly abstraction is precisely that it is not the hardness of the edge that counts, one colour abutting firmly upon another, but the quality of colour. It does not matter whether the colour melts into a neighbouring hue, or is sharply differentiated from it: the meeting is always passive. Albers's squares are crisp enough, but generate no energy from this crispness of outline.

Another painter whose work has something of this quality, without qualifying as Post-painterly abstraction in the strictest sense, is Ad Reinhardt (1913–67), who made a reputation as *the* professional non-conformist of the New York art world during the 1950s, and succeeded in retaining it until his death in 1967. Influenced by the abstract decorative art of Persia and the Middle East, Reinhardt went through a phase in the 1940s when his work came close to the calligraphy of Tobey. But these 'written' marks drew together, and became rectangles which covered the whole picture surface e.g. *Red Painting*. From an orchestration of intense colours, Reinhardt moved towards black. The characteristic paintings of his last phase contain colours so dark,

70 RICHARD LOHSE *Fifteen Systematic Colour Scales Merging Vertically* 1950–67

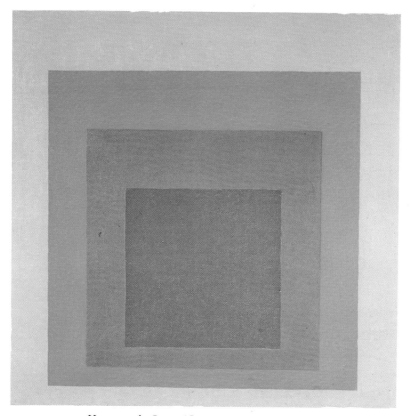

71 JOSEF ALBERS *Homage to the Square 'Curious'* 1963

and so close in value to one another, that the picture appears to be black, or almost black, until it is closely studied, at which point the component rectangles slowly emerge from the surface.

It is interesting to contrast Albers and Reinhardt with 'hard edge' painters who have a more conventional, but still very American, attitude towards composition. Among these are Al Held (b. 1928) – whose large-scale *Echo* is characteristic in its simplified, schematic and geometric form – Jack Youngerman (b. 1926) – whose *Totem Black*, equally monumental as Held's *Echo*, looks like a paper cut-out painted large – and Ellsworth Kelly (b. 1923). Of these, Kelly is probably the best known. His painting consists of flat fields of colour, rigidly divided from one another. Sometimes one colour will contain another completely, so that the picture consists of an image placed upon a

73
74

93

72 ELLSWORTH KELLY
White–Dark Blue 1962

73 AL
HELD
Echo 1966

ground. These are usually Kelly's weakest works, especially when the image itself is derived from some natural form, such as a leaf. At other times it seems as if the canvas, already very large, has not been big enough to accommodate the form, which is arbitrarily sliced by the edge, and continues itself in the mind's eye of the spectator, as, for instance, in *White – Dark Blue*. As a device to impart energy and interest to the painting, this is quite successful, but there is something rather gimmicky and tricky about it. There is also the fact that 'energy' and 'interest' are traditional pictorial concepts which, in the sense in which I have just used them, Albers, Reinhardt, and the Post-painterly abstractionists seem alike determined to reject.

What links Albers and Reinhardt with the so-called Post-painterly abstractionists is, in part, the fascination not with pictorial means, but with aesthetic doctrine. The doctrinaire nature of Post-painterly abstraction is striking. Rather as the logical positivists have concentrated on the purely linguistic aspects of philosophy, so the painters who adhere to the movement have been concerned to rid themselves

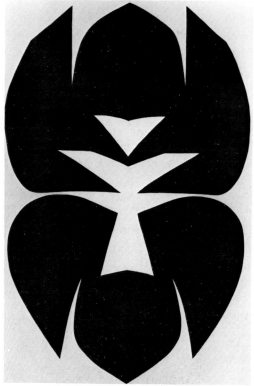

74 JACK YOUNGERMAN
Totem Black 1967

75 BARNETT NEWMAN *Tundra* 1950

of all but a narrow range of strictly pictorial considerations. The American critic Barbara Rose notes that

> in the process of self-definition, an art form will tend toward the elimination of all the elements which are not in keeping with its essential nature. According to this argument, visual art will be stripped of all extravisual meaning, whether literary or symbolic, and painting will reject all that is not pictorial.[1]

Rising out of what Jacques Barzun on one occasion described as the 'abolitionist' nature of Abstract Expressionism (referring to its apparent desire to do away with the art of the past), the new style rejected stratagems even more completely than Albers and Reinhardt.

76 AD REINHARDT
Red Painting 1952

77 JACK TWORKOV
North American 1966

The two painters who can be thought of as its real originators are Morris Louis (1912–62) and the veteran Abstract Expressionist Barnett Newman, though other Abstract Expressionists, such as Jack Tworkov (1900–82), also show some characteristics of Post-painterly abstraction in their later work; an example is the use of thinned paint, which gives a 'flat' look to the canvas.

By 1950 – that is, while Abstract Expressionism was at the height of its success – Newman's aims were already clear. He wanted to articulate the surface of the painting as a 'field', rather than as a composition, as, for example, in *Tundra*, on p. 96 – an ambition which went considerably beyond Pollock. Newman's way of achieving the effect he wanted was to allow the rectangle of the canvas to determine the pictorial structure. The canvas is divided, either horizontally or vertically, by a band, or bands. This line of division is used to activate the field, which is of intense colour, with some small variations of hue

75

from one area to another. The American critic Max Kozloff declares that, in Newman's work, 'the colour is not used to overwhelm the senses, so much as in its curious muteness and dumbness, to shock the mind'. He adds: 'Newman habitually gives the impression of being out of control without being in the least bit passionate.'[2] Whether one agrees with this verdict or not, muteness and lack of passion – 'coolness' in the slang sense of the term – were certainly to be characteristic of the new phase of American art.

With Newman, however, we still get the sense that the canvas is a surface to which pigment has been applied. Morris Louis differs from this, in being not so much a painter as a stainer. The colour is an integral part of the material the painter has used, and colour lives in the very weave of it.

More even than the leading Abstract Expressionists, Louis was an artist who arrived at his mature method by means of a sudden breakthrough. This suddenness is one of the things which has to be taken into account when discussing his work. Louis was not a New Yorker. He lived in Washington, and New York was a place he was notoriously reluctant to visit. In April 1953, Kenneth Noland, a friend and fellow painter, persuaded him to make the trip, both to meet the critic Clement Greenberg and to see something of what was currently being done by the New York artists. Louis was then aged forty-one, and had produced no work of more than minor significance up to that point.

The trip was a success, and Louis was especially impressed by a painting by Helen Frankenthaler, *Mountains and Sea*, which he saw in her studio. The effect on his work was to draw him towards both Pollock and Frankenthaler as influences. Some months of experiment followed, but by the winter of 1954 he had suddenly arrived at a new way of painting. One aspect of its novelty was its technique, which Greenberg later described in this way:

78

> Louis spills his paint on unsized and unprimed cotton duck canvas, leaving the pigment almost everywhere thin enough, no matter how many different veils of it are superimposed, for the eye to sense the threadedness and wovenness of the fabric underneath. But 'underneath' is the wrong word. The fabric, being soaked in paint rather than merely covered by it, becomes paint in itself, colour in itself, like dyed cloth; the threadedness and wovenness are in the colour.[3]

In fact, Louis achieved his originality partly through the exploitation of a new material, acrylic paint, which gave his paintings a very differ-

78 HELEN FRANKENTHALER *Mountains and Sea* 1952

ent physical make-up from those of the Abstract Expressionists. The staining process meant a revulsion against shape, against light and dark, in favour of colour. As Greenberg remarked: 'His revulsion against Cubism was a revulsion against the sculptural.' Even the shallow space which Pollock had inherited from the Cubists was henceforth to be avoided.

One of the advantages of the staining technique, so far as Louis was concerned, was the fact that he was able to put colour into colour. His early paintings after the breakthrough, such as *Untitled*, are veils of shifting hue and tone: there is no feeling that the various colour configurations have been drawn with a brush. Indeed, Louis did not 'paint' even in Pollock's sense, but poured, flooded, and scrubbed the colour into the canvas. This departure from the process of drawing was

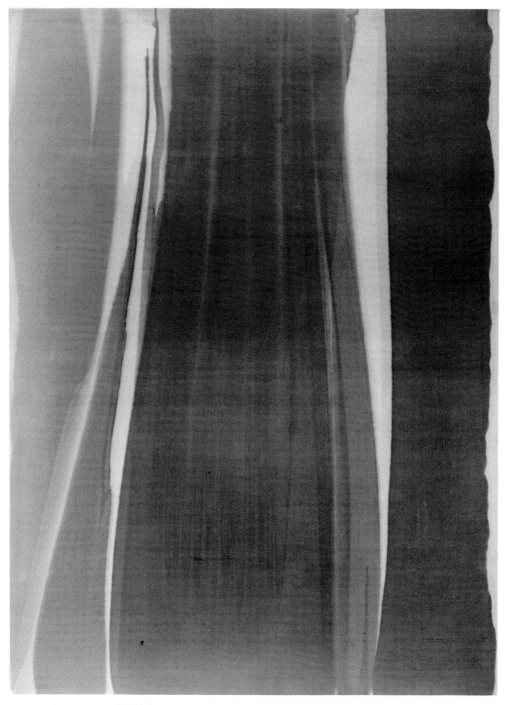

79 MORRIS LOUIS *Untitled* 1959

in some ways rather a reluctant one. In later experiments, Louis was to try and recover some of the advantages of traditional drawing for the stain medium. This is particularly true of the series of canvases called *Unfurleds*, which were painted in the spring and summer of 1961. Irregularly parallel rivulets of colour now appear in wing-like diagonals at the edges of large areas of canvas which are otherwise left unpainted, e.g. *Omicron*. Michael Fried remarks:

81

> The banked rivulets . . . open up the picture-plane more radically than ever, as though seeing the first marking we are for the first time shown the void. The dazzling blankness of the untouched canvas at once repulses and engulfs the eye, like an infinite abyss, the abyss that opens up behind the least mark that we make on a flat surface, or *would* open up if innumerable conventions both of art and of practical life did not restrict the consequences of our act within narrow bounds.[4]

Louis's final period of activity (he died of lung cancer in 1962) resulted in a series of stripe paintings, in which stripes of colour, usually of slightly different thicknesses, are bunched together some distance from the sides of the canvases. Fried feels that these show, as compared to the *Unfurleds* which preceded them, a further strengthening of the impulse to draw. Yet, in their strict, undeviating parallelism, the lines of colour seem inert, and this is true even where, in three paintings of this series, the stripes run diagonally across the canvas. Inertia, strict parallelism, and the constructive impulse (as shown by the paintings with diagonal stripes) were all characteristics which Louis shared with the other Post-painterly abstractionists.

Louis's friend and associate Kenneth Noland (b. 1924) was slower in making his own breakthrough, and therefore belongs to a later stage of the development of this new kind of abstract painting. Noland, like Louis, adopted the new technique of staining, rather than painting, the canvas. And like Louis, he tends to paint in series, using a single motif until he feels that he has exhausted its possibilities. The first important motif in Noland's work is a target shape of concentric rings, e.g. *Cantabile*. The pictures composed on this principle belong to the late 1950s and early 1960s. The target pattern was used, not as Jasper Johns used it contemporaneously, with the deliberate intention of alluding to its banality, but as a means of concentrating the effect of the colour. Often the targets seem to spin against the background of unsized canvas, an effect produced by the irregular staining at their edges. Fried notes:

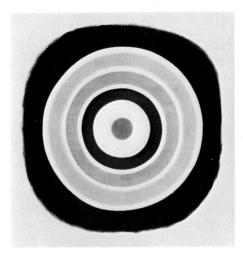

80 KENNETH NOLAND
Cantabile 1962

The raw canvas in Noland's concentric-ring paintings . . . fulfils much the same function as the coloured fields in Newman's large pictures around 1950; more generally, Noland in these paintings seems to have managed to charge the entire surface of the canvas with a kind of perceptual intensity which until that time only painters whose images occupy most or all of the picture-field – Pollock, Still, Newman, Louis – had been able to achieve.[5]

After experimenting with an ellipsoid shape which was no longer, in every case, in the exact centre of a square canvas, Noland began, in 1962, a series which used a chevron motif. *Grave Light* is an example. This was the signal for a growing concern with the identity of the canvas simply as an object. The framing-edge began to have an importance which, on the whole, had not been accorded to it since Pollock. At first, Noland allowed the raw canvas to continue to play its part. But the chevrons suggested the possibility of a lozenge-shaped support – a kind of picture which would be wholly colour, without any neutral areas, with the coloured bands moored to the bands of the frame. These canvases, like the late, diagonally striped paintings by Louis, have an obvious relationship to pictures by Mondrian, where the canvas is designed to be hung diagonally. The Abstract Expressionist and the Constructivist traditions here begin to draw together.

After a while, Noland's lozenges grew narrower and longer, and eventually the chevron pattern was abandoned for stripes running horizontally on enormous canvases, some of them more than thirty feet

82

long. Colour is thus reduced to its simplest relationship, as in the late paintings by Louis, and all pretence at composition is abandoned. These late pictures show the extreme refinement of Noland's colour sensibility. As compared to his early work, the colour is paler and lighter. The tones are close together, which produces effects of optical shimmer, intensified by the sheer vastness of the field, which enfolds and swallows the eye. There is nothing painterly about the way in which the colour is applied; it does not even have the unevenness of Louis's stainings, and the colour-bands meet more crisply and decisively than Louis's stripes. Or, rather, they almost meet: on close examination they prove to be separated by infinitesimally narrow bands of raw canvas, an effect which Noland may have derived from the early paintings of Frank Stella (b. 1936).

Stella, though his work is often grouped with Louis's and with Noland's, is more of a 'structuralist' than a Post-painterly abstractionist. His concern is not so much with colour-as-colour, as with the

81 MORRIS LOUIS *Omicron* 1961

82 KENNETH NOLAND
Grave Light 1965

painting-as-object, a thing which exists in its own right, and which is entirely self-referring. His work, however, does have a direct link to that of Barnett Newman.

The paintings which established Stella's reputation were those which were shown in the Museum of Modern Art exhibition 'Sixteen Americans' in 1960. They were all black canvases, patterned with parallel stripes about 2½ inches wide, a width chosen to echo the width of the wooden strips used for the picture support. Stella went on to execute further series of stripe paintings, in aluminium, copper and magenta paint. With the aluminium and copper paintings, Stella began to make use of shaped supports: from 1967, he turned to brilliantly-coloured shaped works interrelating semi-circles with rectangular or diamond shapes, e.g. *Untitled* reproduced in colour on p. 108. These made the paintings not only objects to hang on the wall, but things which activated the whole wall-surface. There was then a period of experiment with paintings where the stripes were of different colours, followed by one where the shaped canvases fitted together in series to make serial compositions. Then came asymmetrical canvases painted in vivid colours which segmented the shapes, some of which were now curved. These works in turn developed into painted metal reliefs, with freely curved shapes attached to a background. Both these attached strips and the background itself were painted with a fluency which seemed to contradict the rigidity of Stella's earlier work, such

83 FRANK STELLA *New Madrid* 1961

as *New Madrid* reproduced above, but the emphasis on structure as the subject of the painting was nevertheless still present.

If Stella seemed inclined to flirt both with the earliest modernism and with Pop art, another colour painter, Jules Olitski (b. 1922), experimented with what was essentially a critique of Abstract Expressionism. Olitski covered huge areas of canvas with tender stain-87 ings, e.g. *Feast*; these stained areas are often contrasted with a passage at the edge of the canvas in thick, luscious brushwork, reminiscent not so much of Pollock as of a European such as de Staël. The paintings themselves are usually vast. The paradox in Olitski's work is the huge-ness of scale compared with the limitation of content – the pictures hint at an aesthetic position in order to deny it. The sweetness and prettiness are ironic, and yet at the same time truly meant and felt. More even than Noland's and Stella's work, these paintings address themselves to an informed audience.

The same might be said about the work of Larry Poons (b. 1937). Though Poons has sometimes been called an Op artist, his typical work makes it plain where his true allegiance lies. Essentially, his paintings consist of a coloured field, scattered at random with spots of contrasting colour. The eye is offered a multitude of points of focus, and skims about among them, without coming to rest. In Poons's earlier work, the optical effect is enhanced by the choice of tone and hue. The tones are close together, the hues in sharp contrast, which generates an after-image in the eye. Later Poons enlarged the marks to eliminate this effect, as in *Night Journey*, and his work became more 86 gestural.

Another American who was also a second-generation member of the Post-painterly abstractionist group was Edward Avedisian (b. 1936). His work, such as the one reproduced below, has close links with that of Poons of the early 1960s, and functions similarly.

84 EDWARD
AVEDISIAN
At Seven Brothers
1964

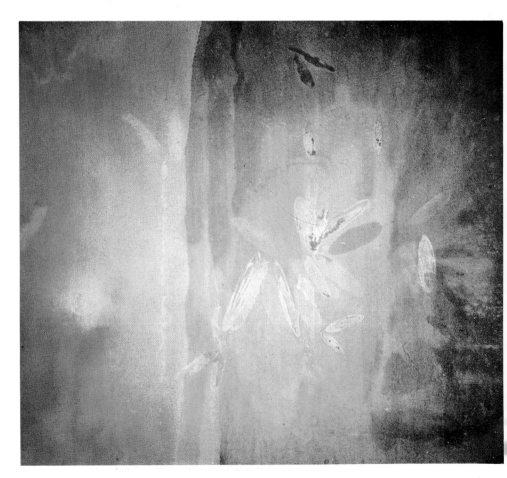

<85 FRANK STELLA
Untitled 1968

<86 LARRY POONS
Night Journey 1968

87 JULES OLITSKI
Feast 1965

88 JOHN HOYLAND *28.5.66* 1966

It is interesting to note that, while both Abstract Expressionism and Pop art scored very considerable triumphs in Europe, Post-painterly abstraction was not nearly so successful in making an impact on the European art scene. When Parisians spoke, sometimes rather bitterly, of the American rejection of 'our' painters, they were talking of the apparent dominance of Post-painterly abstraction in New York. The one country outside the United States where its ideas have gained a considerable foothold is Britain, and this is something which symbolizes the transfer of influence over British art.

88   For example, John Hoyland (b. 1934), one of the few British artists with an American command of scale, is essentially in the tradition of Louis and Noland. His use of the acrylic paint medium is enough to affirm it. Buy Hoyland sometimes gets a hostile reaction from American reviewers for not being sufficiently *pur sang*, sufficiently reductionist. He seems to owe something important to Matisse and to Miró, and his paintings have clearly not abandoned all traditional ideas on the subject of composition. One can even detect references to de Staël, whom Hoyland at one time admired very much.

92   Robyn Denny's (b. 1930) paintings find their starting point in the work of Josef Albers, and especially in the painting Albers produced

in the 1940s. The design tends to be bilaterally symmetrical, while the colours chosen are sharply contrasted in hue but carefully matched in tone. On a large scale, this produces a semi-optical effect, since the oblong colour-patches seem to move backwards and forwards in relationship to the main picture surface.

One of the things which seem to divide these British painters from their American colleagues is the fact that the British remain fascinated by pictoral ambiguity, and continue to juggle with effects of depth and perspective which are quite foreign to American art of the same kind. Work by painters such as John Walker (b. 1939), Paul Huxley (b. 1938), 90 Jeremy Moon (1934–73), and Tess Jaray (b. 1939) all bears out this 89,91 contention. Miss Jaray's work makes the point particularly clearly, as one of its sources is perspective drawings of architecture.

For at least a decade, Post-painterly abstraction represented a kind of modernist orthodoxy – it occupied the kind of position, in terms

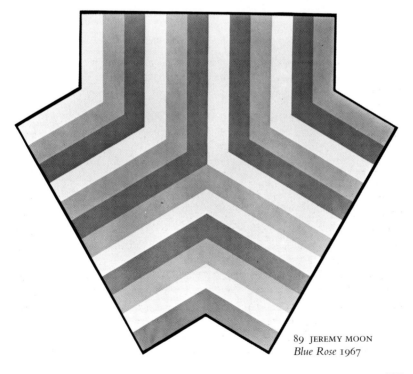

89 JEREMY MOON
Blue Rose 1967

90 JOHN WALKER *Touch – Yellow* 1967

of intellectual prestige, that history painting enjoyed in the eighteenth century. Strong evidence of its success can still be seen in the work of certain Minimalist painters of the 1970s, such as Brice Marden (b. 1938) in the United States, and Bob Law and Alan Charlton in Britain. Because Post-painterly abstraction seemed to bring the possibilities offered by pure painting to a kind of conclusion, artists who wished to find their way forward were for a while inclined to abandon the idea of the painted canvas as a vehicle for what they wanted to do or say. This resulted in a great swing of attention towards sculpture, and also led to an increasing number of experiments with mixed media.

91 TESS JARAY *Garden of Allah* 1966
92 ROBYN DENNY *Growing* 1967

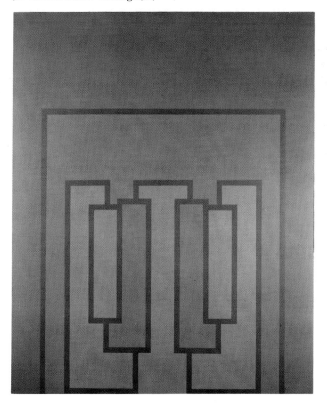

93 JOSEPH CORNELL *Eclipse series* c.1962

94 ENRICO BAJ
Lady Fabricia Trolopp 1964

CHAPTER FIVE

Pop, Environments and Happenings

Post-painterly abstraction, as I have described it, was a continuation of Abstract Expressionism, at least in part. Pop art was a reaction against it, and to begin with it was pop which caused a greater degree of uproar. Pop basically sprang from a shift of sources. Surrealism with its appeal to the subconscious, was replaced by Dada, with its concern with the frontiers of art. But this was not a purely intellectual choice. There were forces within Abstract Expressionism and *art informel* which propelled artists towards the new mode. For example, as Abstract Expressionism began to exhaust its impetus, the prevailing interest in texture led artists to ever-bolder experiments with materials. Some of these – with acrylic paint – were conducted by Morris Louis, and led to Post-painterly abstraction. But most consisted of a re-exploration of the possibilities of collage. Using collage involved an important philosophic step for an artist already familiar with informal abstraction. There, an interesting texture was something which the artist *created*, but collage additions came to his hand *ready-made*; and Marcel Duchamp's idea of the 'ready-made' was one of the central innovations of Dada. Collage had been invented by the Cubists as a means of exploring the differences between representation and reality. The Dadaists and Surrealists had greatly extended its range, and the Dadaists, in particular, had found it especially congenial, and in line with their preference for anti-art. In the hands of the post-war generation, collage now developed into the 'art of assemblage', a means of creating works of art almost entirely from pre-existent elements, where the artist's contribution was to be found more in making the links between objects, putting them together, than in making objects *ab initio*.

In 1961, the Museum of Modern Art in New York staged an important exhibition under the title 'The Art of Assemblage'. William C. Seitz remarked in his introduction to the catalogue:

> The current wave of assemblage . . . marks a change from a subjective, fluidly abstract art towards a revised association with environment. The method of juxtaposition is an appropriate

vehicle for feelings of disenchantment with the slick international idiom that loosely articulated abstraction has tended to become, and the social values that this situation reflects.[1]

Assemblage was important for another reason too. It was not only that it provided a means of transition from Abstract Expressionism to the apparently very different preoccupations of Pop art, but it brought about a radical reconsideration of the formats within which the visual arts could operate. For example, assemblage provided a jumping-off point for two concepts which were to be increasingly important to artists: the environment and the Happening.

Of course, some practitioners of assemblage did not move very far beyond their original sources. The exquisite boxes made by Joseph Cornell (1903–72) – one of which, *Eclipse*, is characteristic – with their poetic, surrealistic juxtapositions of objects, and the witty collages of Enrico Baj (b. 1924), are things which explore the resources of a tradition, without seeking to enlarge them very radically. Other artists were not content with this. Most of them fall into the category which has now been rather slickly labelled Neo-Dada. One would prefer to say, rather, that they are often artists who want to explore the idea of the minimal, the unstable, the ephemeral in what they do.

In America, the two most-discussed exponents of Neo-Dada have undoubtedly been Robert Rauschenberg (b. 1925) and Jasper Johns (b. 1930). Of the two, Rauschenberg is the more various, and Johns the more elegant; elegance has a genuine, if rather uneasy, part to play in any discussion of what these two artists represent.

Rauschenberg was born in Texas in 1925. In the late 1940s he studied at the Académie Julian in Paris, and then under Albers at Black Mountain College. In the early 1950s, Rauschenberg painted a series of all-white paintings where the only image was the spectator's own shadow. Later there was a series of all-black paintings. Neither of these developments was unique. The Italian painter Lucio Fontana (1899–1968) did a series of all-white canvases in 1946; the Frenchman Yves Klein (1928–62) exhibited his first monochromes in 1950 and, closer to home, were of course Ad Reinhardt's 'all black' paintings, also from the 1950s on. After these experiments with minimality, Rauschenberg began to move towards 'combine painting', an early example of which is *Bed*, a mode of creation in which a painted surface is combined with various objects which are affixed to that surface. Sometimes the paintings develop into free-standing three-dimensional objects, such as the famous stuffed goat which has appeared in so many

95 JASPER JOHNS *Numbers in Colour* 1959

96 ROBERT RAUSCHENBERG *Barge* 1962

97 ROBERT RAUSCHENBERG
Bed 1955

exhibitions of contemporary American art. One painting makes use of a functioning wireless set, another of a clock. The artist has also used photographic images, which are silk-screened on to the canvas.

The aesthetic philosophy informing this is essentially that of the experimental composer John Cage (1919–92), whom Rauschenberg met in North Carolina. One of Cage's basic ideas is that of 'unfocusing' the spectator's mind: the artist does not create something separate and closed, but instead does something to make the spectator more open, more aware of himself and his environment. Cage says:

> New music; new listening. Not an attempt to understand something that is being said, for, if something were being said, the sounds would be given the shapes of words. Just an attention to the activity of sounds.[2]

A characteristic painting of Rauschenberg's, such as the enormous *Barge* painted in 1962, is a kind of reverie which the spectators are invited to join; a flux of images which are not necessarily fixed and immutable. Cage remarks on 'the quality of encounter' between Rauschenberg and the materials he uses; one can compare this to the way in which Kurt Schwitters worked. But Rauschenberg is a Schwitters who has passed through the Abstract Expressionist experience.

So, for that matter, is Jasper Johns, though John's work gives one the impression of greater discipline. Johns is also more of an ironist. One work, entitled *The Critic Smiles*, is a toothbrush cast in sculpmetal, placed upon a plinth of the same material. Unlike Rauschenberg, Johns is chiefly known for his use of single, banal images: a set of numbers, e.g. *Numbers in Colour*, a target, a map of the United States, the American flag. The point about these images is largely their lack of point – the spectator looks for a specific meaning, the artist is largely preoccupied with creating a surface. Where the manipulation of paint is concerned, as is evident in *Numbers in Colour*, Johns is a master technician. The way in which Johns operates also suggests links with other things besides Pop art. Like Kenneth Noland, he is interested in pictorial inertia, for example. One of the reasons for choosing banal patterns is the fact that they no longer generate any energy. He is also interested in the idea of the painting as an object rather than as a representation. In some cases, he has used two canvases linked together, with a pair of wooden balls forced between them, so we see the wall behind at the point where they join. Other works have attachments: a ruler, a broom, a spoon.

It is clear from this description of the activities of these two artists that they represent a move away from 'pure' painting. Even to Johns, for all his virtuosity, painting is no more than a means of achieving a certain result, which might possibly be achieved some other way. Rauschenberg was for years associated with the Merce Cunningham dance company: he performed with them as well as devising props and scenery, and clearly this formed as important and central a part of his activity as painting and making objects.

One of the directions suggested by a painting like *Barge* is the move towards the tableau, the work of art which surrounds or nearly surrounds the spectator. The bulky and ferocious assemblages and installations of Edward Kienholz (1927–94) are an example.

Kienholz also represents one aspect of the tendency which is often called 'funk', or Funk art: the liking for the complex, the sick, the tatty, the bizarre, the shoddy, the viscious, the overtly or covertly sexual, as opposed to the impersonal purity of a great deal of contemporary art. Perhaps because if offers this kind of alternative, Funk art proved more than a passing fashion. It was responsible for some of the most alarming images of the 1960s – things such as Bruce Conner's (b. 1933) *Couch* of 1963, which shows an apparently murdered and dismembered corpse lying on a crumbling Victorian sofa, or Paul Thek's (b. 1933) *Death of a Hippie*, or various tableaux by the Englishman, Colin Self (b. 1941). A characteristic one is another corpse, a figure entitled *Nuclear Victim*.

98 EDWARD KIENHOLZ *Roxy's* 1961

99 BRUCE CONNER *Couch* 1963

100 ARMAN *Clic-Clac Rate* 1960–6

101 PAUL THEK *Death of a Hippie* 1967

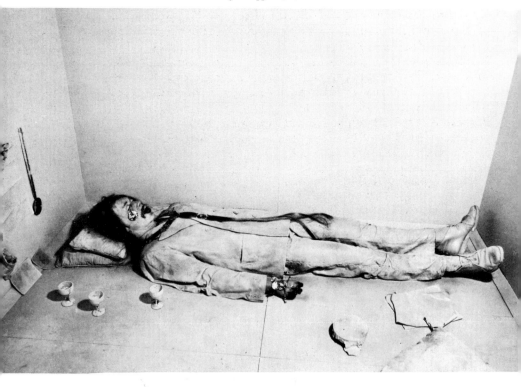

102 CHRISTO *Packaged Public Building* 1961

In Europe, an equivalent of the American Neo-Dadaists was supplied by what is sometimes called New Realism, after the movement founded by the French critic Pierre Restany, in conjunction with Yves Klein and others. Restany claimed that 'the new realism registers the sociological reality without any controversial intention'. What this means one may perhaps deduce from the work of Arman (b. 1928), who was one of the adherents of the group. Arman's most characteristic works consist of random accumulations of objects, e.g. *Clic-Clac Rate*, but objects all of the same sort, encased in clear plastic. These accumulations can exist as panels, or be three-dimensional. For example, Arman has made a plastic torso of a woman, filled with writhing rubber gloves. Another artist attracted by the systematic is Christo (b. 1935), who is best known for his packages, mysterious lumpish objects which sometimes suggest and sometimes wholly conceal what is wrapped up in them, and especially for his spectacular and poetic wrapped public buildings and landscapes.

The major personality among these European Neo-Dadaists was undoubtedly Yves Klein, an example of an artist who was important for what he did – the symbolic value of his actions – rather than for what he made. One sees in him an example of the increasing tendency for the personality of the artist to be his or her one true and complete creation.

Klein was born in 1928. He was a jazz musician, a Rosicrucian, and a judo expert (he studied judo in Japan and wrote a book about it

103 YVES KLEIN *Feu F 45* 1961

which is still a standard text). In judo, the opponents are regarded as
collaborators, and it is this notion which seems to underlie a great deal
of Klein's thinking about art. So does the wish to 'get away from the
idea of art'. Klein said:

> The essential of painting is that something, that 'ethereal glue', that
> intermediary product which the artist secretes with all his creative
> being and which he has the power to place, to encrust, to impreg-
> nate into the pictorial stuff of the painting.[3]

Besides creating the monochromes already mentioned, Klein adopted
various unorthodox methods of producing works of art. For example,
he used a flame-thrower, or the action of rain on a prepared canvas.
(Paintings produced by the action of the elements he labelled
Cosmogonies.) At his direction girls smeared with blue paint flung
themselves on to canvas spread on the floor. The ceremony was conducted in public while twenty musicians played Klein's *Monotone
Symphony*, a single note sustained for ten minutes which alternated
with ten minutes silence. The making of these *Imprints* is recorded in
the film *Mondo Cane*. On another occasion – in Paris in 1958 – Klein
held an exhibition of emptiness: a gallery painted white, with all the

124

furniture removed and a Garde Républicain stationed at the door. Albert Camus came, and wrote the words 'with the void, full powers' in the visitors' book. There were thousands of other visitors to the *vernissage*, so many as to cause a near-riot. Another of Klein's ideas was to offer for sale 'zones of immaterial pictorial sensitivity'. They were paid for in gold-leaf, which the artist immediately threw in the Seine, while the purchaser burned his receipt.

These actions have a certain poetic rightness to them, a quality often absent from the clumsier and more elaborate happenings staged in New York. Klein, at the time of his death in 1962, seemed to stand at the meeting-point of a number of different tendencies. There is the obvious connection with the original Dadaists, and also with certain contemporary artists who stand on the fringes of Dada, such as Lucio Fontana, whose own experiments with monochromes developed into the more familiar slashed canvases. Also reminiscent of Klein's work are the 'lines' of Pietro Manzoni (1933–63): single, unbroken brush-strokes which unroll on long strips of paper. All of these, in turn, are

106

105

104 Yves Klein's painting ceremony

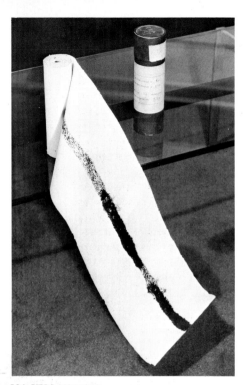

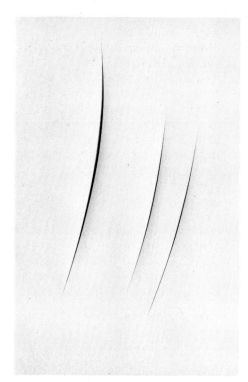

105 PIERO MANZONI
Line 20 Metres Long 1959

106 LUCIO FONTANA
Spatial Concept 1960

linked in a more general way with the tendency towards minimality in sculpture. On the other hand, Klein, as much as Johns and Rauschenberg, is one of the prophets of Pop art. His use of monotony, of the undifferentiated, gives him something in common with Andy Warhol, for instance.

But only *something* in common. Neo-Dada and Pop art are not identical, though Neo-Dada includes Pop. The artists I have so far spoken of in this chapter are not, in my view, genuine practitioners of Pop, though their work has been included in exhibitions and discussed in books under that label. The factors which created Pop art were not universal, but had much to do with the urban culture of Britain and America in the years after the war. Only artists in close touch with that culture caught its special tone and idiom: of all the post-war styles, this is the one which most conspicuously has 'a local habitation and a name'.

After Pop scored its initial success, it did, very naturally, exercise an influence elsewhere. Many of the artists connected with Pierre Restany's New Realism toyed with it. There are, for instance, Michelangelo Pistoletto's (b. 1933) photographic figures fastened to mirror backgrounds in which the spectator sees himself reflected, thus completing the composition; and Martial Raysse's (b. 1936) skilful parodies of painters such as Prud'hon. In a version of Prud'hon's *Cupid and Psyche* entitled *Tableau simple et doux*, Cupid holds a neon heart in his fingers. Another Frenchman, Alain Jacquet (b. 1939), uses photographic images in a way which is reminiscent of both Warhol and Lichtenstein. The Japanese have been almost equally eager to catch up with Pop. Tomio Miki (b. 1938) has made almost as much a speciality of ears in cast aluminium as Warhol has of endlessly repeated images of Marilyn Monroe. In examining these works, however, one is aware

109

107 MICHELANGELO PISTOLETTO
Seated Figure 1962 (with Pistoletto)

108 MARTIAL RAYSSE
Tableau simple et doux 1965

that the involvement with the urban environment is not as immediate as it seems to be in the case of the leading British and American Pop artists.

It now seems to be generally agreed that Pop art, in its narrowest definition, began in England, and that it grew out of a series of discussions which were held at the Institute of Contemporary Arts in London by a group which called itself the Independent Group. It included artists, critics, and architects, among them Eduardo Paolozzi, Alison and Peter Smithson, Richard Hamilton, Peter Reyner Banham, and Lawrence Alloway. The group were fascinated by the new urban popular culture, and particularly by its manifestations in America. Partly this was a delayed effect of the war, when America, to those in England, had seemed an Eldorado of all good things, from nylons to new motor-cars. Partly it was a reaction against the solemn romanticism, the atmosphere of high endeavour, which had prevailed in British art during the 1940s.

In 1956 the group was responsible for an exhibition at the Whitechapel Art Gallery which was called 'This Is Tomorrow'. Designed in twelve sections, the show was designed to draw the spectator into a series of environments. In his book on Pop art, Mario Amaya points out that the environmental aspect probably owed something to Richard Buckle's exhibition of the Diaghilev Ballet, which was held in London in 1954, and which seized on the excuse of a theatrical subject to provide a brilliantly theatrical display.[4] From the point of view of the future, however, probably the most significant part of 'This Is Tomorrow' was an entrance display provided by Richard

109 TOMIO MIKI
Ears (detail) 1968

110 RICHARD HAMILTON *Just What is it that Makes Today's Homes so Different, so Appealing?* 1956

Hamilton (b. 1922) – a collage picture entitled *Just What is it that Makes Today's Homes so Different, so Appealing?* In the picture are a muscle-man from a physique magazine and a stripper with sequinned breasts. The muscle-man carries a gigantic lollipop, with the word P O P on it in large letters. With this work, many of the conventions of Pop art were created, including the use of borrowed imagery.

Hamilton already knew clearly what he thought a truly modern art should be. The qualities he was looking for were, so he said in 1957, popularity, transience, expendability, wit, sexiness, gimmickry, and glamour.[5] It must be low-cost, mass produced, young, and Big Business. These were the qualities which British Pop artists of the 1960s were afterwards to worship. But granted Hamilton's priority, and that of the Independent Group, it is still a little difficult to prove that Pop art sprang directly from their activities. Of all the artists who belonged to the group, Hamilton himself is the only one who can be classified as a Pop painter. In addition, there is the fact that he has always been a very slow worker, and that, at this period, little of his work was to be seen in England.

There were two other British painters who might be labelled 'transitional', both of them, as it happens, among the most interesting that Britain has produced in recent years. Both were students at the Royal College of Art in the mid-1950s. One is Peter Blake (b. 1932), who would classify himself unhesitatingly as a 'realist'. Blake's work represents a reversion to the tradition of the Pre-Raphaelites in the middle of the twentieth century. Like the Pre-Raphaelites, he is nostalgic, but not for the Middle Ages. What he looks back on is the popular culture of the 1930s and 1940s. Unlike other Pop painters, Blake is always concerned to be a little out of date. His house is crammed with memorabilia – postcards, seaside souvenirs, toys, knick-knacks of every sort – and out of these is distilled a very personal poetry.

Richard Smith (b. 1931) represents an attitude which is almost the opposite to this. As a student, he painted in a figurative style which was influenced by the Euston Road School and the Kitchen Sink painters. He was still at the Royal College at the time of 'This Is Tomorrow', and on him, at least, the show had a demonstrable influence. During 1957–9 he shared a studio with Peter Blake, but in 1959 he left for America, and at first divided his time between England and the United States before settling there permanently. Smith's earliest characteristic works were based on packaging. He was also influenced by colour photography, the kind of thing to be found in magazines such as *Vogue*.

His colour sensibility remained unaltered through subsequent changes of direction. He himself describes his colour as 'sweet and tender', and speaks of wanting to give 'a general sense of blossoming, ripening, and shimmering', but the work itself has shed any overt association with Pop. What Smith has done is to pass through the experience of Pop art in order to arrive at a position which approximates to that of the American colour painters. His change to acrylic paint in 1964 was an important step in this process. So was his abandonment of conventional formats in favour of canvases stretched

112

111, 118

111 RICHARD SMITH *Soft Pack* 1963>

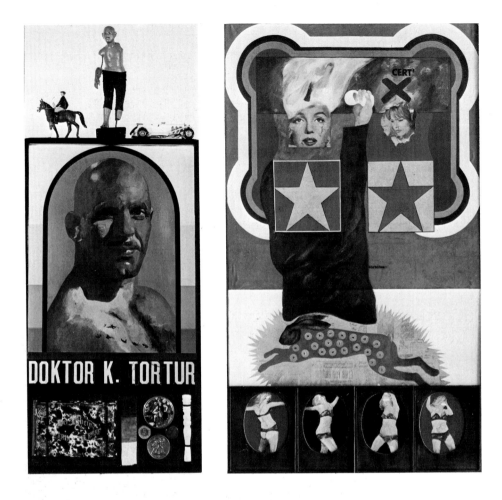

over three-dimensional frames, and his adoption, later, of shapes constructed like kites.

Smith, because he had successfully established himself in New York, meant a lot to his English colleagues, both as an example and as an influence. When he returned to England in 1961, he brought with him on-the-spot information about the activities of artists such as Jasper Johns which had an impact on artists such as Peter Phillips (b.1939) and Derek Boshier (b. 1937). Smith had already absorbed the American indifference to conventional limitations of format, and the American sense of scale, for example.

113
114

132

The key date in British Pop was 1961, not so much because of Smith's resumption of contact with British artists, but because of the Young Contemporaries exhibition which was held in that year. This caused perhaps the greatest sensation of any student show held since the war. The reason was the presence of a group of young artists from the Royal College of Art: Phillips, Boshier, Allen Jones (b. 1937), and David Hockney (b. 1937). Exhibiting with them was a slightly older American student, R. B. Kitaj (b. 1932) who, like Smith, had a first-hand knowledge of American techniques, and he fostered the new obsession with popular imagery among his fellow students.

One of the weaknesses of British Pop art was its easy and rapid success. England, so far as the visual arts were concerned, was at last moving out of its phase of insularity (in literature, insularity was to last much longer). The hedonism of the late 1950s had taken root, and the new artists seemed to offer precisely the gay, impudent, pleasure-

<112 PETER BLAKE
Doktor K. Tortur 1965

<113 PETER PHILLIPS
For Men Only Starring MM and BB 1961

114 DEREK BOSHIER
England's Glory 1961

centred art which fitted the mood of the times. But modern artists of any talent were still thin on the ground, and the young lions of Pop did not meet with much competition.

It soon became clear that the artists who were grouped together after their spectacular début at the Young Contemporaries were temperamentally very different. Phillips was the most genuinely interested in popular imagery, but used it in a rigid and boringly dogmatic way. Boshier came under the influence of Richard Smith and veered away from figurative imagery in the direction of Op art. More capricious and personal than either of these two were Hockney and Jones.

115,116,117   Hockney is an artist who has had an interesting if slightly erratic development. He began as the *Wunderkind* of British art. His life-style was instantly famous; his dyed blond hair, owlish glasses, and gold lamé jacket created – or contributed to – a persona which appealed even to people who were not vitally interested in painting. In this sense, he

115 DAVID HOCKNEY *Picture Emphasizing Stillness* 1962–3 (inscription: THEY ARE PERFECTLY SAFE, THIS IS A STILL)

116 DAVID HOCKNEY *A Neat Lawn* 1967

forms part of the general development of British culture which was symbolized by the sudden and enormous fame of the Beatles. But it was also clear that Hockney was precociously gifted. In his early work, he adopted a cartooning, *faux-naïf* style which owed a lot to children's drawings. Often these early pictures have a delightful deadpan irony.

Some of Hockney's most characteristic work at this time was to be found in his prints. The suite of etchings entitled *The Rake's Progress* chronicles his reactions to the dream-world of America, which he visited for the first time in 1961. They reflect profoundly ambiguous attitudes. The comment is often sharp – the *Bedlam scene*, for instance, shows a group of automata governed by the pocket transistor radios which have become part of their anatomy – but the overall tone of the series is one of avid enjoyment.

Soon, the precarious poise of these early works was threatened. Hockney's painting became increasingly dry, increasingly pre-occupied with naturalism. Some middle-period paintings of the Californian landscape have, it is true, become classics – American critics have compared them to Edward Hopper (1882–1967). Others are disconcertingly dull. Eventually Hockney found naturalism confining, and he made a series of paraphrases of classic modern art, paying especial attention to Picasso. At the same time he became increasingly pre-occupied with photography, made a large series of photo-collages, which he called Cameraworks, and through his photographic experiments which raised issues about the representation of space; later still he returned to quasi-abstract paintings where the viewer wanders in space.

Allen Jones, like Hockney, is an artist whose early work was captivating because it radiated an air of enjoyment not unspiced with satirical humour. The most 'painterly' of all the British Pop painters, he seems to have learned a great deal from Matisse where colour is concerned. There is also a debt to the Orphism of Robert Delaunay. Jones is a less narrative artist than Hockney: he is interest in metamorphoses, 122 transformations, visual ambiguities. A series of *Hermaphrodites* (male/female images melting into one another on the same canvas) seem particularly characteristic of his work. Jones has shown a particularly deft and ingenious fancy with shaped canvases: a series of paintings of *Marriage medals*, done in 1963, is made up of tall vertical canvases to which octagonal canvases are attached.

Jones resembles Hockney rather less happily because he too seems to have had trouble in deepening and developing his work. It has had a tendency to grow increasingly harder and more strident; the colour has left the comfortable 'fine art' tradition of the Fauves. This shows up the extreme thinness of content. The artist insists that the subject-matter of his work has always been of secondary interest to him, but one becomes more and more aware of its insistent banality, a banality that does not seem to have been adopted with any doctrinaire purpose in mind.

121 No one could accuse R. B. Kitaj's work of lack of complexity. The term 'Pop' has to be stretched rather far to cover his work. Kitaj is a hermetic artist; the best comparison is a literary one, in that his paintings are often rather like the *Cantos* of Ezra Pound. In them, one finds dense patterns of eclectic imagery. Often the painter requires that the spectator should try and match his own experience. The catalogue of one of Kitaj's exhibitions tends to pile footnote on footnote, in the

117 DAVID HOCKNEY *Rubber Ring Floating in a Swimming Pool* 1971

118 RICHARD SMITH *Tailspan* 1965

119 PATRICK CAULFIELD *Still-life with Red and White Pot* 1966

endeavour to explain the complexity of his source material. These sources are more likely to be *The Journal of the Warburg Institute* than a favourite comic strip. One's approach to Kitaj's work must be intellectual. He is a dedicated and increasingly excellent draughtsman, and a rather dry colourist. Because his painting is so nearly a form of literature, it sometimes seemed that his prints were more successful than his paintings, and in the 1960s and early 1970s a good deal of his production was graphics, mostly silk-screen prints which used this flexible medium with great ingenuity. From the 1970s his work deepened in meaning and allusion to autobiographical and Jewish themes in increasingly narrative paintings executed in a looser, expressive manner.

There are one or two other artists in Britain who have also been associated by critics with the Pop movement, though they stand a little

120 ANTHONY DONALDSON *Take Away No. 2* 1963>

apart from the rest. One is Anthony Donaldson (b. 1939), who uses Pop imagery – nude or near-nude girls – as components in pictures which are closer to 'hard edge' abstract painting than they are to Pop itself. This is because the girls are usually no more than silhouettes, and the silhouettes take their place among the other shapes in the composition. When the girls are omitted, the effect is still much the same. Another is Patrick Caulfield (b. 1936), who is a little younger than the other members of the 'Pop generation'. He did not leave the Royal College of Art until 1963. Caulfield is better described as a cliché painter than as a Pop painter. His characteristic subject is the department store reproduction, the kind of image that commonly appears in cheap prints, on plastic trays, or in the kits which invite the amateur to 'paint by numbers'. Every shape he uses, every object he depicts, is described by a hard unvaried line, which looks as if it has been printed rather than painted. The colour is equally without modulation. Caulfield is intent on exploring the relationship between fine art and mass culture, and particularly the debased ways of seeing which mass culture seems to encourage. He is thus not fully committed to the Pop ethos, but is, rather, a pitiless critic of it.

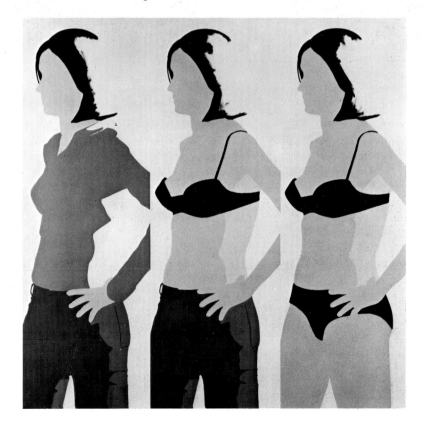

121 R.B. KITAJ *Synchromy with F.B. – General of Hot Desire (diptych)* 1968–9

Before moving on to discuss the American Pop artists, who are in several ways very different from their British counterparts, I must say something about a group of Australian artists who have a much greater relevance to the genesis of Pop art than is generally admitted. The success of contemporary Australian art in London in the years after the war was one of the phenomena of art-dealing. The spearhead of this success was Sidney Nolan (1917–92), and the pictures which created his reputation were a series devoted to the career of the Australian outlaw Ned Kelly. The earliest *Ned Kelly* paintings date from the 1940s, and thus antedate Pop by some years. In them, Nolan, who had been an abstract painter, established a new, *faux-naïf* style as a vehicle for a fairly sophisticated Australian nationalism.

123

140

122 ALLEN JONES *Hermaphrodite* 1963>

123 SIDNEY NOLAN *Glenrowan* 1956–7

Nationalism contributed to the sudden and overwhelming success of American Pop art. Americans found in it a truthful reflection of the society which surrounded them, and they also saw an assertion of the uniqueness of the American vision. It is not too much to claim that Pop led to the construction or reconstruction of American art-history, so as to make a larger place for artists such as Hopper, and even (further back) for painters like Frederick Edwin Church.

The American Pop artists were discovered and promoted by collectors and dealers. The critics and theorists lagged a long way behind these enthusiasts. Indeed, the American art establishment considered, and to some extent still seems to consider, the triumph of Pop art as a rejection of itself and of the direction it had chosen to encourage. A leading advocate of Abstract Expressionism, Harold Rosenberg, had this to say about the new direction:

> Certainly, Pop art earned the right to be called a movement through the number of its adherents, its imaginative pressure, the quantity

124 JIM DINE *Double Red Self-portrait (The Green Lines)* 1964>

of talk it generated. Yet if Abstract Expressionism had too much staying power, Pop was likely to have too little. Its congenital superficiality, while having the advantage of permitting the artist an almost limitless range of familiar subjects to exploit (anything from doilies to dining-club cards), resulted in a qualitative monotony that could cause interest in still another gag of this kind to vanish overnight. . . . Abstract Expressionism still excels in quality, significance and capacity to bring out new work; adding the production of its veterans to that of some of its younger artists it continues to be the front runner in the 'What next?' steeplechase.[6]

In effect, Pop art challenged Abstract Expressionism − or seemed to challenge it − in three different ways. It was figurative, where Abstract Expressionism was mostly abstract; it was 'newer' than Abstract Expressionism; and it was 'more American'.

The principal American Pop artists − Dine, Oldenburg, Rosenquist, Lichtenstein, and Warhol − differed fairly widely from one another. Jim Dine (b. 1935) and Claes Oldenburg (b. 1929) were the closest to the Neo-Dadaists whom I have already discussed. Dine, in particular, has two qualities which link him very closely to Rauschenberg and Johns: he is essentially a combine or assemblage painter, and his subject is the different varieties of reality. In a characteristic work by Dine, a

124

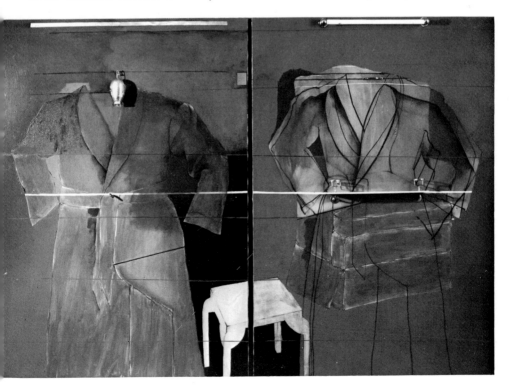

125 ROY LICHTENSTEIN
Whaam! 1963

126 CLAES OLDENBURG
Study for Giant Chocolate 1966

'ready-made' object or objects – an article of dress, a wash-basin, a shower, some tools – is fastened to canvas, and an environment is created for it with freely brushed paint. Often, whatever is presented is carefully labelled with its name.

Oldenburg, too, experimented with efforts of displacement. His objects hover between the realms of sculpture and painting. These objects range from such things as giant hamburgers to squashy models of wash-basins and egg-beaters. Often these things are made of vinyl stuffed with kapok. Oldenburg said: 126

> I use naïve imitation. This is not because I have no imagination or because I wish to say something about the everyday world. I imitate 1. objects and 2. created objects, for example, signs, objects made without the intention of making 'art' and which naïvely contain a functional contemporary magic. I try to carry these even further through my own naïveté, which is not artificial. Further, i.e. charge them more intensely, elaborate their reference. I do not try to make

'art' of them. This must be understood. I imitate these because I want people to get accustomed to recognizing the power of objects, a didactic aim.[7]

Therefore he, too, is interested in reality, with an element of totemism added.

James Rosenquist (b. 1933) and Roy Lichtenstein (b. 1923) differ from Dine and Oldenburg because to a large extent they accept the limitations of the flat surface, and because they are formalists. At the moment, it seems to be Lichtenstein who has been elevated to a status above the others. He is not as hostile to the word 'art' as Oldenburg is. He has said, for example, that 'organized perception is what art is all about'. He adds that the act of looking at a painting 'has nothing to do with any external form the painting takes, it has to do with a way of building a unified pattern of seeing'.

125 Lichtenstein's earlier work was based on comic strips, as in *Whaam!* and *Hopeless*; even the dots which are part of the process of cheap

128 ROY LICHTENSTEIN *Hopeless* 1963

colour printing are meticulously reproduced. The artist once said to
an interviewer:

> I think my work is different from comic strips – but I wouldn't call
> it transformation. . . . What I do is form, whereas the comic strip
> is not formed in the sense I'm using the word; the comics have
> shapes, but there has been no effort to make them intensely unified.

147

<127 ROY LICHTENSTEIN
Yellow and Red Brushstrokes 1966

129 TOM WESSELMANN
Still-life No. 34 1963

131 LARRY RIVERS>
Parts of the Face
1961

130 TOM WESSELMANN
Great American Nude No. 44
1963

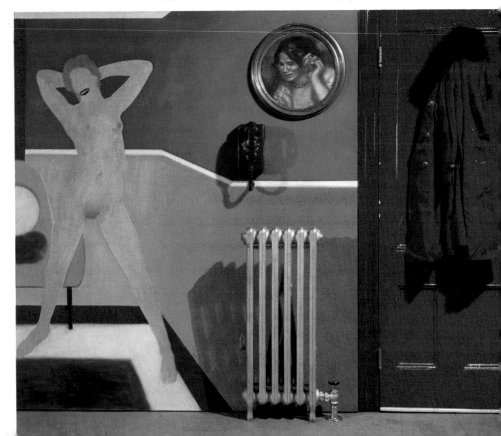

The purpose is different, one intends to depict and I intend to unify. And my work is actually different from comic strips in that every mark is really in a different place, however slight the difference seems to some.[8]

That is, the imagery is in part a strategy, a means of binding together the picture surface. Another aim can be seen most clearly in the series of *Brushstrokes*, e.g. *Yellow and Red Brushstrokes*: meticulous, frozen versions (in comic-strip technique) of the marks which an Abstract

127

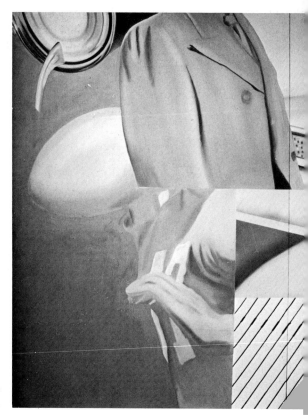

132 JAMES ROSENQUIST
Silver Skies 1962

Expressionist artist might have made with one sweep of the brush. The series is an experiment in 'removal': a word which crops up fairly often in Lichtenstein's discourse. It is also an attempt to make the audience question its own values.

This raises the question of the values put forward by the Pop artists themselves. One of the most characteristic and disturbing aspects of Pop art is the fact that, though figurative, it often seems unable to make use of the image observed at first hand. To be viable, its images must have been processed in some way. Rosenquist declared: 'I treat the billboard image as it is. I paint it as a reproduction of other things. I try to get as far away from it as posssible.'[9] His fragments of billboard imagery were rearranged into virtual abstractions, as in *Silver Skies*. Similarly, the still lifes and nudes of Tom Wesselmann (b. 1931), e.g. *Still-life No. 34* and *Great American Nude No. 44*, are assemblages, or collages of flat, found photographic images of consumer goods;

129, 130

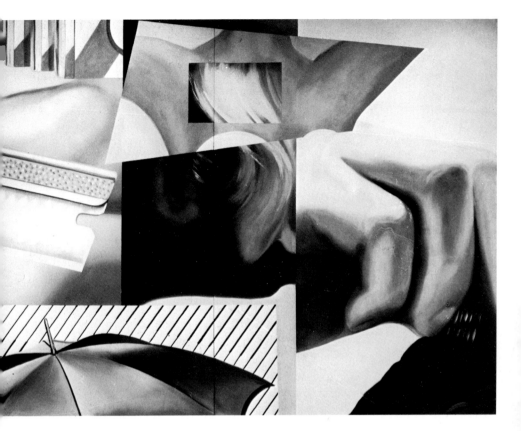

the faceless nudes are silhouettes from which the human presence
fades.

Larry Rivers (b. 1923) is an artist who may be thought of as 'near-
Pop'. Yet he paints in a way which might delight admirers of the
Impressionists, of Manet in particular. The imagery he uses sometimes
recalls Pop subjects, such as product packaging or the design of
banknotes. His rendering of such images, however, is always painterly,
not flat, not like a mechanical reproduction. And he also paints directly
from nature. Some of his paintings, such as *Parts of the Face*, are treated   131
as a vocabulary lesson – a female nude is carefully labelled with the
names of the parts of the body, in French, not in English. Other paintings are fragmented accounts of a particular experience, for example a
street accident. The outstanding visual characteristic of his work is a
kind of glancing obliqueness, as if the artist were unable to focus on
the actual subject for very long at a time.

George Segal (b. 1924) shows much the same helplessness when confronted with an objective reality. His sculptures are made, not by a process of modelling, but by making life-casts of the subjects, almost as if the artist didn't trust his own vision of them.

The most controversial, as well as the most famous, of all the American Pop artists is Andy Warhol (1928–87), whose activities go far beyond the conventional boundaries of painting: he made numerous films, he directed a night-club entertainment, the Velvet Underground, and the kind of notoriety he enjoyed was like that accorded to a famous actor or film star. When the first retrospective of Warhol's work was held, in Philadelphia in 1965, the crush at the private view was so great that some of the exhibits had to be removed, for fear of damage. It was clearly the artist himself, and not his products, whom the visitors wished to see.

Yet Warhol's attitudes towards the notion of 'personality' are ambiguous. On the one hand, he labelled the performers in his films 'super-stars', on the other hand he declared that he himself wanted to be a machine, something which made, not paintings, but industrial products. Samuel Adams Green, in his introduction to the catalogue of the Philadelphia exhibition, remarked of Warhol:

> His pictorial language consists of stereotypes. Not until our time has a culture known so many commodities which are absolutely impersonal, machine-made, and untouched by human hands. Warhol's art uses the visual strength and vitality which are the time-tested skills of the world of advertising that cares more for the container than the thing contained. Warhol accepts rather than questions our popular habits and heroes. By accepting their inevitability they are easier to deal with than if they are opposed. . . . We accept the glorified legend in preference to the actuality of our immediate experiences, so much so that the legend becomes commonplace and, finally, devoid of the very qualities which first interested us.[10]

In fact, more than most Pop artists, Warhol seemed concerned to anaesthetize our reaction to what is put in front of us. Many of his pictures have morbid associations: Mrs Kennedy after the assassination of her husband, Marilyn Monroe after her suicide, 'mug shots' of criminals, automobile accidents, the electric chair, gangster funerals, race riots. The images are repeated over and over again in photographic enlargements which are silk-screened on to canvas. The only modification is an overlay of crudely applied synthetic colour. The repetition and the colour are the instruments of a moral and aesthetic

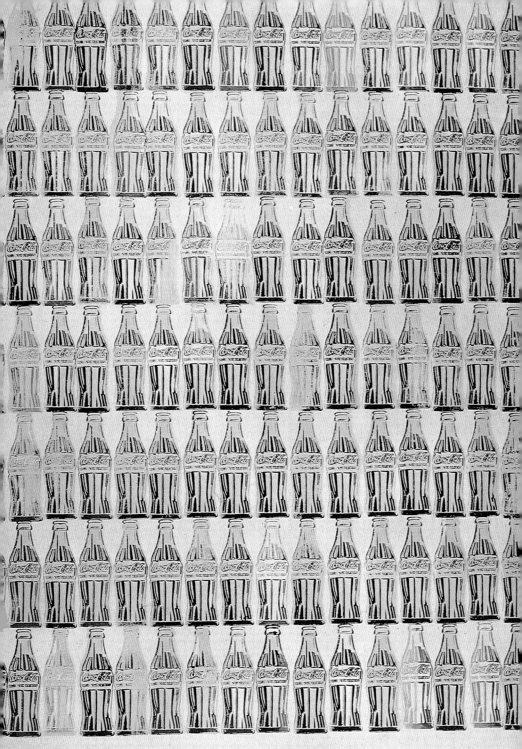

134 ANDY WARHOL *Race Riot* 1964

blankness which has been deliberately contrived. We are aware of
Warhol's narcissism when we look at his pictures, but even this scarcely
touches us. Frank O'Hara, the poet and art critic, once remarked that
much Pop art was essentially a 'put on', a poker-faced attempt to discover exactly how much the audience would swallow. Lichtenstein
also said, speaking of the beginnings of Pop in America, 'It was hard
to get a painting which was despicable enough so no one would hang
it – everyone was hanging everything.'[11] Warhol carried this attitude
to extremes, so that much of what he did was contemptuously private
and aristocratic. This appears in his obsessive concern with boredom,
for example. He made a film of a man sleeping – that and nothing else
– which lasts for more than six hours.

154

135 JIM DINE>
The Car Crash 1960

With the rise of Pop art, both the environment and the Happening took on a new and special importance. There were several reasons for this. One was that Pop specialized in the 'given'; this led artists to experiment with the literal reproduction of reality. Edward Kienholz's more ambitious works fall into this category. There was, too, the consuming interest taken by Pop artists in the phenomena of popular culture, among them such enfolding experiences as amusement arcades and side-shows in circuses: the 'Tunnel of Love', for example. Yayoi Kusama's (b. 1940) *Endless Love Room* of 1965–6 uses pure fair- 136 ground techniques, with a space bewilderingly enlarged by multiple mirrors.

136 YAYOI KUSAMA *Endless Love Room* 1965–6

135   The classic Pop art Happenings, such as Jim Dine's *The Car Crash* and Claes Oldenburg's *Store Days*, took place in environments specially constructed by the artists. The Happening involved the extension of an 'art' sensibility – or, more precisely, a 'collage-environment' sensibility – into a situation composed also of sounds, time-durations, gestures, sensations, even smells. Its roots remained in the artist's studio and not in the theatre. The spectator was not supplied with a matrix of plot and character; instead, he was bombarded with sensations which he had to order on his own responsibility. *The Car Crash* was a subjective reconstruction of the sensations produced by a traffic accident, and in this is comparable with the very different environmental piece by Beuys illustrated in Chapter One.

The events put on by Europeans differed from the American Happenings which preceded them in several ways. They were more abstract, less specific even than their predecessors. Much of their energy went into the exploration of extreme situations. Sometimes, indeed, the artists who took part in them seemed to engage in a desperate search for the unacceptable, for behaviour which would

156

137 CLAES OLDENBURG *Store Days* 1965

restore them to a position as rebels and enemies of society. At the same time there was less disposition to regard this kind of activity as a kind of art-world romp. For one event, the English artist Stuart Brisley (b. 1933) spent many hours almost motionless in a bath full of water and animal entrails. Even more extreme was the work done by various members of the Vienna Group in Austria – among them Hermann Nitsch (b. 1938), Otto Muehl, Gunter Brüs (b. 1938) and Rudolf Schwarzkogler (1941–69). Many of their events and actions were unbridled expressions of sado-masochistic fantasy. Nitsch claimed that he took upon himself 'the apparent negative, unsavoury, perverse, obscene, the passion and the hysteria of the act of sacrifice so that YOU are spared the sullying, shaming descent into the extreme.'[11]

But not all the work done in Europe was deadly serious. The Englishmen Gilbert and George (b. 1942) made their names with a

138 STUART BRISLEY
*And For Today –
Nothing* 1972

139 RUDOLF
SCHWARZKOGLER
Action, Vienna
May 1965

piece called *Singing Sculptures* in which the two participants, with gilded faces, stood on a plinth and mimed to the music-hall song 'Underneath the Arches'. The point was a concern with the idea of style and stylishness. Style was plucked from its context and examined as a separate entity. And, finally, the question of the division, or the lack of it, between the creator and what he creates was brought up. Gilbert and George described themselves as 'living sculptures', and there was more than an implication that everything they did was to be looked upon as art.

140 GILBERT AND
GEORGE
Singing Sculpture
1970

CHAPTER SIX

Abstract Sculpture, Minimal Art, Conceptual Art

During the 1960s radical changes took place in the development of contemporary sculpture. Concurrent with the creation of Pop objects by such artists as Claes Oldenburg, there was the rise to prominence of David Smith (1906–65), whose career as a sculptor in many ways paralleled that of Jackson Pollock in painting. Smith began his career as a painter, a close associate of Arshile Gorky and Willem de Kooning, who were to become leading Abstract Expressionists. He did not view his abandonment of painting for sculpture in the early 1930s as marking a sharp break in his career. Yet there is also a striking opposition between Smith's attitudes and those of the Abstract Expressionist painters. Pollock's work was an assertion of the rights of the individual, of the interior world of dream opposed to the exterior world of fact; the paintings themselves were a rejection of the mechanistic. Smith's mature work, on the contrary, could be the product only of a highly developed technological civilization. He relied heavily on industrial techniques, borrowing these from the metal sculptures of Picasso and Julio González, which he knew only from books and magazines, but adding an element of American industrial know-how. As the poet and critic Frank O'Hara said of him:

> From the start, Smith took the cue from the Spaniards to lead him towards the full utilisation of his factory skills as an American metalworker, especially in the aesthetic use of steel glorifying rather than disguising its practicality and durability as a material for heavy industry.[1]

By the end of World War II, Smith was already a respected artist in mid-career. In January 1946 there was a full-scale retrospective of his work, shared by the Willard and Buchholz galleries in New York. His originality became even more apparent, however, in the late 1950s, when his work became larger in scale and broke free of the conventions of contemporary American sculpture. The techniques he now adopted enabled him to work very rapidly and freely, even when using

161

<141 JOHN McCRACKEN *There's No Reason Not To* 1967

massive forms and heavy materials such as steel. In 1962, he was invited by the organizers of the Spoleto Festival to spend a month in Italy, and was offered an old factory as a workshop. He made twenty-six sculptures in thirty days, many of them gigantic. He was one of the first sculptors to think not in terms of individual works but of the permutations of a single idea in a series, until the artist felt that it had been taken far enough. Initially, he still made references to the human figure, as in the *Agricola* and *Tank Totem* series of the 1950s. Later, he moved towards a more completely abstract style, in the series he labelled *Zig* (1961–4) and *Cubi* (1962–5). The *Cubi* series, in particular, has an unstable, dynamic quality which characterizes Smith's most accomplished work.

Smith was a revolutionary artist in a number of ways. His work, despite its massive scale, has a lack of sculptural density which can seem disconcerting, wth basic shapes taken ready-made from industrial forms, placed in seemingly provisional arrangements. One sculpture, seen in isolation, is usually less effective than several from the same series, viewed together or in sequence. The fact that Smith sometimes painted his work, or at other times gave it a rough polish, the raw glitter of metal which is only part of the way through the process of manufacture, reinforces these reactions. Like the Post-painterly abstractionist painters of the 1960s, Smith tended to eschew associations; in this he is very different from a sculptor such as Moore, who seems to want to summon up the powers of nature – rocks, water and wind – to help him in his task. All of these procedures and preferences were to be influential upon younger men.

The only other sculptor to enjoy anything like Smith's international prestige and influence in the 1960s and early 1970s was the British Anthony Caro (b. 1924), who made similar use of ready-made steel parts – I-beams, sheet-steel, pieces of coarse metal mesh – assembled in sprawling compositions. His welding together of industrial elements, the original identity of which remained intact, followed on from the assemblages made by artists in the 1950s, but now treated in a more purely abstract way. Caro said, in an interview with Andrew Forge in 1966:

> I would really rather make my sculpture out of 'stuff' – out of something really anonymous, just sheets maybe, which you cut a bit off . . . Much of the sculpture that I'm doing is about extent, and might even get to be about fluidity or something of this sort, and I think one has to hold it from becoming just amorphous.[2]

142 DAVID SMITH *Cubi XVII* 1964

From this statement, and from the appearance of the work itself, it is clear that Caro did not share Smith's sculptural preoccupations, despite the debt he owed to him. To take the most obvious difference first: Caro's work of the 1960s usually has a horizontal emphasis, as opposed to the verticality of most of Smith's late sculpture. Caro's sculptures could be described as being both space-devouring and ground-devouring. The traditional base has been abolished, and each piece has taken possession of a certain territory and modifies the spectator's reactions to the surrounding space. While Smith preferred to have his work shown in the open air, Caro, on the contrary, favoured enclosed spaces that could be occupied and activated by the sculpture.

At the time when they were made, Smith's late sculptures, and contemporaneous and slightly later ones by Caro, seemed to indicate the main line of sculptural development for the future. This, however, did not prove to be the case, and it is perhaps significant that Caro, in work made in the 1980s and early 1990s, has more and more tended to revert to traditional techniques, such as bronze-casting, and to the incorporation of figurative references, as in a recent series, *The Trojan War* (1993–4), devoted to the personages and events of Homer's *Iliad*. The series consists of semi-abstract representations of the Olympian Gods (*Athene*, *Aphrodite*, *Apollo*), of Greek and Trojan actors in the story (*Ajax*, *Hector*, *Paris*, *Helen*), of groups of people (*The Achaians*), and even of landscape (*Mount Ida*). The materials are ceramic, bronze and wood as well as steel, and the organic forms look back to the sculpture of the early 1950s – to early sculptures by Eduardo Paolozzi or even by the French sculptor César (b. 1921).

There are, nevertheless, features significant for the future in the work of both men, and in that of Caro in particular. For instance, though both were still interested in creating complex forms, these forms were often composed of very simple industrial units. Both, but Caro in particular, tended to abolish the bases traditional with sculpture, and to turn each piece into another object added to a pre-existing world of objects. Caro, too, tended, during the 1960s and 1970s, to 'dematerialize' his sculptures by choosing to paint them a unifying and often tonally ambiguous colour, one which heightens our uncertainty about the object's visual weight.

Neither sculptor, however, is the primary source of the radical changes which were to overtake sculpture, and with it all of avant-garde art, in the course of the 1960s and 1970s. The development of Pop art was paralleled by continuing radical changes in the realm of abstraction. At the height of Pop art's popularity, commentators were

143 ANTHONY CARO *Sun-feast* 1969–70

inclined to oppose it to a phenomenon which they labelled Op art –
that is, to a kind of abstraction, operating in both two-dimensional and
three-dimensional form, which relied on optical and kinetic effects.
What the viewer saw, when confronted with works of this kind, was
either something which relied on the physiological reactions of the eye
– the mechanism of seeing – to contrasts of hue and tone which produced an illusion of motion; or else objects which actually made use
of real motion. Both of these ways of working had deep roots in the
history of modernism. Their real originators were the Russian
Constructivists, such as Aleksandr Rodchenko, who made a series of
suspended *Spatial Constructions*, based on the forms of armillary
spheres, in 1920–21; and artists who had been associated with the
Bauhaus, such as Moholy-Nagy (*Light-Space Modulator*, 1921–30; a
Kinetic Sculpture using glass rods filled with mercury, 1930–36).

If post-war optical painting is to be traced back to a single source,
that source is unquestionably Victor Vasarely (b. 1908), who had
studied in 1928–9 at the Mühely Academy (the Budapest offshoot of
the Bauhaus, directed by Alexander Bortnyik), and who then settled

in France. Characteristically, Vasarely remarked that it was during this period at the Budapest Bauhaus that 'the functional character of plasticity' was first revealed to him. Kineticism was important to Vasarely for two reasons, one personal – the fact that the idea of movement had haunted him from his childhood; the other the more general idea that a painting which lives through optical effects exists essentially in the eye and mind of the spectator, not merely on the wall. Vasarely concerned himself with paintings, with works composed in separate planes, and with screens and three-dimensional objects. Static works rely for their kineticism on the action of light and on well-known optical phenomena, such as the tendency of the eye to produce after-images, when confronted with very brilliant contrasts of black and white, as in *Metagalaxy*, or the juxtaposition of certain hues. The

144 VICTOR VASARELY *Metagalaxy* 1959

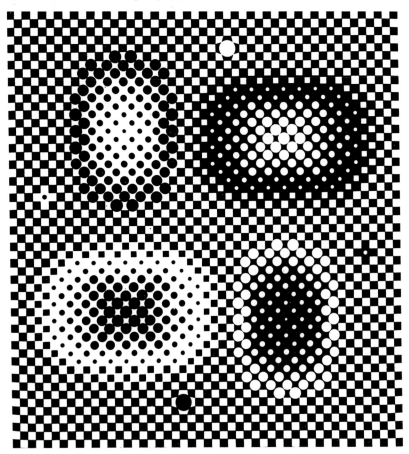

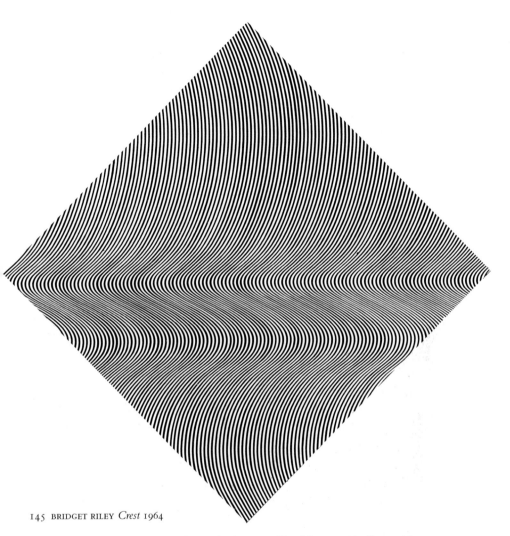

145 BRIDGET RILEY *Crest* 1964

completion of the painting through the act of looking was in line with the view taken earlier in the century by Duchamp concerning the interdependence of the object and the spectator within the framework of the creative act, and foreshadowed what came to be called Conceptual art. Vasarely's chief rival for dominance in this field is the British artist Bridget Riley (b. 1931). Her black-and-white painting *Crest* is typical of her earlier work. A much less austere, more deeply instinctive artist than Vasarely, her work often seems to attempt to render natural forces, in this case the flow of water, without making specific landscape references. Her development has led her through austere black-and-white, through muted grey and pastel hues, to her current interest in brilliant colour.

Three-dimensional kinetic art objects made a wider range of choices available to the artist. They could either, as did optical painting, remain static, while relying on the action of light and on well-known optical phenomena to produce an illusion of movement, or they could actually move, with or without the aid of mechanical power. 'Mobiles', which move at random, without mechanical aid, were essentially the invention of two men – first made by the Russian Constructivist Aleksandr Rodchenko, they were then, after a lapse of some years, re-invented and perfected by the American Alexander Calder. Mechanically-powered art objects can be traced back to Duchamp (who made use of a gramophone turntable), and to another Russian Constructivist, Naum Gabo.

The revival of objects of this type was largely the work of Latin American artists, among them the Argentinian members of the Madí Group, founded in Buenos Aires in 1944, and Venezuelans such as Carlos Cruz-Diez and Jesús Rafael Soto. The political situation in Venezuela, then under the Pérez Soto dictatorship, brought the Venezuelans in particular to Europe, and these experiments, made in Latin America in the 1940s and 1950s, at a time when Constructivism was out of favour in Europe and the United States, became widely influential in the 1960s. The 'physichromies' of Carlos Cruz-Diez (b. 1923), such as *Physichromie No. 1*, are works in very slight relief. Often this extra dimension is used to provide planes of colour which move as the spectator shifts his position in relation to them.

147

A more important artist who sometimes made use of effects of somewhat the same kind is Jesús Rafael Soto (b. 1923). Soto's original influences were Mondrian and Malevich. In the early 1950s he made paintings which created their effect by repetition of units. The units were so disposed that the rhythm which linked them came to seem more important to the eye than any individual part, and the painting was therefore, by implication at any rate, not something complete in itself, but a part taken from an infinitely large fabric which the spectator was asked to imagine. Soto then became interested in effects of superimposition, just as Vasarely did. Two patterns painted on perspex sheets were mounted very slightly apart, and seemed to blend together in a new space which hovered between the front and back planes supplied by the sheets. Later, Soto began a series of experiments with lined screens. These had metal plaques which projected in front of

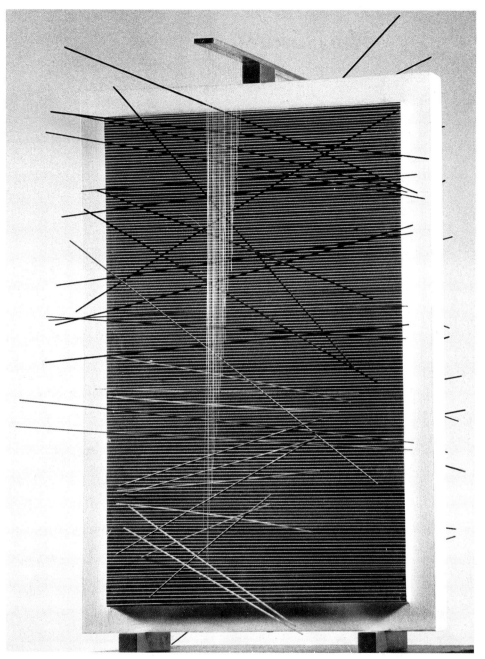

146 JESUS RAFAEL SOTO *Petite Double Face* 1967

147 CARLOS CRUZ-DIEZ *Physichromie No. 1* 1959

146 them, or else metal rods or wires are freely suspended before this vibrating ground, such as *Petite Double Face*. The vibration tends, from the optical point of view, to swallow up and dissolve the projecting or suspended solids. Each instant, as the spectator moves his eyes, a new wave of optical activity is set up. The most intense of all Soto's works are large screens of hanging rods. Hung along the length of a wall, these layers of rods seem to dissolve the whole side of a room, calling into question all the spectator's instinctive reactions to an enclosed space.

Because Op art is so commonly treated as a completely closed, self-contained phenomenon, little has been made of its possible relationship to other developments in the abstract art of the period. Essentially, these developments were the two related phenomena which came to be labelled Minimal and Conceptual art.

Minimal art once again can be traced to the experiments made by the Russian artists of the early Revolutionary period – to the work of the Constructivists, and even more precisely to the Suprematism of Malevich, most notably to paintings such as his *White on White* of 1917. These experiments were taken up again in the 1950s and early 1960s – by the young Robert Rauschenberg, with a series of all-white canvases, made when he was at Black Mountain College in the early 1950s; by Ad Reinhardt, most radically in paintings of 1960–66 producing an all black effect through a subtle layering of dark colours; and in Europe by Yves Klein (1928–62) with completely monochrome works in IKB (International Klein Blue), and by Piero Manzoni (1933–63) in his series of *Achromes*. Other painters working in minimal or near minimal ways included Robert Ryman (b. 1930), who experimented both with unstretched canvases and with baked enamel on copper, and Agnes Martin (b. 1912), who used almost invisible grids on monochrome grounds.

In the United States, Minimalism made its greatest impact, and established itself as a major new art phenomenon, through the activity of artists working in three dimensions rather than in two. A kind of transitional stage, with Minimal overtones but still some relationship to the work of David Smith, is represented by the work of Richard Serra (b. 1939). Serra's weighty leaning pieces of 1968–71 have a dynamic quality which derives from their apparent physical instability. They are also often asymmetrical in form. His outdoor sculptures, notably the notorious *Tilted Arc* (1989), have been a focus of controversy because the public found them threatening. There is a suppressed element of Expressionism in much of Serra's work which makes it untypical of Minimal art taken as a whole. The main line of descent in American Minimalism must be looked for elsewhere. The architect-turned-sculptor Tony Smith (b. 1912), who had been an apprentice of Frank Lloyd Wright, was one of the first to make an impact. He gave up architecture for sculpture because he felt that buildings were too impermanent and vulnerable to alterations contrary to their creators' intentions. His sculptures have been described in an oversimplified way as examples of the 'single unit Gestalt' which came to be thought of as typical of Minimal art, but the artist himself spoke of some of them as:

> Part of a continuous space grid. In the latter voids are made up of the same components as the masses. In this sense they may be seen as interruptions in an otherwise unbroken flow of space. If you think of space as solid, they are voids in that space. While I hope they have form and presence, I don't think of them as being objects

148 TONY SMITH *Playground* 1962

among other objects; I think of them as being isolated in their own environments.[3]

Much of Smith's work seems to reflect his experience of architecture. He said of one piece, called *Playground* (1962): 'I like shapes of this kind; they remind me of the shapes of ancient buildings made with mudbrick walls.' Characteristically, many of the sculptures consist of rectangular boxes fitted together; sometimes this is varied by using tetrahedrons. One, called *The Black Box* (1962), was suggested by a box for index cards which the artist saw on a friend's desk. Seen one night, the shape became an obsession, so Smith telephoned his friend the next morning and asked for the dimensions.

I asked him to take his ruler and measure the box. He was so out of it that he didn't even enquire about why I wanted to know the size. I multiplied the dimensions by five, made a drawing, took it to the Industrial Welding Co. in Newark, and asked them to make it up.[4]

Obviously, there is in this a strong element of the Conceptual as well as of the Minimal. The sculpture existed notionally as a set of measurements written down on paper, before it is given material form by the fabricator whom the artist employed to make the object to his specification. There is, in addition, a concentration on the deliberately inexpressive, which is not present in the work of Tony Smith's namesake David, nor in that of Caro. These two characteristics indicated the direction that the new American sculpture more and more tended to take.

Minimal art was not simply a question of the activity of one artist, but of a whole school of artists, among them Carl Andre (b. 1935), Dan Flavin (b. 1933), Robert Morris (b. 1931), Sol LeWitt (b. 1923) and John McCracken (b. 1934). One of the most articulate of these artists was Donald Judd (1928–94), who spoke of his practice thus:

141

> Three dimensions are real space. That gets rid of the problem of illusionism and of literal space, space in and around marks and colours – which is one of the most salient and objectionable relics of European art. The several limits of painting are no longer present. A work can be as powerful as it is thought to be. Actual space is intrinsically more powerful and specific than paint on a flat surface.[5]

149 ROBERT MORRIS *Untitled (circular light piece)* 1966

Judd's interpretation of this credo was less liberal than the words themselves might lead one to suppose: a string of galvanized iron boxes strung out at regular intervals across a wall.

Judd's colleague, Robert Morris, defended Minimal art in equally emphatic terms:

> Simplicity of shape does not necessarily equate with simplicity of experience. Unitary forms do not reduce relationships. They order them. If the predominant, hieratic nature of the unitary form functions as a constant, all those particularising relations of scale, proportion, etc., are not thereby cancelled. Rather they are bound more cohesively and individually together.[6]

These justifications are in some ways beside the point, because it became increasingly clear that the Minimal artist did not really wish to express himself, or express some meaning, in the old way. There was, it is true, a sense of *ordering*, which often took the form proposed by Tony Smith: the artists provided a partial image of a complete order throughout all the space which could be imagined, and left the spectator to fill in the rest, in his or her imagination.

This is exactly what happens, for example, in much of the work of Sol LeWitt. In April 1968 LeWitt had an exhibition in New York which consisted of a single sculpture, descriptively entitled *46 Three-part Variations on Three Different Kinds of Cubes*. The cubes were boxes of standard size. Some were closed, some open on one side only, some open on two facing sides. These were piled together in groups of three. The cubes were regularly aligned in stacks, and the stacks regularly aligned with one another. Each of the eight rows set out the possible solutions in a fixed order of permutation, beginning with a row which established all the possible permutations when each stack contained just one of each of the three kinds of cubes.

Another form of Minimal art relies not on placing unitary objects within a space, but on the alteration of the space itself. One of the best-known examples is the work of the Frenchman Daniel Buren (b. 1938), who makes use of patterns of stripes to emphasize the character of a room or a set of rooms, or to alter the visitor's perception of their character. Thus Buren's installation *On Two Levels with Two Colours*, made for the Lisson Gallery, London, in 1976, emphasizes the irregularity of the spaces available, and their slightly unexpected relationship (due to the fact that they formed part of two adjacent converted buildings with floors on slightly different levels), by providing them with striped skirtings in contrasting hues.

151

150 DONALD
JUDD
Untitled 1965

151 DANIEL BUREN
*On Two Levels with
Two Colours* 1976

152 DAN FLAVIN
*Untitled (to the
'Innovator'
Wheeling
Beachblow)* 1968

153 LARRY BELL *Untitled* 1971

Some Minimal art is less dour – and perhaps also less naïve. Dan
Flavin's work, for instance, makes use of straight lengths of fluorescent
tubing, and is the point at which Minimalism meets Kinetic art. Flavin
regards not only light, but space, as his material, and in this sense his
work is related to that of Buren. 'I knew,' he says, 'that the actual space
of a room could be broken down and played with by planting illusions
of real light [electric light] at crucial junctures in the room's composition.'[7] His *Untitled (to the 'Innovator' Wheeling Beachblow)* of 1968 is an
example of this. A framework of fluorescent tubes, pink, old, and 'day-
light', are set in a corner of the gallery space. Some of the tubes are
shielded, and reflect light back on the adjacent walls; others are bare.
The space is washed with different hues, which alter the visitor's perception of the space he or she stands in.

Taking Flavin's art as a point of reference, it is possible to look in
several directions. One direction points towards the California artists
of the so-called 'Light and Space' group, one of whose members is
Larry Bell (b. 1939), who has made glass cubes and also larger sculptures consisting of coated glass sheets placed at right angles. The coat-
ings used are the product of the California aerospace industry. The

177

154 ERIC ORR *Prime Matter* 1990

specially treated glass both reflects the spectator and allows him or her to see what is beyond, revealing and concealing reality in unexpected ways. The art object is not the cube itself, or the glass screen, but fleeting effects of reflection and transparency. An example of this was the untitled installation Bell exhibited at the Hayward Gallery, London, in 1971. Basically, this consisted of a number of large sheets of glass placed in pairs, at right angles to one another, together creating a labyrinth though which the visitor was invited to wander. The installation was animated, and at the same time made mysterious, by other visitors in the space, reflected or concealed by the coated glass.

153

178

Other artists of the same group, such as Robert Irwin (b. 1928) and Eric Orr (b. 1939), made works where the effect of dematerialization was almost complete, and the spectator's perceptions were manipulated by the subtle use of light. One of the most ambitious practitioners of this genre is James Turrell (b. 1943), best known for his on-going *Roden Crater* project, which involves the excavation and alteration of an extinct volcano at Sedona in the Arizona desert. Work on this started in 1972 and is still in progress. Turrell's aim is to create a series of experiences which, while relying on well-known optical phenomena, have a quasi-mystical impact on the viewer. For example, the crater, while retaining its outward appearance intact, is being excavated in such a way as to turn it into a giant camera obscura, which will throw the image of the moon or the sun on to the walls of an underground chamber.

Turrell has created similar, if less ambitious light effects by making installations in museums and commercial galleries – for example, a series of rooms (entitled *Light Spaces*), each filled with a different colour of light, made for the Stedelijk Museum in Amsterdam in 1976. Later, for example at the Venice Biennale of 1988, he devised enclosed

155 JAMES TURRELL *Roden Crater,* work in progress, conceived 1974

156 ROBERT SMITHSON *Spiral Jetty* 1970

spaces divided by an illusory diagonal plane – a shimmering wall which seems solid until the spectator walks up to it and tries to touch it.

Turrell's work, while bordering on the mystical and reliant on the action of light, also has links with the form of expression which has been labelled Earth art. Much of this is Minimal art executed on a gigantic scale. The best-known example is Robert Smithson's (1928–73) *Spiral Jetty* of 1970 – a giant spiral structure of stones and earth projecting from the shore of the Great Salt Lake in Utah. The remote location, and the fact that the lake itself has now risen to swallow up the structure, means that the piece, for all its gigantism, is in fact known almost entirely through the photographic documentation made of it when it was new.

A similar situation exists with many other examples of Earth art, either created on distant sites, or deliberately ephemeral, or both. Some of the better-known artists in this field are British, and their

157 RICHARD LONG>
A Line in Ireland 1974

work can perhaps be seen as an extension of the tradition of Romantic landscape which has played such an important role in the history of British art. Richard Long's (b. 1945) work consists of a range of activities, including direct interventions in the landscape, often on remote sites, and installations such as stone circles, made in galleries using material found in a particular location; like another British artist, Hamish Fulton (b. 1946), he also uses photographs, diagrams and/or

written texts to document his movement through a particular tract of country. Andy Goldsworthy (b. 1956) works in a related fashion, piling up a cairn of loose stones, or covering a rock in a stream with a blanket of leaves of a particular colour, and then photographing the result. In each case, it is the pattern of activity which counts, far more than the actual physical result.

Long's work in particular, since it can consist simply of a diagram or a map, or even of a simple written statement, has as many links with what has been called Conceptual art as it does with Minimalism. Conceptual art is a form of expression which tries to abolish the physical as completely as possible, and which aims to bypass optical stimulation in favour of intellectual processes which the audience is invited to share with the artist. That is, it is essentially an art of mental patterns, embodied by any means which the maker sees fit to employ. Like Minimal art, it first made its appearance in the second half of the 1960s. A classic early example is Joseph Kosuth's (b. 1945) *One and Three Chairs* of 1965. It consists of a wooden folding chair, a photograph of a chair, and the photographic enlargement of the dictionary definition

<158 ANDY GOLDSWORTHY *Tree Cairn* June 1994

159 JOSEPH KOSUTH *One and Three Chairs* 1965

of a chair. The artist asks his audience in which of these three the true identity of the object is to be found – in the thing itself, the representation, or the verbal description? Can it be discovered in one, some, all, or in the end none of them?

Sometimes, paradoxically, Conceptual art became totally physical – an idea expressed in the most literal sense through flesh and blood. Dennis Oppenheim's (b. 1938) *Reading Position* of 1970 consists of two photographs which record the effects of sunburn on the artist's own torso – part of it sheltered by an open book, and part left exposed. This

160 DENNIS OPPENHEIM *Reading Position for Second Degree Burn* 1970

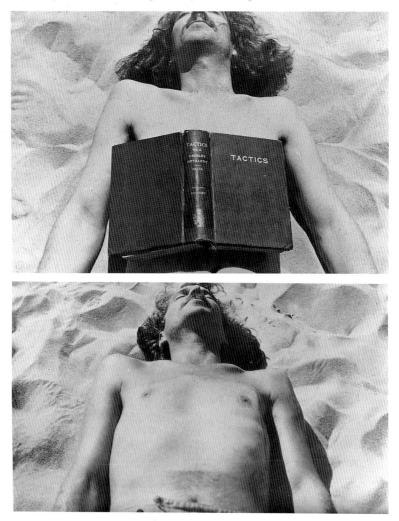

161 JENNY HOLZER *The Survival Series: Protect Me From What I Want* 1985–6

kind of expression is often classified as body art or performance art. To create his piece Oppenheim had to do something at least mildly painful. Masochism is a frequent characteristic of body art – something it shares with the post-pop 'actions' or Happenings of such artists as Stuart Brisley (b. 1933) or the Austrian Rudolph Schwarzkogler (b. 1941). The idea of artistic dematerialization here comes full circle, and is linked to physical actions and gestures which in turn are often yoked to the old Romantic notion of art as an expression of personal suffering or sacrifice. When this happened it was difficult to say that the art so created remained 'subjectless'. Its subject is the artist – his or her relationship to both the idea of making art and the idea of society.

Because its basic material was ideas – and also language – Conceptual art experienced a strong revival at the end of the 1980s, when the attention of the avant-garde art world turned to issue and

162 BARBARA KRUGER
*Untitled (Your Gaze Hits
the Side of my Face)* 1981

161   content based work. The activity of Jenny Holzer (b. 1950) spans both periods. Her *Truisms*, which owe something to the text-based work of Lawrence Weiner (b. 1942), date from the end of the 1970s; her work with light-emitting diodes (as seen at the Venice Biennale of 1990) is a further elaboration typical of the late 1980s. Holzer's work, with its often feminist content, is related to that of Barbara Kruger (b. 1945) whose photomontages also rely heavily on language rather than visual imagery for their effect.

CHAPTER SEVEN

Arte Povera, Post-Minimalism and their Heritage

While art which embraced Minimalism in the 1960s and 1970s often claimed to be totally purified from subject-matter, just as it was purified from the demands of complex form, it did in fact usually have a recognizable if partly hidden agenda. The basic assertion made by every Minimal artwork was that the business of art was with art itself – art for art's sake. Other considerations were rigorously excluded, in spite of the fact that the references were often to everyday objects and activities. In a paradoxical way, this exclusion could be perceived as being in its own way a recognizable theme or subject. Conceptual art, too, grew out of aesthetics, and, as with Minimal art, declared its status as art in relation to its context in the museum setting. Joseph Kosuth's examination of the relationship between the object itself, a representation of the object, and a written description of the same object, as presented in *One and Three Chairs*, can be seen as a practical demonstration of one aspect of what was an aesthetic or philosophical impulse. Yet, simply because its materials were ideas, and the words which embodied these ideas, an art of concepts nevertheless found it difficult to remain within the strict boundaries which were set for it by its original inventors. Thus, if one takes a second look at the work of artists such as Long and Goldsworthy, one sees that it does, in fact, have a definable subject-matter which reaches beyond the boundaries of the world of art, and that this subject is the relationship between man and nature.

159

The conflict between subject and not-subject is one of the major topics in the work of one of the most influential American artists of the 1970s and 1980s, Bruce Nauman (b. 1941). Nauman's neon pieces, which are some of his most typical works, are a kind of hybrid: a compromise between Conceptual and Pop impulses. *Life Death/Knows Doesn't Know* (1983) uses a technique familiar from advertising signs to pose a universal question which reaches well beyond any narrowly aesthetic framework. Nauman's work in this vein provided themes for a number of other artists, chief among them Jenny Holzer, with her

163

elaborate installation pieces using light-emitting diodes which formed phrases and sentences: an example, like Nauman working in this way, of advertising technology moving across into the territory of high art.

Another important aspect of Nauman's work is its extreme variety of means. Unlike the work of Pop painters like Warhol, or even that of Minimal sculptors such as Judd, Nauman's work possesses no immediately recognizable stylistic or even physical identity, not even one created by a particular and characteristic choice of materials. Each piece exists as an independent entity. In this Nauman resembles an earlier artist of major stature, Marcel Duchamp. Yet Nauman differs from Duchamp, and indeed from members of the Dada movement, such as Francis Picabia, because his work, though sometimes ironic, is not inherently negative. What it represents is not the violent rejection of all previous art, but a questioning of the stylistic straightjacket which had remained a salient characteristics of much Pop art and Minimalism, though in the Pop artists' widespread stylistic borrowings one can witness the birth of attitudes now termed 'postmodern'. Despite Pop's apparently greater variety, however, it had much in common with Minimalism, notably a 'hands off' look and the use of certain formal devices (the grid, repetition, box forms). There was also a common reference to industrial production.

Scepticism about style as an end in itself became apparent in Europe at the beginning of the 1970s, with the appearance of Arte Povera. This took its name from an exhibition organized in 1970 by the Italian critic Germano Celant. Celant characterized the kind of art he selected for the show as being anti-formal, private, elusive, and interested in the essential nature of the materials used.

There was, however, more to it than simply this. The originators of Arte Povera saw it as being as much the child of American Pop art as it was that of the Minimal and Conceptual influences which were the contemporaries and rivals of Pop. The Italian critic Marco Meneguzzo notes that Pop art was read, in Europe, as something which had 'a direct contact with the social'.[1] That is, art was endowed with a new moral and political significance: 'The new subject [was] no longer only the artist, but who brings life into being, who retrieves the militant "poverty" of art vis-à-vis an opulent and alienating society.'[2] There was, as he points out, a repudiation of the sanctity of the object and a feeling of alienation which was strengthened by the rebellious anarchist upheavals which swept Europe in 1968 and 1969. Treating Arte Povera, as its name suggests, as being primarily an Italian rather than a totally pan-European phenomenon, he notes that it was significant

163 BRUCE NAUMAN *Life Death/Knows Doesn't Know* 1983

that its main centres were Turin and Rome. Turin, one of the chief industrial cities in Italy, was, at the end of the 1960s and the beginning of the 1970s, the theatre of violent social conflict. Rome, the capital, was less tense, but here the artists had constantly before their eyes the example of the Baroque with its promiscuous intermingling of forms and materials and its refusal to make firm distinctions between artistic genres.

Celant, in a history of the Arte Povera movement published in 1985, notes that it was this complex, heterogeneous quality which tended to upset American observers. He cites the attacks on European 'complexity' which were being launched as early as 1964 by artists such as Frank Stella (then still in a Minimalist phase) and Donald Judd. For supporters of American Minimalism, the new European art seemed muddled and compromised. Celant retorts: 'In reality one has the affirmation of artistic variety and relativism, and of the wonder and

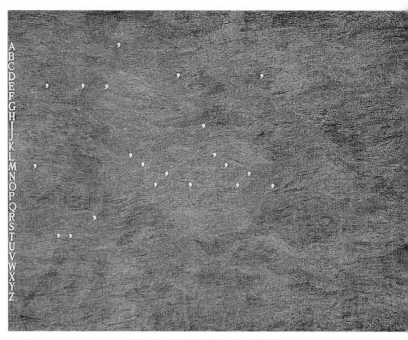

164 ALIGHIERO E. BOETTI *Bringing the World into the World* 1973–9

coherence of the incoherent, where what counts is the overflowing sense of fusion and metamorphosis with history.'[3]

Among the artists closely associated with various phases of the Arte Povera movement were Giovanni Anselmo (b. 1934), Alighiero E. Boetti (1940–93), Luciano Fabro (b. 1936), Jannis Kounellis (b. 1936), Mario Merz (b. 1925), Giuseppe Penone (b. 1947) and Giulio Paolini (b. 1940). Each of these interpreted the already vague credo of the movement in his own way. Anselmo and Penone make installations in which rough or 'poor' materials are used to evoke the poetry of nature. Kounellis's work often has a darker, more deliberately industrial tone, but he also makes use of 'natural' elements, including live animals and birds. One of his most famous early pieces was a work staged at the Galleria l'Attico in Rome, in 1969. In this twelve live horses were tethered to the walls (*Untitled*, 1969). Kounellis saw in this both a conjunction between the formal (the horses spaced at regular intervals) and the completely unpredictable (the actual movement of the animals) and a way of turning the work into a complete sensuous experience, which

167

190

165 GIUSEPPE PENONE *Breath* 1978>

166 LUCIANO FABRO *Golden Italy* 1971>

167 JANNIS KOUNELLIS
*Work Incorporating Classical
Fragments*

168 GIULIO PAOLINI>
Apotheosis of Homer 1970–1

169 MARIO MERZ>
610 Function of 15 1971–1989

appealed to the spectator's hearing, touch and sense of smell, as well
as to the sense of sight. Working in a somewhat similar fashion, Paolini
alludes both to Greek myths and to modern interpretations of them.
Merz has produced a long series of works which are variations on the
theme of Fibonnacci's series – a sequence of numbers in which each
number is the sum of the previous two. Fibonacci, otherwise known
as Leonardo of Pisa, was an Italian mathematician of the thirteenth
century, who is said to have anticipated a number of the scientific and
mathematical discoveries usually attributed to the Renaissance.

The link between the work of the Arte Povera group and that of
Joseph Beuys, made of similarly 'poor' or humble materials, is often
noted. Less commonly noticed is their link to the British sculptors of
the 1970s and 1980s, such as Tony Cragg (b. 1949), Richard Deacon
(b. 1949), Richard Wentworth (b. 1947), Bill Woodrow (b. 1948) and
Anish Kapoor (b. 1954). The link is the more interesting because Arte
Povera, despite a considerable success within Europe, and eventual
acceptance in the United States,did not seem to make much impact in
the British Isles. There are similarities between artists like Anselmo and

170 TONY CRAGG
African Culture Myth 1984

Penone and the work of British Land art sculptors such as Long and
Goldsworthy, but these have often been ignored on the grounds that
Arte Povera, for all its improvised quality, remained an essentially
gallery-based art – where it alludes to nature, this continues to be seen
within an essentially Claude-like framework, poeticized, but also
deliberately constructed. Even more significant, however, is the likeness between some of the early sculptures of Cragg, made from fragments of urban detritus (scraps of plastic, for instance) and Arte Povera.
Cragg expresses similar social concerns and a like-minded rejection of
the consumer society, and he does it in much the same fashion, by res-
cuing or 'redeeming' materials formerly considered too degraded for
artistic use.

172,173   In the work of Wentworth and especially Woodrow, there is a more
specific relation to Pop, through the employment of items of familiar
174   domestic use. Woodrow, and the Scottish sculptor David Mach (b.
1956), both transform junked consumer durables – items such as television sets, washing-machines or supplies of unsold magazines – into
fantastic new images, often with considerable wit, but also with some

171 RICHARD DEACON
Two Can Play 1983

172 RICHARD WENTWORTH
Jetsam 1984

loss of the moral force which characterizes Cragg's best inventions. Items which the original Pop artists of the 1960s set up as icons of contemporary culture are now treated with sardonic contempt by a newer generation of artists.

Anish Kapoor, half Jewish and half Indian, brought up in India, but living and working in Britain, has used the legacy of both Arte Povera and Minimal art in a different fashion. His simple shapes, covered in intense powdery colour, are often reminiscent of ritual objects connected with Hindu Tantrism (the most refined and mystical form of Hindu worship). Kapoor is also fascinated by the idea of absence – of the sculptured form as being essentially the container for a mysterious void, and seems indebted in this sense to Lucio Fontana. Efforts have often been made to align Kapoor's work with other contemporary artists of Indian origin, but Kapoor has always resisted any tendency to categorize his work in this way, pointing out that his affinities are essentially European. In fact, the most striking similarity is with the work of artists like Anselmo and Penone. He represents a renewal of some of the basic ideas of Arte Povera within a British context.

One important aspect of Arte Povera, largely ignored when it was new, and little analysed since, was the way in which it displaced the spectator's attention from the single object to the setting. Environmental or installation art had been practised as early as the

175

<173 BILL WOODROW
Self-Portrait in the Nuclear Age 1986

<174 DAVID MACH
Thinking of England 1983

175 ANISH KAPOOR
Passage 1993

1920s by the Dadaist Kurt Schwitters, and further elaborated by the Surrealists and by the pioneers of Pop. The practitioners of Arte Povera took it a stage further: since their materials were often so flimsy, or at least so lacking in solid presence, it was the total ambience which counted. The link between the Roman branch of Arte Povera and the Italian Baroque, shrewdly noted by Meneguzzo, is something which deserves further investigation. Spectators increasingly came to think of avant-garde exhibits as a hall of mirrors, places to enjoy a series of illusory effects, with or without some thought-provoking moral or philosophical dimension. Arte Povera can be perceived not simply as a closed 'art movement', organized very much along the lines of the other art movements of the same epoch (the later 1960s and early 1970s), but as the initiatory phase of an attempt to alter the nature of art, to remove its dependence on the idea of identifiable stylistic quirks, and to change its relationship with its public.

In recent years, the word 'sculpture' has been released into a whole new series of meanings, unknown to the pre-modern era and equally unknown to the pioneer modernists of the first half of the twentieth century. This has given a special prominence to artists who have used artistic activity as a way of making points about their own obsessions or past histories, creating a series of private yet deliberately theatrical effects. An important precursor in this respect was the short-lived Eva Hesse (1936–70). Though her work is generally associated with that of the Minimalists and Land artists such as Smithson and LeWitt who were her New York contemporaries, her soft sculptures and ladder-like structures seem like mysterious echoes of her own psychological traumas. An artist who has a resemblance to Hesse in some of her output is another foreign-born but American-domiciled sculptor – Louise Bourgeois (b. 1911), selected, when already in her early eighties, as the American representative at the Venice Biennale of 1993. Bourgeois's work is a meditation on the past, and also a release of anger – chiefly, it seems, anger about a blocked and frustrated childhood, the sadistic teasing to which she was subjected by an anglophile father, and the presence in her childhood home of her father's mistress, a young Englishwoman who officially served as governess to the young Louise and her sister. Bourgeois makes these feelings the subject-matter of a striking series of quasi-Surrealist allegorical tableaux, replete with sexual allusions of various kinds. Also concerned with ideas of memory and loss is the American environmental artist Ann Hamilton (b. 1956). Hamilton, like Hesse and Bourgeois, makes use of organic materials, but her choice among these of such substances as honey and wax also reflects perhaps references to Beuys. Rebecca Horn (b. 1944), the German installation, performance, action and video artist and film maker, similarly evokes in her work the transformative power of materials, such as carbon and mercury, and of the interaction of the body and machines in metaphoric narratives about desire and vulnerability.

Younger artists working with psychologically loaded subject-matter and making free use of metaphor include the much discussed, but otherwise very different, Robert Gober (b. 1954), who is American, and the British Damien Hirst (b. 1965). Gober is the more reticent of the two – his work has a deliberately disturbing, yet elusive quality. Some of its typical ingredients are as follows: realistic models of human legs, sticking out of the wall at about knee-height; a dressmaker's dummy wearing a wedding dress; a paper bag filled with doughnuts, placed on a pedestal; a baby's cot with slanting sides; wallpaper showing a pattern of male and female sexual organs, or else a repetitive design where a

176 ROBERT GOBER
Untitled 1991

sleeping man is paired with a lynch-mob victim hanging from a schematic tree. Since Gober is known to be an openly gay man, this system of imagery has been connected by commentators with the impact of the AIDS crisis on the New York art world. Examined objectively, however, it is much less specific. To say flatly that Gober's work is 'art about AIDS' requires a good deal of energetic reading in. What it does undoubtedly convey is a general feeling of disturbance, of restless unease. This comes not from single objects, but from the relationships between them.

Within a few years of graduating from Goldsmiths' College in London, Damien Hirst became the most notorious artist of his generation in Britain. His fame rests chiefly on work involving various dead animals and fish preserved in tanks of formaldehyde. Writing of one of these, a vast basking shark which floats in perfect equilibrium in the tank built to contain it, the critic Charles Hall remarked that it 'functions almost as an allegory of the fallibility of believing that one can impose order on a system which, quite literally, has to keep moving in order to stay alive. The more permanent something is, the more absolute its death.'[4] Significantly these words were written after the piece had been conceived by the artist, but before it had actually been

177 DAMIEN HIRST *Away from the Flock* 1994

178 BILL VIOLA *The Sleep of Reason* 1988

made. As with earlier Conceptual art, the making process was simply
a matter of giving incontrovertible physical form to a visual metaphor.

Extreme subject-matter presented in a dispassionate way has also
featured in the work of video artists in the 1980s and 1990s. The
American Bill Viola (b. 1951), for instance, has made elaborate
environmental pieces which offer intimate insights into his own
psyche presented with public panache. In one of these, *Nantes Triptych*
(1992), a triptych of three projection screens showed, on the left, his
wife giving birth, in the middle himself floating, and on the right, his
mother on her deathbed. It was the impalpable, almost ectoplasmic
nature of the medium itself which produced the requisite effect: the
spectator, despite the very non-private nature of the space in which
the event was taking place (an art gallery) felt that he or she had
become a privileged intruder.

CHAPTER EIGHT

Neo-Expressionist Tendencies in the 1980s

The radical assaults made on traditional painting by Arte Povera, Conceptual art, Performance art, Video art, Land art and other developments continued to meet with resistance from both within and outside the art world. While promoters of the avant-garde had proclaimed that painting, the chief medium of expression in western art since the Renaissance, was now dead and buried, painters established by the 1960s, and by the 1970s many younger artists as well, had turned to painting as their preferred medium. The return to an atmosphere receptive to painting was marked by an important survey exhibition held at the Royal Academy of Arts in London from January to March 1981. Its title, 'A New Spirit in Painting', carried polemical overtones for the cognoscenti, if not for the public at large. One of the curators of the show noted in his introductory essay that: 'The artists' studios are full of paint pots again and an abandoned easel in an art school has become a rare sight.'[1]

'A New Spirit in Painting' consisted mainly of four tendencies. First there were abstract painters who were practitioners on canvas of varieties of Minimalism, among them artists like Robert Ryman, Brice Marden and Alan Charlton, already mentioned. There were survivors from the various art movements that had flourished in the immediate past – Willem de Kooning and Cy Twombly carrying on the traditions of Abstract Expressionism, Andy Warhol and David Hockney as standard bearers for Pop. There were isolated 'masters' of figurative painting who were aligned to no particular movement, among them Bacon, Balthus and Lucian Freud.

The art world's rediscovery of Freud (b. 1922), as the result of a retrospective held in 1974 by the Arts Council of Great Britain, was an example of the way in which important artists could apparently drop from view when their work did not fit the particular vision of the avant-garde held by those who had the power to shape opinion in the world of contemporary art. Freud's inclusion in 'A New Spirit in Painting' was part of a process of rehabilitation which culminated in

179 LUCIAN FREUD *Double Portrait* 1985–6

an exhibition held at the Hirshhorn Museum and Sculpture Garden, Washington DC, in September to November 1987, which was seen subsequently in Paris, London and Berlin. These exhibitions turned Freud from an artist of strictly local interest into one of world rank. The point here was that he was himself quite unchanged by the process. He remained what he had always been – a figurative painter of a traditional kind, dependent upon the presence of the model in the studio, interested only in what could be observed in those circumstances. Freud's rehabilitation was not a completely isolated event. The 1970s, 1980s and 1990s have been marked by series of similar re-emergences. Another example (in this case a painter not included in 'A New Spirit') is that of the French figurative painter Jean Rustin (b. 1928), six years younger than Freud, and the subject of a major retrospective exhibition at Oberhausen in Germany in January 1994.

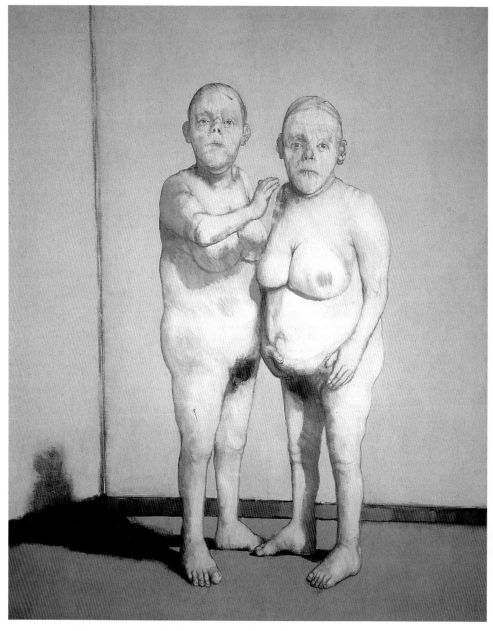

180 JEAN RUSTIN *The Twins* 1987

Rustin's extraordinary nudes – geriatric, sexually obsessed, making obscene gestures – are not painted from the life, like Freud's figures. But they are the reflection of a somewhat similar world: bleak, isolated, apparently deprived of hope. His work, like that of Freud, has found a response with contemporary audiences because it seems to offer a truthful reflection of important aspects of the world as they know it. The acceptance since the early 1980s of the coexistence of the kind of divergent approaches represented by Freud and Rustin, in contrast to the succession of dominant styles and movements earlier in the century, is itself symptomatic of a much greater plurality of attitudes.

The main thrust of 'A New Spirit in Painting', however, was the promotion of a Neo-Expressionist tendency in art which was closely identified with the culture of the Federal Republic, the larger, more prosperous, committedly capitalist portion of a Germany which was at that point still politically divided. It was significant that much of the funding for the exhibition came from West German sources. Neo-Expressionist painting was not, in 1981, an entirely new invention. One of the leading figures in German Neo-Expressionism, Georg Baselitz (born Georg Kern, 1938), had begun his career in the DDR, moving to West Berlin in 1956 and evolving a fully formed Expressionist figurative style by the early 1960s. Though Baselitz had proved a rebellious student when in the DDR, his Neo-Expressionism was to some extent based on East rather than West German practice. In the immediately post-war years, Expressionism had been favoured as the 'official style' by the Communist East German regime because of the hostility shown by the Nazis to the original group of German Expressionists, who flourished both before World War I and during the Weimar period. Baselitz's close friend and ally A. R. Penck (born   181 Ralf Winkler, 1939) was also born in East Germany and, though he never formally attended an art school, was subject to the same cultural influences.

Baselitz and Penck, though pioneers of the new tendency, were at least in some respects untypical of it. Both were more interested in the 'how' of painting rather than the 'why', in method rather than in content. Penck created a language of graphic signs which owed something to Picasso, and which looked forward to the work of artists connected with the New York Graffiti movement, such as Keith Haring.   182 In 1967 Baselitz began painting his images upside-down, in order, as he claimed, 'to set the imagination free'. A characteristic example is *Die Mädchen von Olmo* of 1981. The effect was to focus attention on   188

205

181 A. R. PENCK
T3 (R) 1982

183 RAINER FETTING >
Dancers III 1982

182 KEITH HARING
Ignorance = Fear 1989

the somewhat perverse way in which the work was done rather than on what the pictures actually represented.

Other members of the Neo-Expressionist group focused directly on Germany and her problems. Anselm Kiefer (b. 1945) evolved a complex system of imagery which incorporated elements taken from German legend, from esoteric philosophy, from the history of World War II, and from the poetry of the great Romanian-Jewish poet Paul Celan (who wrote in German). Some of his most effective images, e.g. his *Untitled* of 1978, were inspired by the designs of Hitler's Inspector-General of Buildings (and later Minister for Armaments) Albert Speer. Since Speer in turn was the heir of the great German classicist Karl-Friedrich Schinkel (1781–1841) this enabled Kiefer to set up a series of cultural variations and parallels which in turn illuminated some of the darker corners of recent German history. His work can be compared to the political paintings made by some of the artists of the early Romantic epoch, and perhaps most fruitfully to Theodore Géricault's *Raft of the Brig 'Medusa'*, which is similarly ambiguous and complex in its use of traditional formulations in order to comment on contemporary events.

190

German Neo-Expressionism also embraced overtly political art,
189 such as Jörg Immendorf's (b. 1945) *Café Deutschland* series, initiated in
the late 1970s, which comments directly on the division of Germany,
and a nostalgic revival of motifs used by the original Expressionists.
183 Rainer Fetting's (b. 1949) *Dancers III* (1982) is a reprise of imagery first
used by Emil Nolde in paintings inspired by his visit to the German
colonies in the Pacific, shortly before the outbreak of war in 1914.

Although Neo-Expressionism, for obvious reasons, became firmly
associated in the public mind with a post-war revival of German art,
it was paralleled by developments elsewhere, notably in the United
States and in Italy. In the USA the seminal figure is Philip Guston
(1913–80), originally a member in good standing of the post-war
Abstract Expressionist movement. In the late 1960s Guston shocked
the American art world with a sudden return to figurative work,
making paintings which were deliberately bold and rough: their
cartoon-like simplicity of line serves as reminder that Guston began
his artistic career as a young boy by taking a correspondence course in
cartoon drawing. The cartoons they most resemble, however, are those

184 PHILIP GUSTON *The Rug* 1979

185 LEON GOLUB *Mercenaries V* 1984

produced from the mid-1960s onwards for 'underground' magazines such as the *East Village Other*, the *Berkeley Barb* and the *Los Angeles Free Press*. There is a particularly close resemblance to the work of Robert Crumb, creator of the anarchic beast-fable *Fritz the Cat*, and progenitor of the white-bearded Zen Master, Mr Natural, who had been everything from a bootlegger under Prohibition to a taxi-driver in Afghanistan. One detail which reinforces the comparison is the fact that both artists have a fascination with hobnailed boots at the end of spindly legs – these feature prominently in Guston's painting *The Rug* (1979). By working in this way, Guston seemed to reject his own generation in favour of a younger one; at the same time he turned his work into an autobiographical vehicle for savage criticism of what was happening to American society. Guston had in fact begun his career as an admirer of the Mexican muralists, visiting the studios of both Orozco and Siqueiros and producing a mural of his own (in collaboration with Reuben Kadish) for the Emperor Maximilian's summer palace in Morelia, Mexico.

The political paintings – the *Vietnam* series (1973) and the *Mercenaries* (1976–80) – produced by Leon Golub (b. 1922), usually

186 JULIAN SCHNABEL *Humanity Asleep* 1982

categorized as a social realist, also reflect a deep distress about what was happening to the world, and to the American dream in particular. Like Kiefer, Golub made direct allusion to political and historical events that provided evidence of a sickness in their respective societies.

The Neo-Expressionist and painterly strains in American art took a whole series of new directions with the emergence of a younger generation of painters such as Julian Schnabel (b. 1951), Susan Rothenberg (b. 1945) and Terry Winters (b. 1949). Schnabel is an artist who has been greatly praised and greatly abused in equal measure. His signature works are those in which the surface is covered with fragments of broken crockery – a device originally borrowed from some of the decoration in Gaudi's Parque Güell in Barcelona – e.g. his *Humanity Asleep*. Schnabel uses this not only as a way of producing a richly textured surface but of subverting the possibility of any fluency of drawing. This is another version of the search for awkwardness which one also discovers in Baselitz's insistence on painting his images upside-down. One can also look somewhat further back, to Dubuffet's fascination with so-called 'outsider' art (graffiti, children's drawings, images produced by the mentally ill). The images Schnabel uses, however, are those of the great humanist themes – the Crucifixion, the fate of man, mankind's relationship with nature. Critics have seen something overweening in this, and have not been mollified by the bombast of the artist's pronouncements. Yet it cannot be doubted that Schnabel, at his best, is one of the most richly talented artists of his generation: one of the most inventive, one of the most various, and finally one of the most decorative – an adjective he would probably repudiate with some violence.

Neither Rothenberg nor Winters is as various as Schnabel. Both tend to be monochromatic. Rothenberg paints archetypal images – a horse, a body, or part of a body, e.g. the outstretched arm in *Beggar* – in deliberately simplified outline. These are endowed with symbolic

187 SUSAN ROTHENBERG *Beggar* 1982

188 GEORG BASELITZ *Die Mädchen von Olmo* 1981
189 JÖRG IMMENDORFF *Eigenlob stinkt nicht* 1983

190 ANSELM KIEFER *Untitled* 1978

191 TERRY WINTERS *Caps, Sterns, Gills* 1982

force. Winters achieves a similar effect in accomplished paintings featuring hugely enlarged mushrooms and other fungi, e.g. *Caps. Sterns, Gills*. The tendency to fragmentation in these paintings demonstrates the pressure on the contemporary artist to make the part stand for the whole. An artist of the pre-modern epoch would have felt able to express the same meanings in a much more elaborated way. Now, even when working in a deliberately expressive fashion, the painter hints and leaves the spectator to guess.

It is perhaps a surprise to find a group of Neo-Expressionist painters in Italy, since Expressionism, from the time of Edvard Munch onwards, had always been considered a quintessentially northern or even nordic style, the contrary impulse to southern classicism. The four Italian artists most closely associated with the tendency are the so-called 'three C's' – Sandro Chia (b. 1946), Francesco Clemente (b. 1952) and Enzo Cucchi (b. 1949) – and Mimmo Paladino (b. 1948). They are often discussed as members of the so-called 'trans-avant-

214

garde', a term invented by the Italian critic Achille Bonito Oliva and first used by him in an article which appeared in the periodical *Flash Art* in 1979. In the following year Bonito Oliva published a book, *La Transavanguardia italiana.*

The idea – one closely related to contemporary postmodernism in architecture – was to find a means of escape from the shibboleths of avantgardism, and thus, by implication and in an Italian context, from some of the more puritanical aspects of Arte Povera. It is not surprising, therefore, to find a strong element of parody in Italian Neo-Expressionist painting which surfaces particularly in the work of Chia, with its mock-heroic figures, as, for example, in *Crocodile Tears*. These look back to the work done by Giorgio de Chirico, at the time – from the mid-1920s onwards – when he attempted to lead a traditionalist revolt, and also to the paintings of de Chirico's lesser-known brother, Alberto Savinio.

192 SANDRO
CHIA
Crocodile Tears
1982

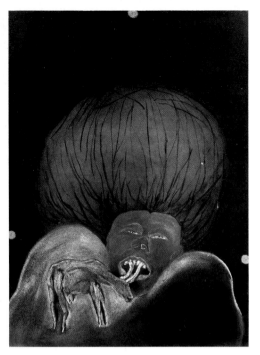

The most eclectic of the other artists in the group is Francesco
193 Clemente – see, for instance, *Toothache* – who commutes between
Italy, New York and India. He has a studio in Madras and many images
borrowed from Indian art appear in his work. The most traditionally
Expressionist, and therefore the closest to his German confrères, is
Cucchi, as, for example, in *A Painting of Precious Fires*, and the most
individual, and at the same time the most visibly Italian is Paladino
who comes from southern Italy; he was born near Benevento and
spent his childhood in Naples, and has rooted much of his work in
ancient but non-classical sources. His imagery seems to owe much to
Italian pre-Romanesque and Romanesque fresco painting, and also to
types of sculpture – Sardinian and primitive Italic – on the very fringes
of the main classical tradition. This gives his work a distinctively hier-
atic, other-worldly quality, as can be seen from *It's Always Evening*
reproduced here. Of all the artists who have been classified as Neo-
Expressionists he is perhaps the one, apart from Guston, whose
imagery lies right at the other end of the scale of reference, who makes
the most coherent and powerful impact.

194 MIMMO PALADINO
It's Always Evening 1982

195 ENZO CUCCHI
A Painting of Precious Fires 1983

CHAPTER NINE

America in the 1980s

From the mid-1970s, especially in the United States, there was a feeling that the old system which had governed the development of modernism almost from its beginnings was starting to disintegrate. In particular, commentators began to feel that the old hierarchical structure of styles and movements was being put under serious strain by new developments in art. Indicative of this new way of thinking was the appearance of books such as Alan Sondheim's *Individuals: Post-Movement Art in America* (New York, 1977), and Corinne Robins's *The Pluralist Era: American Art, 1968–1981* (New York, 1984). Neither of these texts was nearly as comprehensive as their respective titles imply, and both remained New York orientated. Nevertheless, their appearance was a symptom of the deep unease which was beginning to infect the art world. This feeling was, however, concealed to some extent by the art-boom of the 1980s, which made rapid fortunes for a number of artists who happened to catch the fancy of a new generation of collectors coming into the market with a great deal of spare cash in their pockets. Many of these collectors lived outside New York. A powerful group was based in Los Angeles and another group in Texas. There were Germans, Swedes, Swiss, Italians (such as Count Panza di Biumo, who began accumulating a major collection of avant-garde art long before this activity was truly fashionable), and even Englishmen (such as the advertising magnate Charles Saatchi). Though these collectors bought the work of European artists as well as American ones – the German and Italian Neo-Expressionists were for a while very popular, and there was also some enthusiasm for British art and for the artists associated with Arte Povera – the collectors, and following their lead the museum curators and exhibition organizers, continued to look to New York as the ultimate arbiter of what was important. Indeed, the European artists they favoured were more likely to be those who had made the obligatory pilgrimage to New York. The only flaw in the New York art world's record was the comparatively slow recognition it accorded to Joseph Beuys.

Creatively, the situation was rather different. Though New York remained the arbiter of taste, it was no longer inveitable that major artists would find it necessary to live and work in the city. Foreign artists, it is true, did continue to come to New York, settling there either permanently, or at least for long periods, in order to enjoy its cultural excitements and also to remain in close touch with the museums and commercial galleries who had so much influence over their careers. Two well-known examples are the Italian Sandro Chia and the German Rainer Fetting.

American artists were rather less mesmerized by New York, for several reasons. One was that every time the city boomed, spaces where artists could live and work became harder to find and also increasingly expensive. Sculptors making work on a major scale were priced out of Manhattan comparatively early. Some based themselves in the immediate hinterland – in upper New York state or in New Jersey. Others preferred to work in California or in Texas, where they were in any case close to some of their most important patrons. In addition, there was the fact that many American artists, even those most closely attached to the idea of an avant-garde, now made at least part of their income through teaching, chiefly at universities. Small, prosperous university communities provided pleasanter and less stressful places to live than New York itself. More important still was the growing regional support system for much American art. Those artists who now lived and worked outside of the metropolis responded to local tastes and standards, found themselves local dealers and patrons, and exhibited at local museums (some of which were also institutions of major importance). The growth in collecting was matched by a growth in the number of museums, and the vast majority of these new or revamped institutions regarded giving support to contemporary art as being a large part of their mission. In pursuing this course, they had to consider the tastes and wishes of those who immediately surrounded them.

Despite the erosion of New York's pre-eminent position, artists, curators and critics based there continued to look for new ways to grow and develop, conscious of the city's long tradition of innovation, and reluctant to see it relegated to the role of a powerless forum, where ideas which originated elsewhere would be sifted and debated, but left in the end unchanged.

As a result of their efforts, numerous exhibitions and publications have been devoted in recent years to the subject of 'new New York art', which has nevertheless proved rather resistant to critical analysis.

196 ERIC FISCHL
Sleepwalker 1979

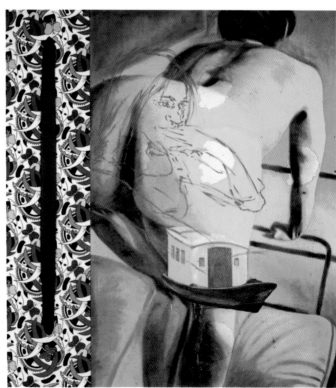

197 DAVID SALLE
His Brain 1984

One reason is comparatively simple. If the new phenomena in New York were no longer to be described in terms of 'styles' and 'movements', how then were they to be defined?

A first attempt was made with the appearance of such artists as David Salle (b. 1952) and Eric Fischl (b. 1948). What linked these two artists was the notion of what was sometimes labelled 'bad painting'. This was more than an American version of Neo-Expressionism, and indeed neither of the artists named is particularly Expressionist in style. As a concept, 'bad painting' implied a use of traditional techniques in a fashion barely adequate to the strains the artists imposed on them – see, for example, Fischl's *Sleepwalker*. Fischl made a much-quoted comment on this in a statement written for a solo exhibition held at the Edward Thorp Gallery in New York in 1982:

196

> I would like to say that central to my work is the feeling of awkwardness and self-consciousness that one experiences in the face of profound emotional events in one's own life. These experiences, such as death, loss, or sexuality, cannot be supported by a life

198 PETER HALLEY *Yellow and Black Cells with Conduit* 1985

style that has sought so arduously to deny their meaningfulness, and a culture whose fabric is so worn out that its public rituals and attendant symbols do not make for adequate clothing. One, truly, does not know how to act! Each new event is a crisis, and each crisis is a confrontation that fills us with much the same anxiety that we feel, when in a dream, we discover ourselves naked in public.[1]

Fischl's models for his queasy examinations of American bourgeois life – supported by his statement quoted above – might have been the Socialist Realist painters of the 1930s, most specifically the work of the brothers Raphael, Moses and Isaac Soyer. Salle turned to models which were nearer at hand. His work is a rehashing of ideas borrowed from Pop art – Rosenquist's colliding realist images, Warhol's interest in appropriated photographs taken directly from magazines and news-papers. He also, in his use of conflicting images occupying the same apparent space, seems to have been influenced by new photographic techniques such as holography. It is hard to like Salle's work because of its anaesthetized, deadened handling of the artist's materials, but there is no doubt that his role was extremely prophetic, in its willing-ness to use an eclectic range of clashing imagery and subtly ill-matched stylistic conventions. A good example is *His Brain* (1984). This has at least four layers of imagery: first the applied fabric strip to the left; then the primitive houseboat, seemingly floating in space; then the outline sketch of a woman putting her hand to her mouth; finally the female nude bending over. The female nude seems to be borrowed from a soft-core pornographic magazine; the artist is perhaps trying to indi-cate the way in which different thoughts and images, some erotic, some not, jostle for position in the male psyche. None of the images, however, has much energy or distinction in itself.

In 1988, the critic and art impresario Jeffrey Deitch made a brave stab at a definition of what was taking place in New York, but he could not avoid falling back into the old vocabulary:

> In art historical terms, the new art is a somewhat mannerist evolu-tion from Pop, Minimalist and Conceptual trends, a 'new and improved' synthesis of these earlier styles. The cultural awareness of Pop, the materials and presentation strategies of Minimalism, and the Conceptualists' explorations into the context of the art object are its immediate artistic heritage.[2]

This definition of what was happening allowed room both for the apparent total abstraction of artists such as Philip Taaffe (b. 1955) and

197

Peter Halley (b. 1953), and also for the Neo-Pop of Jeff Koons (b. 1955), Haim Steinbach (b. 1944) and Allan McCollum (b. 1944). What, if anything, did these artists have in common: that is, apart from the fact that a certain section of the critical and museum community became excited by their work at about the same moment? One clue to a possible link can be found in a statement made by Peter Halley, perhaps the most articulate of this generation of New York artists:

> The history of abstract art is the history of a real progression in the social. It is the history of the organization of the compartmentalized spaces and the formal systems that make up the abstract world.[3]

Halley's own paintings, which superficially look to be derived from late Mondrian, e.g. *Yellow and Black Cells with Conduit*, are not to be   198
read in a traditionally formalist way, but as social diagrams. The 'cells' and 'conduits' which make up his abstract designs are in fact derived from his perception of New York buildings – the spaces bound together by the energy systems which service and make them habitable. Taaffe's work, e.g. *Four Quad Cinema*, which sometimes looks like a revival, if not direct appropriation, of the 1960s Op art associated with Bridget Riley, is presumably also meant to be construed as a diagrammatic representation of social and economic patterns.

199 PHILIP TAAFFE *Four Quad Cinema* 1986

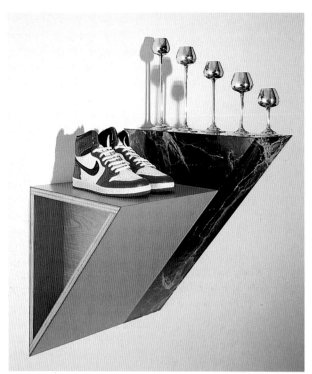

200 HAIM STEINBACH
Related and Different 1985

201 ALLAN McCOLLUM
25 Perfect Vehicles 1986

202 JEFF KOONS *Michael Jackson and Bubbles* 1988

The objects on formica shelving of Haim Steinbach, as in *Related and Different*, and the simulacra or substitutes of Allan McCollum are similarly things meant to be examined within a social context, not for their own sake. Steinbach raises questions about our attitudes to objects, to the possessions which fill our lives. He suggests, slyly, that we make altars even to the simplest and humblest of these, because they supply us with a large part of our identity; in the process he also makes ironic references to his artistic forbears, notably Judd, hinting at the commodification of avant-garde art itself. McCollum takes a slightly different tack. His characteristic serial works of the 1980s – *Perfect Vehicles* (non-functional ginger-jar forms made of cast and painted plaster or concrete, 1985–7) and *Surrogate Paintings* (1978–82; equally non-functional arrays of 'pictures', where every image is solid black) – arise from an examination of the process whereby we learn to take our surroundings for granted. The object loses its functional identity, and becomes no more than a sign.

The quintessential New York artist of the 1980s is undoubtedly Jeff Koons, who, at least in terms of the personality cult surrounding him,   202 has firmly established himself as Andy Warhol's successor. Koons's effect on the sophisticated New York audience has been well described by the American art historian Robert Rosenblum:

> In terms of first-person experience, I still recall the shock of my initial confrontation with Koons's lovingly hideous and accurate reconstructions of the lowest levels of three-dimensional kitsch, from porcelain Pink Panthers and Popples to painted wooden bears and angels. We all, of course, have been seeing this kind of thing for years in every shopping centre and shopping trap, but never before have we been forced, as one is in a gallery setting, to look head on and up close at its mind-boggling ugliness and deliriously vapid expressions.[4]

What Rosenblum expresses here is the reaction of someone well-versed in reading the codes through which the art world expresses itself. Behind Koons's vulgarity, he immediately supposes, there must lie something else, some higher didactic purpose.

In general, this is the supposition which attaches to most of the work produced by leading New York artists of the younger generation. It is, for example, vital to the work of Robert Gober, who replaces Koons's upfront aggression with a teasing elusiveness. In both cases, the audience has to agree to play the game by the artist's rules, to accept the conditions which he or she has laid down. Interestingly enough, those younger generation artists who make art in a more solidly traditional fashion, while still being prominent figures in the New York art environment, are generally women. That is, the work of such artists as Elizabeth Murray (b. 1940) and Jennifer Bartlett (b. 1941), though adventurously experimental, has a much stronger link to the world of direct perception, one might even say to the universe as most people see it when operating in a quotidian 'non art' context, than that of their male confrères.

Various strategies have been popular as ways of navigating around the blockage between art and life, two realms which coincide but which are now (in the New York art world at least) separated by apparently unbreachable barriers. Some of these turn around the fashionable terms 'postmodernism', 'deconstruction' and 'appropriation'. Postmodernism, in this context, was used to imply that the emphasis on originality and authorship, so much identified with the Modern Movement, is now *passé*: the work of art only acquires meaning according to the context within which it is placed. Deconstruction is the process whereby these contextualized meanings are revealed.

203, 204

203 ELIZABETH MURRAY *Small Town* 1980

204 JENNIFER BARTLETT *Yellow and Black Boats* 1985

Appropriation of existing images is entirely permissible because their meaning changes when the original context is removed and exchanged for another. The art of the past thus becomes an inexhaustible quarry.

For the Starn Twins (b. 1961), for instance, Hans Holbein's image of the Dead Christ in the Öffentliche Kunstsammlung in Basel is material for a photo-piece, a *Stretched Christ* (1987). What has struck the artists is what most observers notice about the original: the fact that Christ's recumbent body is enormously enlongated. They have set out to produce the same effect by slicing apart, then reassembling, photographs of a live model. The result is curious: it isolates the image from its original cultural and religious context, that of the birth of Protestantism in the merchant cities of northern Europe. Yet it is not endowed with many additional meanings to take the place of those it has lost. The only additional perception it offers is a banal one about the literalism of the photographic image. Jeffrey Deitch's description of the new New York art as 'mannerist' takes on a more pejorative connotation here than perhaps he intended.

Tim Rollins (b. 1955) and K.O.S. (the initials are an acronym for Kids of Survival), and the South Bronx Hall of Fame devised by John Ahearn (b. 1951) and his collaborator Rigoberto Torres (b. 1961) illustrate a different and perhaps worthier approach – an attempt to mate a visibly avant-garde art with the kind of social concern fashionable in the 1930s. Rollins, a teacher with background in Conceptual art, works with a group of deprived adolescents from the South Bronx on collective pictures which are almost invariably illustrations of literary classics. The texts chosen range from Lewis Carroll's *Alice's Adventures in Wonderland* to Franz Kafka's *Amerika*. The images are painted on a surface made up of the actual pages of the chosen book. Rollins is emphatic that the team does not try to find illustrations to the text in any conventional sense – the 'kids' are encouraged to interpret it in relation to contemporary issues and to their own situation in particular. He also asserts that he censors input from his own store of knowledge:

206

> Usually I don't bring in the historical references until we know we're right on the track of where we're going, because sometimes art history can be very intimidating, and influence us too much to repeat something. So it's really great to have them develop it in their own voice and then to say that history's not just to legitimate what we're doing, but to emphasize that this stuff comes from a tradition, and that we're not just playing around and making it up. I say 'Here's

205 THE STARN TWINS *Stretched Christ* 1985–6

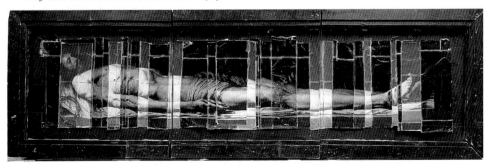

206 TIM ROLLINS AND K.O.S. *Amerika II* 1985–6

the tradition, and we should know about it, but we should also know how we're going to go beyond it.'[5]

The immediately identifiable and consistent style of many of the resulting paintings seems, however, to argue that Rollins himself exerts a strong influence over the work, and that the paintings are ultimately individual rather than collective creations, unthinkable without a strong personality at the centre of the enterprise.

Like Rollins, Ahearn moved to the South Bronx, rather than growing up there. He uses the life-casting technique pioneered by the Pop sculptor George Segal to make portraits of neighbourhood characters. The whole process often takes place in public. Torres, who began as Ahearn's assistant, and who does come from the community, now works to some extent as an independent creator. The sculptures have won acceptance from their subjects for three reasons: first,

207 RIGOBERTO TORRES
Mermaid 1993

208 JOHN AHEARN
Audrey and Janelle 1983

because of their direct verisimilitude; second, because they single out their subjects in a positive and acceptable way; and third because the whole process of casting in plaster was already familiar from local workshops where popular religious sculptures were made.

The acceptance of Ahearn and Torres in the wider art world is due to a different kind of contextualization: the link to Pop art, and to Super Realist sculptors such as Duane Hanson (b. 1925) and John De Andrea (1941), plus the fact that the work is seen as community oriented and directed towards social amelioration. Rollins's work with the K.O.S., and that of the Ahearn-Torres partnership, represents two of the points where the current New York avant-garde marches in step with the current fascination with 'issue-based' art. It is significant that both are to some extent collective enterprises. Working collectively flattens out individual stylistic quirks, but does not necessarily dilute the actual subject-matter.

Despite the attention given to artists like Jeff Koons and Robert Gober, the 1980s saw, as I have previously suggested, a weakening of the power of New York over the rest of the American art world. Some of the more directly practical reasons for this have already been discussed. Rebellions against the hegemony of New York were not, of course, altogether new. One of the most celebrated had been the work of the American Regionalists. Thomas Hart Benton garnered a great deal of publicity when he ostentatiously shook the dust of New York from his feet at the beginning of the 1930s. In April 1935, the New York *Sun* interviewed Benton and quoted his forthright views of the subject:

> Since the depression it has lost its dynamic quality. On the upswing New York is grand – when it is building buildings, tearing down buildings, making and spending money, its life is irresistible, and in its drive it's a grand show. But when it is on the downswing it gets feeble and querulous and touchy. The place has lost all masculinity . . . The zest for real life has gone out of thinking. It is no longer experimental or observant, but has gone scholastic, monkish and medieval.[6]

Benton blamed it all on the pernicious influence of European modes. Forty and fifty years later, a number of American artists were inclined to echo his words, without necessarily trying to fix the blame outside the United States. They received some encouragement for the desire to return to the regions from developments within the history of recent American modernism. There had, for example, been visible

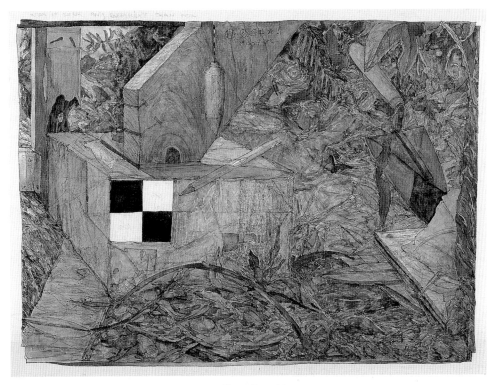

209 WILLIAM T. WILEY *Was It Ever Any Different From Now* 1987

deviations from a New York-imposed norm in both California and in Illinois. The earliest of these was the rebellion staged in the 1950s, in and around San Francisco, against the then current New York obsession with non-figurative art. The 'Bay Area Figuration' of such artists as David Park (1911–60), Elmer Bischoff (1916–91) and the young Richard Diebenkorn (1922–93) was a conscious gesture of defiance directed against the orthodoxies of the dominant Abstract Expressionist school on the East Coast.[7] The return to figuration, partly under the influence of the Beat poets, who also flourished in San Francisco at that time, developed further into the kind of 'funk' art made by Bruce Conner and others, which has already been briefly mentioned in Chapter Five. From this in turn sprang the kind of narrative art, strongly influenced by personal fantasy, which is typical of much recent San Francisco painting.[8] Painters typical of the tendency are Roy De Forest (b. 1930) and William T. Wiley (b. 1937); the latter received most of his art education in northern California and his work

210, 209

210 ROY DE FOREST *Untitled* 1990

remains very characteristic of the local sensibility, even though he no longer lives in the area. It is evident that one powerful influence on the work of De Forest, Wiley and others was the imagery invented by the underground cartoonists who flourished in the 1960s and whose work has already been cited in connection with Philip Guston's later development.

Whereas Guston remained isolated within his context (and was made to feel this isolation by the reception his exhibitions received when the new work was first shown and before it was discovered by a younger generation of artists), in northern California the anarchic humour of Robert Crumb and his peers was assimilated without effort into the realm of 'serious' painting and sculpture. Assimilativeness and a tendency to breach boundaries were leading characteristics of northern California art in general. One major frontier which was often ignored by Bay Area artists was the accepted division between fine art and craft. Craft enjoyed a prestige, and also a seniority, in the structure of northern California culture which was denied to it on the East

Coast. San Francisco and its environs had been a major centre for the turn-of-the-century Arts and Crafts Movement. Especially typical of the northern California art scene in the 1960s, 1970s and 1980s was a group of ceramic sculptors whose members included Robert Arneson (1930–92), David Gilhooly (b. 1943) and Viola Frey (b. 1933). In the earlier part of their careers the first two of these had close links with the funk art movement.

213

The art of southern California tended to take a different direction from that typical of the area around San Francisco, but still remained visibly different from that produced in New York. The painting of Californian Pop painters, such as Billy Al Bengston (b. 1934) and Ed Ruscha (b. 1937) to some extent parallels that done by New York colleagues in the Pop movement. However, Ruscha's work shows a much more sophisticated understanding of the techniques of both still photography and film than that of New York-based painters mining the same aspects of popular culture. The most generically southern Californian art, however, is the work of artists deliberately manipulating the audience's perception of light and space, whose work has

211 DAVID GILHOOLY
An Excessive Dragwood Sandwich 1987

212 ROBERT ARNESON
Californian Artist 1982

213 VIOLA FREY
*Artist/Mind/Studio/World
Series I* 1993

already been discussed in Chapter Six. Though many of the most
important monuments of the Light and Space movement, chief among
155 them Turrell's *Roden Crater* project, are not located within the boundaries of the state of California, the sensibility which informs them has
long been recognized as typical of the region. Another, and very
214 different tendency is summed up in the work of Mike Kelley (b. 1954).
Born in Detroit, and originally a student at the University of
Michigan, his career seems to have been based, as Thomas Kellein
remarks,[9] on his rejection both of his place of origin and of his
Catholic working-class background (he shares the latter with Robert
Mapplethorpe, another notable iconoclast). Kelley savagely mocks
Southern Californian infantilism. Among his chosen means of expression are desecrated soft toys (old teddy bears, stuffed cloth animals),
and brutal cartoon drawings. He is the candid chronicler of a degraded
culture.

In Illinois, the breakaway from New York tastes and standards was
led by the Chicago Imagists. These were artists affiliated to Pop art yet
approaching popular culture in a rather different spirit from that which
inspired their East Coast confrères. Since the 1950s Chicago had had

major private collections of classic European Surrealist art, including the home-grown American Surrealist, Joseph Cornell, and these exercised a major influence. Other, and very important influences were 'outsider' art – the product of untutored painters and sculptors, chief among them the black visionary Dwight Yoakum (1886/8–1976), a circus artist and hobo who at one point in his career had been personal valet to the circus tycoon John Ringling; and the work, simultaneously playful and threatening, of the sculptor H. C. Westermann (b. 1922), as well as the psychedelic images associated with rock music in the late 1960s. Among the best known Chicago Imagists were Ed Paschke (b. 1939) and Roger Brown (b. 1941). Their 215,218 work, with its tinge of Expressionist intensity and (in Brown's case in particular) its frequent use of insistent repetitive patterning, was in its own turn widely influential. So too was the combination of Surrealist and Pop influence in the work of Chicago painters such as Jim Nutt (b. 1938) and Gladys Nilsson (b. 1940). There is a striking difference between the work of this generation of Chicago artists and that of Leon Golub, also from Chicago, whose work was mentioned in the 185 previous chapter. Golub was from his beginnings deeply serious in

214 MIKE KELLEY *Center and Peripheries #5* 1990

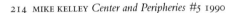

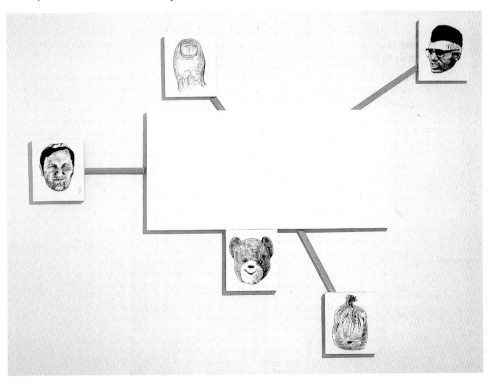

tone. The Chicago painters just cited were, by contrast, playful, sardonic and deeply involved in popular culture. The impact they made on the rest of American art was to be much more specific and easily visible than that of the leading New York artists of the same epoch, perhaps because the openness, exuberance and energy of the midwestern artists' work, and its lack of heavy theoretical baggage, made it easier to assimilate.

219   It made itself felt in Texas, in the work of such artists as David Bates (b. 1952) and Peter Saul (b. 1934, a pioneer of Pop art in the early 1960s); and also in Louisiana, in that of Robert Warrens (b. 1933) and the late Robert Gordy (1933–86), In each instance, however, the already established Chicago idiom was given a regional twist. The paintings of David Bates deliberately pay homage to an established

215 ED PASCHKE
Minnie 1974

216 ROBERT WARRENS *When I Grow Up –*
the Fireman 1993

217 PETER SAUL *Jeffrey Dahmer* 1993

tradition of folk painting in Texas, paraphrasing and affectionately par-
odying typical aspects of its imagery. Peter Saul is a social and political
satirist whose work supports the Texan reputation for spinning tales
while at the same time undermining the Lone Star state's reputation
for rock-solid political conservatism.

The city of New Orleans offers an especially interesting example of
the way in which the American art world is creating new regional
centres. It now possesses the greatly enlarged New Orleans Museum
of Art (a rival in size to the perhaps better-known museum in Dallas),
a Contemporary Art Center with a regular programme of avant-garde
exhibitions, a major collection of contemporary sculpture (corpo-
rately owned but publicly accessible and featuring an array of major
international names), and a lively group of commercial galleries which
attract both local patrons and those from outside the city. Since New
Orleans makes so much of its income from tourism, its visual arts programme has attracted steady support from City Hall. This gradual
growth in the area of the contemporary visual arts has not, however,
led to excessive homogenization. Robert Warrens, who lives and
works in the neighbouring city of Baton Rouge, the state capital, but

239

who exhibits frequently in New Orleans, is very typical of one aspect of Louisiana art in both his paintings and his constructions, which are exuberantly carnivalesque.

Tourism, and a pronounced consciousness of regional identity, seem to be two factors often required for the creation of a viable regional art scene in some area of the United States. There is a striking contrast to be drawn, for instance, between Indianapolis, a large and prosperous midwestern community with a fine art gallery and good universities but very little in the way of a regional art scene (attested by the lack of many commercial galleries supporting local artists) and the much smaller resort city of Santa Fe in New Mexico. The healthy climate of the region, and the existence of a still flourishing Native American culture, had from the beginning of the century tended to attract artists to come and live and work in the region. The most celebrated of these settlers was Georgia O'Keeffe (1887–1986) but other celebrated artists worked there at various times, among them John Marin, Stuart Davis, Andrew Dasburg and Marsden Hartley. Today, it continues to be an artists' colony, with a large number of commercial galleries representing both artists who live locally and others with national or international reputations. One regional speciality is the work of artists of Native American descent, such as Jaune Quick-to-See Smith and Emmi Whitehorse, who are now moving into the modernist mainstream. Both artists make use of traditional images and symbols (for example, in Jaune Quick-to-See Smith's work one finds representations of Indian petroglyphs; in that of Emmi Whitehorse, a form taken from the shape of her father's branding iron). And both are influenced by the distinctive hues of the New Mexican desert landscape.

The first attempt to define a separate artistic identity for the far northwestern city of Seattle and the region surrounding it was made by the French critic Michel Tapié, author of *Un Art Autre*, in 1954. Tapié saw what he felt was a unique situation there – a relationship to Europe, but also direct cultural links with China and Japan. For him the work of Mark Tobey (1890–1976) summed up the distinctive flavour of Seattle art. Tobey moved to Europe in the very year Tapié came to this conclusion, and spent the rest of his career in Switzerland. However, a group of artists associated with him remained in the region. They included Morris Graves (b. 1910), Kenneth Callaghan (1905–86), Guy Anderson (b. 1906) and the sculptor George Tsutakawa (b. 1910), who had studied with Archipenko. It was these artists who created the idea of a distinctive local style, with much use

240

218 ROGER BROWN *Randie's Donuts with Hollywood Junipers and Ranchhouses* 1991>

219 DAVID BATES *Sheepshead* 1985>

of flat pigment on delicate paper surfaces, a preference for tempera rather than oil, and a preference for abstraction in delicately graded tones rather than for figurative work. Where figuration did appear, as in Graves's modest but wonderfully skilful drawings of animals and birds, it tended to have oriental overtones. Seattle art of the late 1950s and early 1960s has been described as having 'the aesthetics of mist'.

Since that time there has been a huge diversification, and the Seattle school, if it continues to exist, represents an attitude to life-style, rather than a unified stylistic language. In 1986, the magazine *Art in America* estimated that there were over 30,000 artists living and working in Washington State, with 4000 of them resident in the Seattle metropolitan area.[10] Seattle had the most ambitious range of public art projects in the United States, some the work of well-established artists from out-of-state, such as Robert Morris, Michael Heizer and Robert Irwin, while others were commissions offered to local artists.

Seattle art in the 1980s and 1990s covers a broad gamut, with the same bias towards an art/craft alliance as can be observed in Northern California. If there is a noticeable local influence it comes less from the Far East than from the indigenous art of the Northwest Coast Indians. Traces of this can be found, for example, in the colourful work of Sherry Markovitz (b. 1947). Few locally-based artists have recently made any international impact, with the notable exception of the video artist Gary Hill (b. 1951), who had a series of major international shows in Europe in the early 1990s. What is impressive is that so many professional artists should have found nourishment and support in the local environment. Since many are incomers, it is clear that a high percentage made a conscious decision to opt out of the competitive New York scene, or anything resembling it.

It is all too easy to dismiss American art which is not New York-centred as being inherently less sophisticated than the metropolitan product. In the sense that it is less immediately influenced by artistic fashions of the moment, this is probably true. However, it is also noticeable that it is often readier to deal with complex human and social issues, and does so in ways which make sense to the specific communities which it both confronts and addresses. Furthermore, as will become apparent in the following chapters, the hegemony of certain metropolitan art centres, whether New York, Paris or London, as *the* centres of modernism, had been eroded by the end of the 1980s.

CHAPTER TEN

Questioning the Western Modernist Canon
from the 'Margins'

A striking feature of developments in art since the mid-1960s has been the acknowledgment given to art which used to be regarded in Europe and the United States as coming 'from the margins', and thus being scarcely worthy of consideration within the modernist canon. While the Modern Movement made claims to being of universal significance, and while it also plundered freely from non-European cultures (as Picasso did from African art in *Les Demoiselles d'Avignon* in 1907), it remained in all essentials a strictly Western European phenomenon. The art which was considered truly modernist was produced either in Europe or else (through an extension of European cultural hegemony) in the United States.

The sole, even partial, exception was art produced in Latin America. During the first half of the twentieth century this went through two phases: first, one in which modernism tentatively established itself as a viable form of cultural expression in South and Central America, the Spanish-speaking Caribbean, and in Mexico; and second, one in which the Mexican mural painters established themselves as the type-figures of Latin American modernism, and at the same time achieved a temporary cultural foothold elsewhere, especially in the United States. The first phase is typified by the Brazilian painter Tarsila do Amaral (1886–1973) and the Anthropophagist Movement to which she belonged. It was named for the manifesto *Antropófago*, written by the Brazilian poet and critic Osvado de Andrade, and published in 1928. The central doctrine of Anthropophagism was that the Latin American artist must devour all outside influences and transform them into something completely new. In Tarsila's case these came from the French painters André Lhôte, Fernand Léger and Alfred Gleizes, all allied to Cubism, with whom she had studied in Paris, and from the proto-Surrealism of her friend the poet Blaise Cendrars. The second phase is associated with Diego Rivera, José Clemente Orozsco and David Alfaro Siqueiros. Muralism's claims to be a form of modern art

243

220 JACOBO
BORGES
The Betrothed 1975

in good standing, as well as an effective instrument of Mexican nationalism and political radicalism, were seldom challenged when the
founders' energy was at its height. Seen now, from the vantage point
of the 1990s, it more and more looks like an attempt to achieve nineteenth-century populist aims in modernist guise.

During the 1940s, when the Abstract Expressionist movement was
getting under way in the United States, a novel form of
Constructivism appeared in Latin America. These Constructivist
impulses have only recently begun to attract the sort of attention they
deserve: they were not unified; they were little publicized in Europe
and America during and just after World War II; they often arose in
countries which were then in the grip of dictatorial regimes, a situation that ran counter to the established modernist myth that a truly
progressive art must be the product of political democracy. However,
with hindsight, the art produced by members of the Madí and Arte
Concreto-Invención groups, both founded in Buenos Aires in 1945,

221 ANTONIO BERNI>
Juanito in La Laguna 1974

can be seen to anticipate many of the Minimalist and Conceptualist experiments of the mid-1960s, albeit with different intent.

The full reaction against Muralism, by the 1940s more or less a spent force, had to wait until the early 1960s. In its most effective form, the war was waged by the Colombian critic Marta Traba, founder in 1962 of the Museo de Arte Moderno in Bogotá, who allied himself with the Mexican artist José Luis Cuevas. Traba argued that the makers of the political revolution of the second decade of the century in Mexico, and the artists who later became their allies, were no better than political reactionaries, because of their intolerant determination to democratize the arts by force and put them at the service of politics. The two allies opened a new era in Latin American art, in which a multiplicity of artistic experiments became possible.

Despite the preconception – largely imposed by European critics – that Latin-American art was 'fundamentally surrealist' in orientation, the art produced by a new generation of Latin Americans, who now saw themselves as heirs legitimately entitled to all the riches of modernist experiment, was extremely various, and followed no set pattern. Traba, in her critical writing, offered a useful distinction between culturally 'open' and culturally 'closed' countries. Culturally open countries, she said, tended to face towards the Atlantic, and were receptive to foreign, and especially European influences. Among them she numbered Argentina, Brazil and Venezuela. Culturally closed countries are either landlocked, like Bolivia and Paraguay, or face towards the Pacific. Other commentators have placed great stress on the question of possible Pre-Columbian origins for Latin American art, often failing to realize that the so-called Indigenist Movement was largely a literary creation, with its roots in the writing of the Peruvian Marxist critic José Carlos Maríategui, and in that of the Guatemalan novelist Miguel Angel Asturias. It is, however, certainly true that artists in countries which were the seat of great Indian civilizations, such as Peru and Mexico, have looked to these remote predecessors for inspiration, though both the actual formats and the intellectual formulations of new Latin American art have remained essentially Western. The result has been an eclectic, unpredictable outpouring of visual images, which shows scant respect for the stylistic categorizations favoured by European and North American commentators.

Among the more important achievements of Latin American painting and sculpture in the years since the breakdown of the Muralist hegemony have been the late collage-paintings of the Argentinian artist Antonio Berni (1905–81), which use the debris of modern

221

222 FERNANDO BOTERO
*The House of the Arias
Sisters* 1973

industrial civilization to create detailed narratives of the lives of some
of his country's poorest inhabitants; the pictorial meditations on the
nature of memory made by the Venezuelan artist Jacobo Borges (b.   220
1931), and the wonderfully ironic narrative work of the Colombian
Fernando Botero (b. 1932), whose lively paintings of Medellín broth-
els, made in the 1970s, are like illustrations to an unwritten novel by
his equally ironic fellow countryman, Gabriel García Márquez. Yet,
strangely, the Latin American artist who did most to bring the region
into the general consciousness was Frida Kahlo (1910–54), much of   223
whose work was completed before this book begins, and who was, in
her own lifetime, regarded somewhat condescendingly as the gifted
but semi-amateur painter wife of the leading Muralist Diego Rivera
(1886–1957). What changed the responses to Kahlo's art were, first, the

rise of the feminist movement in the United States, and second, the publication of Haydn Herrera's brilliant biography of her in 1983. These brought into focus the extraordinarily vivid and personal nature of Kahlo's paintings, many of which were self-portraits. Though she possessed considerable powers of self-assertion, Kahlo would have been as surprised as anyone to find that her reputation now overshadows that of her husband.

In the 1970s and 1980s Latin American artists became fascinated with Conceptual art and with installation. One of the leaders of this tendency in Argentina was Víctor Grippo (b. 1936). Interest in Conceptual art of a rather hermetic kind was perhaps encouraged by the political and economic situation in Argentina at this time: there was a period of military rule from 1966 to 1970, Juan Perón's second, feeble presidency from 1973 to 1976, and a further period of military rule from 1976 to 1984. During this time inflation rose as high as four hundred per cent, and from 1976 onwards the so-called 'dirty war' raged in the country, with many disappearances of supposed left-wing sympathizers. Even after the restoration of democracy, Conceptualist tendencies continue to be visible in the work of younger members of the Argentinian avant-garde. The work of Guillermo Kuitca (b. 1961), for example, with its preoccupation with maps and building plans, shows not the slightest trace of indigenist or Pre-Columbian influence. It is an examination of the urban Argentina of the present day, and of Europe as the artist has come to know it through widespread travels.

225

<223 FRIDA KAHLO *Self-portrait* 1940

224 VÍCTOR GRIPPO *Analogía I* 1971

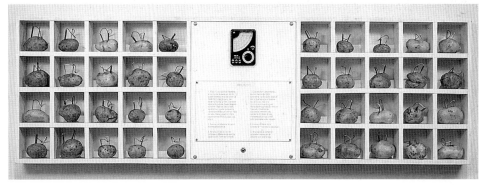

225 GUILLERMO KUITCA *Triptych of Mattresses* 1989

226 TUNGA *Lizart 5* 1989

227 LYGIA CLARK
Rubber Grub
1964

In Brazil, there has been a rich production of Conceptual and site-specific work. This, with its disregard for conventional formats, and its liking for unexpected and often insubstantial materials, has a kinship with Italian Arte Povera, but its deepest roots are in the work done in the 1960s by Brazilian Neo-Concretists such as Lygia Clark (1921–88) and Hélio Oiticica (1937–80), who had already anticipated many of Arte Povera's most typical ideas. The chief heirs of this way of working in Brazil today are such artists as Tunga (Antonio José de Mello Mourão, b. 1952), whose extraordinary environmental works, often filled with gargantuan locks of braided 'hair' (tresses made of lead wire) combine sexual fetishism with imagery reminiscent of Lewis Carroll's *Alice's Adventures in Wonderland*.

Chile, an exception to Traba's rule that culturally closed countries face the Pacific, has seen the appearance of a new avant-garde. This began under the Pinochet dictatorship and has achieved recognition as a new 'School of Santiago' under the democratic regime of Patricio Aylwin, elected president in 1989. Its chief members are Eugenio Dittborn, Gonzalo Díaz (b. 1947), Arturo Duclos (b. 1959) and the Australian-based Juan Dávila. The three participants who live in Chile

227
226

228 GONZALO DÍAZ *The Founding Father*, 1994

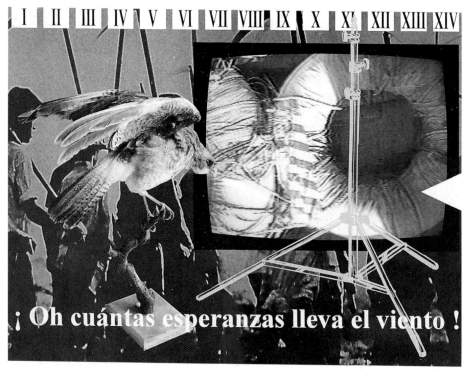

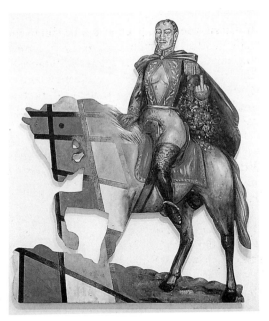

229 JUAN DÁVILA
The Liberator Simon Bolivar
1994

230 EUGENIO DITTBORN *The Car of the Dead Spy* 1994

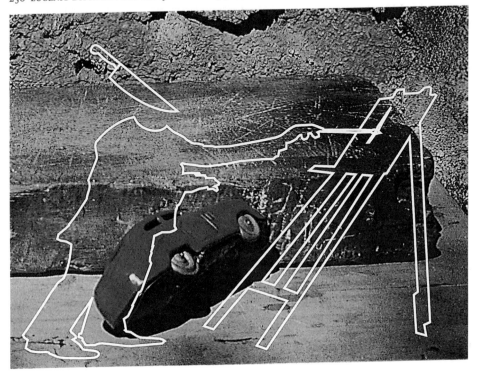

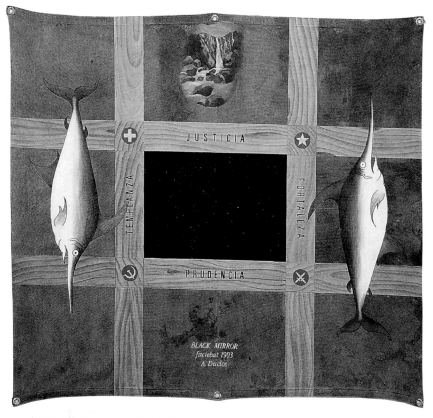

231 ARTURO DUCLOS *Black Mirror* 1993

230, 228 all work in different ways – Dittborn is famous for his 'postal art', Díaz
is chiefly known for installations, and Duclos makes cryptic symbolic
assemblages. What their work has in common is not a similarity of
appearance – what would formerly have been called a style – but
certain attitudes: an approach to the business of making art. The spectator's thought processes are directed down certain pathways, and
across those pathways shadows are cast: those of the Catholicism of the
colonial period; those of the fear and violence of Pinochet's seizure of
power.

There are real, if elusive, resemblances between the new Chilean art
and other kinds of modernist art which have made their appearance in
parts of the globe away from traditional centres of innovation such as
Paris and New York. For example, the *perestroika* art which appeared

254

in Russia in the closing years of Soviet communism looked, at first sight, like a revival of the old Russian avant-garde – the group of artistic experimentalists which had cast in its lot with the October Revolution, which had flourished until the mid-1920s, then lost much of its energy before being finally snuffed out by Stalin's imposition of the creed of Socialist Realism in the early 1930s. Some of the more prominent of these *perestroika* artists, among them Ilya Kabakov and Eric Bulatov, had been associated with the shows of so-called 'unofficial art' from the Soviet Union which were seen in Western Europe in the late 1970s. Though these exhibitions received a sympathetic reception from political journalists, western art critics often dismissed the participants as feeble imitators of already outdated modes. In the 1980s, however, it became apparent that the more interesting of the new Russian artists were dependent, not on an imperfect knowledge of the development of the avant-garde in the West, but on their own intimate acquaintance with the establishment codings of Soviet official art. That is, in order to 'read' the new Russian art correctly, the spectator had to understand its love–hate relationship with the more artistically degraded aspects of Socialist Realism, and with the rhetoric of Soviet official art. Painters like Bulatov have continued to develop this ambiguously coded language even after the demise of the regime which gave it birth. The Soviet way of life has been examined in detail by Ilya Kabakov, in a series of evocative installations. *He Lost His Mind,*

232 ERIC BULATOV
Perestroika 1989

233 ILYA KABAKOV *My Mother's Life II* detail from the installation *He Lost His Mind, Undressed, Ran Away Naked* 1989

Undressed, Ran Away Naked (1989) is an example – an autobiography in the form of a labyrinth. The detail shown here – *My Mother's Life II* – is a recreation of a corridor in a shabby Soviet apartment block. The black-and-white landscape photographs hanging on the wall, taken by the artist's uncle, allude to the unquenchable Russian love of nature, which survives even in the direst urban conditions.

The new Japanese avant-garde of the 1980s has also concerned itself with the idea of cultural coding. After Japan's defeat in World War II, and the American occupation of the country that followed, it seemed natural, because the occupation brought with it many cultural influences from across the Pacific which were assiduously fostered by the occupiers, that contemporary Japanese art should seek to follow an American path. There were, nevertheless, also powerful influences from Europe. The first major post-war group in Japan, the Gutai Group, showed the impact of both sets of influences. Founded in December 1954, Gutai was the child of the painter Jiro Yoshihara (1905–72). Yoshihara, in addition to being an artist, had made a substantial private fortune in the oil industry, and it was essentially his money which sustained the activities of the group. Early Gutai activities were directed at least as much towards creating artistic events, including groups of temporary outdoor sculptures, as they were towards making paintings which could be displayed in galleries. It was essentially the need to make money which drove the other members of the group, who were not nearly as rich as Yoshihara himself, into making work in more conventional formats. Their paintings, abstract and freely brushed, are a fusion of traditional oriental calligraphy and the dominant tendencies in abstract painting of the 1950s in New York and in Paris. The current revival of interest in Gutai, however, is based on the early environmental works and art-events which make the participants, like some of the Neo-Concrete artists in Brazil, look like precursors of Italian Arte Povera.

More recent Japanese avant-garde art, for example the work of Yasmasu Morimura (b. 1951), or that of Yukinori Yanagi (b. 1959), takes a very different tack. Basically conceptual, they present ideas with a mocking irony directed in part against the Japanese tendency to run after western ideas, but largely, too, against western culture, and in particular at western pomposity in defending what are perceived as immutable cultural and moral values. Morimura's *Playing with Gods* 235 series (1991) is photo-based. The artist himself plays every role, female as well as male, in a series of tableaux based on western masterpieces of painting, such as one of Lucas Cranach's *Crucifixions*. At first glance it looks as if the artist is making fun both of the Japanese custom of using male actors in female roles and of Japanese cultural tourism. Only on a second look does it become apparent that he is also questioning western hierarchies as well. Yanagi's *Flag Ant Farms*, such as the 236

234 JIRO YOSHIHARA
Untitled 1971

version shown at the Venice Biennale in 1993, are plastic boxes in which coloured sand has been arranged to form the designs of various national flags. These boxes are linked by lengths of plastic tubing, and a colony of ants is introduced. As the ants move back and forth between the boxes, they gradually blur the designs, so that one symbol of national identity crumbles into another. Yanagi presents this as an allegory of the futility of nationalism.

One of the things Yanagi's work has in common with Morimura's, in addition to its ironic stance, is exquisite craftsmanship. This quality is associated with much traditional Japanese art, but is viewed with disfavour by many modernist artists and art critics as evidence of a lack of true creative spontaneity. The new generation of Japanese artists have found a way of making this refinement work within a modernist, or what some would insist on calling a postmodernist context.

Both contemporary Latin American and contemporary Japanese art show keen awareness of modernist ideas, though a somewhat uneasy relationship with them. The situation is different with the art now emerging from modern Africa, though this is nevertheless attracting a good deal of attention from western commentators and has been the

235 YASMASU
MORIMURA
Playing with the Gods,
No. 1 Twilight 1991

236 YUKINORI YANAGI *Union Jack Ant Farm* 1994

subject of a number of recent survey exhibitions. African art of a 'classical' – that is to say traditional – kind, played a seminal role in the genesis of the Modern Movement and has been correspondingly idealized by modernist art critics. This led to the idea that all African art which showed traces of reciprocal western influence was *ipso facto* weak and corrupt, and unworthy of serious notice. It is only recently that such attitudes have begun to change, though some western commentators remain distressed by the lack of familiar social and institutional signposts. Jan Hoet, the Belgian-born curator of the 1992 Kassel Documenta (Documenta IX), gave a vivid, if also slightly naïve description of his reactions when looking for art in contemporary Africa, lamenting that there was no trace of the familiar western infrastructure which supports the activity of contemporary artists: 'I did not find any houses of the well to do containing contemporary art. Nor any press providing artistic and cultural information.'[1] Yet he was constrained to add:

> And in spite of everything there is art. Isolated traces of expression, without any suggestion of academic references, or artisan traditions and Western influences. Its basis consists of spontaneous commentaries and personal experiences, or else it is the product of adaptation mechanisms.[2]

259

In fact, one of the fascinating characteristics of the art of modern Africa is that it is a reaction to the situation as it actually exists, not as westerners would like it to exist. Where it looks back to traditional forms, more often than not it is because these find a profitable market with western tourists. Where it is most itself, it owes much to things which enthusiasts for 'Africanism' prefer to overlook, such as the activity of Christian missionaries or the availability of new materials (linoleum for making prints, concrete for making sculptures), which are nevertheless very much part of the fabric of the new Africa. The Namibian printmaker John Muafangejo (1943–87) was born in a purely tribal context in Ovamboland, across the border in Angola, moved to Windhoek in what was then South West Africa as a result of political disturbances in the region, and came under the protection of the Anglican mission there. It was the members of this mission who discovered his talent as an artist and sent him to Rorke's Drift in South Africa, then the only school in South Africa where a black man could receive an artistic education. Muafangejo's prints deal with many themes: his tribal background, African proberbs, the political situation, his own Christian faith. All of these are vividly rendered. There is one major underlying theme, and that is the process of detribalization. Muafangejo's images are not the product of a collective consciousness, as seems to have been the case with traditional African art, but those of a man who is slowly being forced to recognize his own individuality, his own isolation. The catalogue raisonné of Muafangejo's prints, published in South Africa in 1992, bears the

238 CHÉRI SAMBA>
Pourquoi un contrat?

237 JOHN MUAFANGEJO
Lonely Man,
Man of Man 1974

appropriate title *I Was Loneliness*. It is this concern with individuality, the shape of the self, which makes him in a broad sense a recognizably modern artist. The fact that his linocuts often bear a startling resemblance to woodcut images produced by the first generation of German Expressionists is on the other hand no more than a coincidence – he cannot be aligned with the German Neo-Expressionists who were his exact contemporaries.

Another African artist whose work has recently made a considerable impact in the West is the Zairean painter Chéri Samba (b. 1956). If Muafangejo's prints are sometimes anguished, Samba's work is satirical and often cheerfully cynical. It shows the strong narrative thrust typical of African culture, but bears little if any resemblance to traditional African art. It does, however, spring from a recognizable background. Samba, who comes from a small village in Lower Zaire, left this for the capital, Kinshasa, and began his career in a studio making hand-painted advertising signs. From this he graduated to drawing strip cartoons for a newspaper. Eventually the two forms were integrated in his paintings. His work is a vivid reflection of the African life of the present day. It may not be specifically modernist, but it is undoubtedly contemporary: one could scarcely apply the adjective more precisely.

Samba's paintings, which are a spontaneous expression of Zairean urban culture, make a striking contrast with the paintings by Australian Aborigines which have also recently been co-opted into the universe of western contemporary art. These were not absolutely spontaneous in origin. In the form in which they are now known, they originated in the promptings of a white art teacher, Geoffrey Bardon, who arrived to teach children at the outback settlement of Papunya in 1971. Bardon, having first encouraged adult members of the community to paint murals in his school, then provided them with the materials – synthetic paint and boards – to create independent works based on traditional Dreamings, the traditional images and symbols which formed part of a complex tribal network of ownership and interrelationship, and which had previously figured in ritual sand paintings and also in body decoration. The paintings, marketed through a Papunya Tula Artists' Collective, found a welcome from white Australians living in the great cities of the coast, and eventually became known abroad. As they became more popular they increased in size, and the artists began to work on canvas rather than on small boards, thus creating work which was directly comparable with the abstract paintings made in the West almost from the beginning of the Modern Movement.

The real question raised by Aboriginal painting, in the context of a general survey such as this, is not that of how the makers view it – they perceive it as an extension of traditional activities, one which both expresses and conceals tribal meanings and secrets and which at the same time makes a very welcome cash contribution to the depressed economy of the outback. It is how non-Aboriginal spectators see and assimilate it. The answer is a little unsettling: basically they can only view it in a western context. What makes it assimilable is a tradition of abstract art which is now the best part of a century old, but which has little or nothing to do with Aboriginal culture. Aboriginal art has become modernist by default, just as African tribal sculpture did before it.

The different cultures dealt with in this chapter are obviously only a selection of the kinds of modernist art from non-western milieux which are now making an impact in the West and being, though sometimes only with difficulty, absorbed into an international system of art-making. The kind of work these countries produce is affected

239

239 PETER BLACKSMITH JAPANANGKA
Snake Dreaming 1986

by their own traditions, by their recent political, social and economic histories, and by the attitudes of the regimes in power. China and South Korea, for example, have much in common with one another culturally, but extremely different political regimes. South Korea, like Japan, but unlike China, has been exposed for a long period to western, and specifically American, cultural ideas. There are, nevertheless, certain areas where modern Chinese and modern Korean art have much in common. Painting in traditional ink-and-brush style continues to be important in both. So-called 'western-style painting', however, tends to be very different in the two countries. Korean art has been largely abstract, and has tended to found itself, as the Gutai group did, on the abstract painting made in both the United States and in Europe in the 1950s. The senior generation of Korean artists, such as Ha, Chong Hyun (b. 1935) have tended to produce exquisitely 240 refined monochromatic abstracts, with surface markings reminiscent of traditional calligraphy. It is only when one looks at Ha, Chong Hyun's work more closely that one realizes that it is created in a very different way from western work of superficially the same sort. In his case, the foundation is a very coarse hemp cloth (a traditional Korean material), and the pigment is actually pushed through the hemp mesh from behind. Other Korean monochromists of the same generation layer the canvas with paint, then with Korean mulberry-bark paper, then with more paint. Their work rejects technology while that of the expatriate Korean, Nam June Paik, embraces it enthusiastically. Younger Korean artists have only gradually and rather tentatively moved towards making figurative work.

In China, western ideas were theoretically banned during the period of the Cultural Revolution, though in fact one type of art favoured by

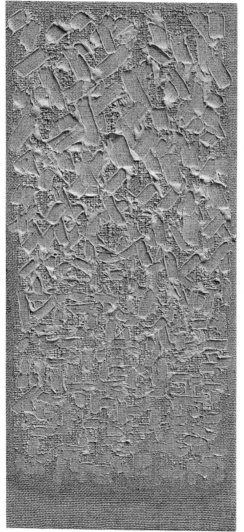

240 HA, CHONG-HYUN
Conjunction 94–07 1994

descent, Ralph Hotere (b. 1931), wishes to be perceived as an artist without ethnic trappings, and has devoted much of his work to a consideration of ecological perils to the New Zealand environment, most strikingly in his *Aramoana* series (1983), which makes use of 'typical' New Zealand building materials, such as corrugated iron. Another artist, this time of *pakeha* background, also concerned with the defence of the ecology, is the sculptor Chris Booth (b. 1948), perhaps best known for his *Rainbow Warrior Memorial* (1988–90), erected on a headland overlooking Matarui Bay in New Zealand's North Island, where the Greenpeace ship of that name was eventually scuttled, after damage inflicted by French saboteurs.

This by no means exhausts the list of countries where something resembling modern art exists, or is beginning to emerge. In India, for instance, it has existed since the time of Amrita Sher-Gil (1913–41), the daughter of a Sikh father and a Hungarian mother, who studied in Paris before returning to live and work in India. Sher-Gil's chief models were Gauguin and Modigliani, and she interpreted what she saw on her extensive travels around the subcontinent through their eyes. Nevertheless, Indian modernist artists have had a uphill struggle for survival, because of the lack of local patronage, and many of the best-known, such as Francis Newton Souza (b. 1924) and the late Avinash Chandra (1931–92) have been forced to make their careers outside the country. Bhupen Kakhar (b. 1934), probably the best-known Indian artist now living in India itself, and the leading figure in the so-called 'School of Baroda', was not free to paint full-time until he was in his fifties. After training in a western-style art school, he spent many years working part-time as a bookkeeper in a small factory. His work is a blend of eastern and western elements: among his influences are the Douanier Rousseau, Sienese painting of the fourteenth and fifteenth centuries, and David Hockney; but also Indian bazaar oleographs, Nathwadra paintings devoted to celebrating the cult of Krishna, and the work of late eighteenth- and nineteenth-century Company School painters – Indian artists working for the British. Kakhar's work is significant for more than one reason: amongst other things it demonstrates the immense range of visual information now available to even a comparatively poor painter, living and working in what is, from a European or American perspective, a remote region.

Meanwhile, new artists continue to emerge in areas which were once completely off the modernist map. Modern art from China, Japan and Korea is now being followed onto the international stage by work from the Philippines and Vietnam.

243 JOHN SCOTT *Women's House* 1993

CHAPTER ELEVEN

Issue-based Art: African-American, Afro-Caribbean, Feminist and Gay Art

The ever increasing emphasis on the importance of subject-matter in art, as opposed to individual or expressive style, led in turn to the notion that one of the specific tasks of the contemporary artist was to give a voice to groups which in some way felt themselves to be disadvantaged. This was not altogether a new idea – African-American art and its supporters and promoters had played at least an intermittent role of this sort in the history of American art almost from the beginning of the century. From the 1920s onwards art by African-Americans was seen as one of the ways in which an oppressed minority could find a voice. Its development along this road can be traced through several successive stages – first the work of the painters of the Harlem Renaissance (Aaron Douglas, Palmer Hayden and William Henry Johnson), who made up the first coherent grouping of African-American artists. Then that of Jacob Lawrence (b. 1917) and Romare   245
Bearden (1914–88). Then the African-American art of the 1960s and   244
the Civil Rights Movement. Statements made at this period were often full of political rhetoric. One curator, writing in 1970, defined the situation thus:

> Black art is a didactic art form rising from a strong nationalistic base
> .and characterized by its commitment to (a) use the past and its
> heroes to inspire heroic and revolutionary ideas, (b) use recent
> political and social events to teach recognition, control and
> extermination of the 'enemy', and (c) to project the future which
> the nation can expect after the struggle is won.[1]

Exhibitions of African-American art were reasonably frequent in the early and mid-1970s, in the wake of the Civil Rights Movement, and under a shifting array of titles. The most important were the following: 1971, 'Contemporary Black Artists in America', Whitney Museum of American Art, New York; 1975, 'Jubilee: Afro-American artists in Afro America', Museum of Fine Arts, Boston; 1976, 'Two Centuries of Black American Art', Los Angeles County Museum of

244 ROMARE BEARDEN
The Family 1948

245 JACOB LAWRENCE *One of the
Largest Race Riots Occured in East St.
Louis* from the series *The Migration
of the Negro* 1940–1

Art. Significantly, there seems to have been only one major enterprise of this sort in the 1980s – 'Black Art: Ancestral Legacy – The African Impulse in African American Art', mounted by the Dallas Museum of Art in 1989.

The Dallas exhibition was somewhat coolly received, as by this time a great many leading African-American painters and sculptors preferred to emphasize the essentially independent nature of their art. This had always been the case, for example, with Sam Gilliam (b. 1933), the leading African-American abstract painter of his generation, whose off-stretcher paintings represent a continuation of the tradition of Morris Louis. It was also the case with leading African-American sculptors such as Martin Puryear (b. 1941) and John Scott (b. 1940). Puryear, one of the very few African-American artists to have direct experience of Africa – as a young man he served in Sierra Leone as a member of the Peace Corps – has always denied that either African art or the desire to assert African-American rights are main motivations for his work, which falls within the tradition of Brancusi but has also been influenced by Minimalists such as Donald Judd.

Scott's brightly painted kinetic sculptures are part of a line of descent which stems from the work of George Rickey and Alexander Calder. The artist, however, does say that part of the inspiration for their thin, spidery forms comes from the African legend of the diddley bow – the hunter's bow which, after the kill, was turned into

247

246, 243

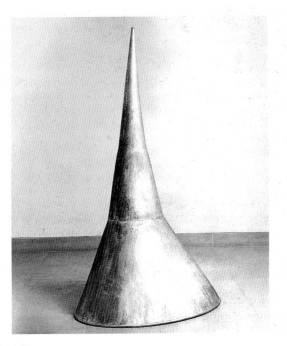

246 MARTIN PURYEAR
Noblesse O. 1987

247 SAM GILLIAM *Horizontal Extension* 1969

an improvised one-string fiddle and played to appease the spirit of the slain animal.

The most discussed African-American artist of the 1980s was the painter Jean-Michel Basquiat, who died in 1988 at the age of twenty-seven. Basquiat, of mixed Haitian and Puerto Rican origin, came from a middle-class family which had no close links with the main tradition of African-American culture, as this had developed since the early 1920s. His beginnings as an artist were in the urban graffiti craze which mesmerized many of his New York contemporaries, and which briefly became fashion in the New York art world. Basquiat was perhaps the only one of these untutored graffiti artists to transfer his energies successfully to the mainstream. In 1983 he even made paintings in collaboration with Andy Warhol and Francesco Clemente: the ultimate sign of hip acceptability. The collaboration with Warhol was of a curious sort. Paintings created jointly by the two artists, such as *Collaboration* (1984) often look like a battle for dominance over the

248 JEAN-MICHEL BASQUIAT and ANDY WARHOL *Collaboration* 1984>

picture space, with essentially incompatible images struggling to make a stronger impact. Basquiat's frenetic energy generally, as here, triumphs over the more laid-back approach of his senior partner, and the result is more visibly Basquiat than Warhol.

While Basquiat certainly made paintings which referred to aspects of African-American culture (notably to music), and to black hero figures, his interests were as widespread as his ambitions were unbounded. He was as likely to allude to Leonardo da Vinci or Homer as he was to turn to specifically 'ethnic' subject-matter. He did, however, enjoy challenging liberal values by using images and inscriptions which referred to his own racial origins in a fashion which in other hands would certainly have been perceived as racist. Basquiat's work is not an attempt to raise black consciousness or to assert specifically African-American values, but through it he often conducted an unsettling dialogue with the audience about what it meant to be a young black man in the American urban context.

The one area where African-American artists maintained a much more militant stance during the 1980s was in work done by women. One of the most politically committed figures on the American art-scene during the period was Adrian Piper (b. 1948). Piper's installa-

tions and environments aim to confront spectators with the true nature of their own attitudes. Some titles give the flavour of her work: *Aspects of the Liberal Dilemma* (1978), *Four Intruders Plus Alarm System* (1980), *Cornered* (1988) and *What It's Like, What It is, No 1* (1991). It is an important aspect of Piper's work that she is very light-skinned – this gives her Performance work in particular a special edge. Other women working in this field, with somewhat similar attitudes, are Faith Ringgold (b. 1930) and the mother and daughter Betye (b. 1929) and Alison Saar (b. 1956). In each case the work seems as much concerned with the special position of black women in American society as it does with African-American identity in general. Its links to feminist tradition are therefore at least as strong as its links to the development of a uniquely African voice for American artists of African descent.

Afro-Caribbean art in Britain, which has similar parameters and a somewhat similar relationship to the society that surrounds it as African-American art in the United States, contrasts with the latter because it has a much shorter history. Essentially it is the product of the great West Indian migration to Britain which took place in the years after World War II. Like African-American art it attempts to deal with issues such as slavery, racial discrimination and identification with an idealized Africa (a location in the mind which differs widely from

252

249 BETYE SAAR
The Liberation of Aunt Jemima 1972

250 HEW LOCKE *Ark* 1992–4

its counterpart in everyday reality). Far more than African-American art it is still in a state of formation. Some artists, such as Keith Piper (b. 1960) make paintings and elaborate environmental works with forthright political messages, thus resembling the more militant African-American artists of the 1970s. Others, such as the Guyanese sculptor Hew Locke (b. 1959) are experimenting with a self-invented 'folk' tradition. Locke's *Ark*, a large, richly decorated papier-mâché model of a boat, symbolizes both the transition from one culture to another and the brutal Middle Passage which brought the slaves from Africa.

The most conspicuous content-based art being produced within the contemporary art world is not racially orientated but feminist. The first feminist art work to catch the imagination of a wide public was Judy Chicago's (b. 1939) installation *The Dinner Party*, which dates from 1979. By the time it was created, feminist art already possessed quite a substantial history: it had started to manifest itself as a discernible force in the early 1970s. Women artists and women art historians started to ask themselves a series of questions: why were women so

254

251 KEITH PIPER *The Nanny of the Nation Gathers her Flock* 1987

undervalued as artists? (This was the question posed in Linda Nochlin's influential essay 'Why have there been no great women artists?', *Art News*, LXIX, January 1971).[2] In what ways could women's art advance the feminist cause? Should women's art be fundamentally different from that produced by members of the opposite sex? In December 1976, just over two years before Judy Chicago unveiled *The Dinner Party*, Ann Sutherland Harris and Nochlin were responsible for a major exhibition at the Los Angeles County Museum of Art, 'Women Artists: 1550–1950'. This was a first step towards the rediscovery of role-models such as Artemisia Gentileschi (1593–1651), Paula Modersohn-Becker (1876–1907) and Frida Kahlo. Meanwhile, feminist theoreticians elaborated new critical approaches to the artwork and its function within an aesthetic and social context. Many of these were derived from French structuralist and post-structuralist philosophy – that is, the work of art was seen not as an end in itself, nor as a complete, self-sufficient entity, but as something which modified the situation in which it was put, and which changed character and meaning as the situation itself changed. Feminist art theory, because it was a coherent system, largely lacking in the contemporary art world

276

252 FAITH RINGGOLD *The Wedding: Lover's Quilt No. 1* 1986

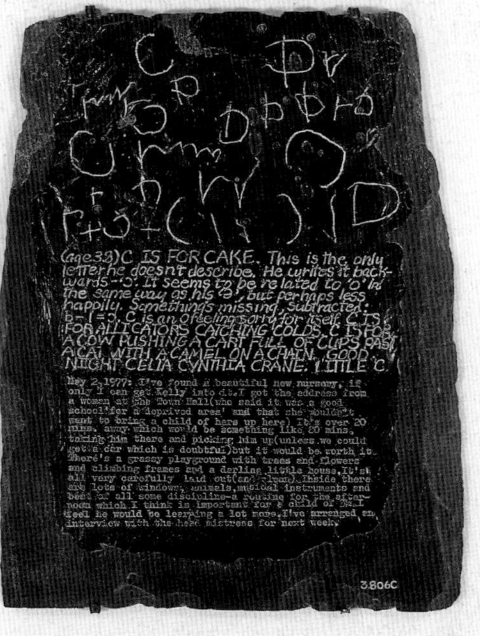

253 MARY KELLY
Post-Partum Document,
Documentation VI 1978–9

since the decline of Marxism, had a profound impact on the development of art criticism in general: it seemed to offer a point of reference for all writers on contemporary art.

The new feminist art differed quite widely from what had been till then the prevailing situation in the contemporary art world. Rather than emphasizing the artist's ego, it was often collaborative. *The Dinner Party*, though conceived by Judy Chicago and made under her direction, was the work of many hands, and highlighted what were traditionally regarded as women's skills, such as stitchery and china-painting. The piece was a triple eucharist in celebration of feminist heroines, and each woman was symbolized by a plate with a different design placed on an embroidered runner. Like many feminist works, *The Dinner Party* was an environmental piece, with a strong theatrical element. Feminist artists also specialized in video and performance. They often avoided using media which invited direct comparison with male traditions in painting and sculpture.

Typical feminist works include Mary Kelly's *Post Partum Document* (1973–9), an anthropological analysis of a mother's relationship with her son (their initial closeness and the inevitable separation imposed by society); the *Untitled Film Stills* of Cindy Sherman (b. 1954), a

256

278

254 JUDY CHICAGO *The Dinner Party* 1979

255 ROSS BLECKNER *8,122+ as of January 1986* 1986

256 CINDY SHERMAN
from *Untitled Film Stills* 1979

series, begun in 1977, of role-playing photographic self-portraits in
which the artist shows herself in poses and situations borrowed from
B-movies; and the photo-collages and installations of Barbara Kruger
(b. 1945), which adopt many devices from the propaganda posters produced by Russian Constructivist designers, such as the Shternberg
Brothers, in the early 1920s.

Feminist art developed in step with another kind of issue-based art:
the art of gay liberation, which was soon transmuted into art which
was a response to the AIDS crisis. When homosexual art gradually
emerged from the ghetto of pornographic illustration, its first impulses
were hedonistic. The 'Rodeo Pantheon' series (1980–90) by the
American painter Delmas Howe (b. 1935), for example, combines   257
Western, Greek classical and homosexual themes in a celebration of
male beauty. There is a similar celebration in Robert Mapplethorpe's   258
series of photographs 'Black Males', first exhibited together at the
Galerie Jurka, Amsterdam, in November 1980. Mapplethorpe boasted
to his lover and memorialist Jack Fritscher that he had seldom or never
received a bad review.[3] He also expressed his contempt for, but also

281

257 DELMAS HOWE *Theseus and Pirithoüs at the Chutes* 1981–2

complete indifference to, the idea of censorship, in a conversation which Fritscher says took place in 1982: 'He cared little really about sexual politics, racial equality, established religion or government grants.'[4]

The censorship controversy which engulfed Mapplethorpe's work immediately after his death, when the Corcoran Gallery of Art in Washington DC cancelled a showing of a touring retrospective, and when the same exhibition was later the subject of a criminal prosecution on its appearance at the Cincinnati Contemporary Arts Center, was therefore nothing to do with the photographer's own intentions. He was not a militant, and his work was an expression of purely personal preferences and tastes. He profited from the loosening of restrictions which formed part of the cultural climate of the late 1970s and early 1980s, but did nothing either to bring it about or to defend it once it had taken place. The thing which would have pleased him about the Corcoran affair was the added notoriety it brought with it.

One finds a similarly personal approach in the work of another photographer of male nudes (many of them black), the New Orleans-

282

based painter George Dureau (b. 1930). Dureau's work has been cited as one of Mapplethorpe's most important sources,[5] and certainly wherever their images resemble one another Dureau has the priority. His photographs, however, differ from Mapplethorpe's in important respects. His interest in cripples and in physically disadvantaged people (particularly dwarfs) had led to comparisons with Diane Arbus. Yet Dureau is very unlike Arbus and also unlike Mapplethorpe in the profound sympathy he brings to his subjects. For Mapplethorpe his black men are beautiful objects, or at best beautiful male animals, representations of sexual power purged of almost any trace of human individuality. Dureau, on the contrary, empathizes with his subjects. For him,

258 ROBERT MAPPLETHORPE *Thomas* 1986

259 GEORGE DUREAU
Wilbert Hines 1972

each is a complete, complex personality, and nudity is one way of revealing that complexity, in addition to satisfying the photographer's own erotic interest, which is undoubtedly present.

This attitude is greatly modified in the work of such artists as Robert Gober, David Wojnarowicz (1954–92), and Ross Bleckner, who deal

176 not simply with homosexual preferences but with AIDS. Gober's sculptures and environmental pieces, already cited in a previous chapter, are so elusive that to call them AIDS-art without much qualification falsifies the artist's intent. Yet they do often have a feeling of muffled lamentation, of obscure grief, which critics have linked to Gober's situation as an 'out' gay man, living and working in New

255 York. Bleckner's paintings are by no means all of them about AIDS – others play elaborate postmodernist games with abstract and figurative conventions. There is, however, a long series of canvases featuring chalices and vases of flowers, often amid rays of light, which are commemorations of the victims of the disease. Bleckner claims that in these he is 'degrading the sublime. I want my paintings to attempt a belief and a sincerity which I, as an artist, don't necessarily feel, and certainly don't feel continuously.'[6]

284

Wojnarowicz, together with his fellow AIDS-victim, the British painter and film-maker Derek Jarman (1941–94), was one of the fiercest polemicists associated with the fight against AIDS. Jarman's later paintings, for example those included in his exhibition 'QUEER' in 1992, shortly before his death, and in the posthumous show 'EVIL QUEEN' in 1994, are violent inscriptions and graffitoed emblems; Wojnarowicz's are more frequently complex personal narratives, often with overlapping systems of imagery which the spectator is forced to decode. However, they too spring from urban graffiti. Wojnarowicz began his career spray-painting emblematic designs on walls and in abandoned warehouses (notorious for clandestine homosexual encounters) along the Hudson River waterfront. There is in fact no real frontier between Wojnarowicz's work as a visual artist and his work as a writer, though (paradoxically enough) his fierce autobiographical book *Close to the Knives* (New York, 1991) has little to say about art itself, though much to impart about the author's disturbed adulthood

260 DAVID WOJNAROWICZ *Bad Moon Rising* 1989

and damaged childhood. What the two artists have in common, besides their fate, is an urgency of utterance which has little or nothing to do with the idea of conscious stylistic gesture. In AIDS art, the actual subject-matter is primary. Another homosexual artist and AIDS-victim who fits into this category is the British painter David Robilliard (1952–89), whose wry inscriptions decorated with mock-naïve drawings put him in a neighbouring category to that occupied by Jenny Holzer with her 'Truisms'.

Lesbian art has achieved much less public visibility than gay male art. What is currently the fullest account of the activity of 'out' lesbian artists, the second edition of Emmanuel Cooper's *The Sexual Perspective: Homosexuality and Art in the Last 100 Years in the West*,[7] makes it clear that a great deal of what he describes has had to rely on 'alternative' spaces to achieve visibility, and has thus remained somewhat out of the mainstream (in marked contrast to the enormous commercial success achieved by Robert Mapplethorpe, whose estate, after his death, was valued for probate at $228 million).

There is also the fact that lesbian artists have been divided between the wish to focus on women's issues, and focusing on purely lesbian ones. Nancy Fried's (b. 1945) sculptured torsos in clay are about suf-

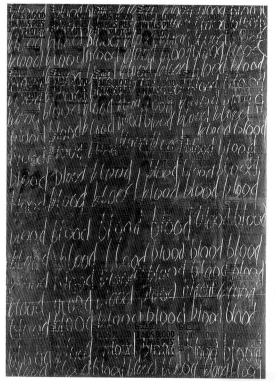

261 DEREK JARMAN
Blood 1992

262 NANCY FRIED
The Hand Mirror 1987

fering from cancer, and the need to undergo a mastectomy: these are subjects that, in the same circumstances, any women artist might feel the need to tackle. Lesbian identity is often affirmed through appropriation, for example, in Sadie Lee's (b. 1955) witty version of the Mona Lisa, showing Leonardo's iconic woman wearing a collar and tie. This image is an addition to a long series of Mona Lisa variants in twentieth-century art, beginning with Duchamp's *L.H.O.O.Q.*

One problem with a purely issue-based art is that it tends to devalue universal human emotions. Some of the most moving comments on the AIDS crisis, for example, have been made by the American performance artists Karen Finley, who is heterosexual, but who has lost many friends to the disease. Her installation piece *The Vacant Chair* (1993), a throne-like seat covered with flowers, foliage and moss, confronting two plain chairs, is a comment on grief and loss. The spectator takes one of the plain chairs and is asked to contemplate the fact of absence. Though triggered by a situation specific to the 1980s and 1990s, this looks at something much larger: our relationship as human beings to all those who have passed through our lives and are now 263

263 KAREN FINLEY *The Vacant Chair* 1993

departed from us. Finley points out that the symbolism of the chair or
seat left vacant on some social occasion is in fact very old.

Another problem is that it has increasingly tended to squeeze out
aesthetic feeling and to replace it with arid, aggressively moralistic
didacticism. Everything we know about what we call art – and as I
pointed out in my first chapter what we call art is in fact a variable,
which changes according to context – suggests that the impulse to
make it and the desire to become engaged with it traditionally have
much to do with the workings of the pleasure principle. The pursuit
of morality as an end in itself eventually becomes wearisome. Shock
tactics, which go hand in hand with the new moralism (Andres
Serrano's *Piss Christ*, mentioned in my first chapter, is a case in point)
notoriously offer only diminishing returns. These are problems which
the artists of the first decades of the new millenium are going to have
to work out, as the original modernists worked out a way to escape
from the straightjacket of nineteenth–century academicism.

8

288

Text References

Chapter One

1 See, for example, Irving Sandler's *The Triumph of American Painting: A History of Abstract Expressionism*, New York, 1970.

2 On this subject, see Marcel Duchamp's unequivocal letter to Hans Richter, dated 10 November 1962, condemning Pop art. Duchamp says: 'This Neo-Dada, which they call New Realism, Pop Art, Assemblage, etc., is an easy way out and lives on what Dada did. When I discovered ready-mades I thought to discourage aesthetics. In Neo-Dada they have taken my ready-mades and found aesthetic beauty in them. I threw the bottle-rack and the urinal in their faces and now they admire them for their aesthetic beauty.' Hans Richter, *Dada – Art and Anti-Art*, London, Thames and Hudson, and New York, McGraw-Hill, 1966, pp. 207–8.

Chapter Two

1 André Breton, *Manifestes du Surréalisme*, Paris, J.-J. Pauvert, 1962, p. 40.

2 Maurice Nadeau, *The History of Surrealism*, New York, Collier Books, 1967, and London, Jonathan Cape, 1968, p. 202.

3 Barbara Rose, *American Art Since 1900*, New York, and London, 1967, pp. 127 *et seq.*

4 Harold Rosenberg, 'Arshile Gorky: the Man, the Time, the Idea', *Horizon*, New York, 1962, p. 106.

5 *Arshile Gorky: Paintings, Drawings, Studies*, catalogue of an exhibition held at the Museum of Modern Art, New York, in collaboration with the Washington Gallery of Modern Art, 1962, p. 45.

6 Talcott B. Clapp. 'A painter in a glass house', quoted in *Arshile Gorky: Paintings, Drawings, Studies*, catalogue of an exhibition held at the Museum of Modern Art, New York, in collaboration with the Washington Gallery of Modern Art, 1962, p. 43.

7 Jackson Pollock, 'My Painting', *Possibilities* 1, New York, George Wittenborn, winter 1947–8.

8 André Breton, op. cit., p. 44.

9 Harold Rosenberg, *The Tradition of the New*, London, Thames and Hudson, 1962, p. 31.

10 Ibid., p. 30.

11 Frank O'Hara, *Jackson Pollock*, New York, George Braziller, 1959, p. 116.

12 Patrick Heron, 'The Ascendancy of London', *Studio International*, London, December 1966.

Chapter Three

1 From interviews with Francis Bacon by David Sylvester, recorded and filmed in London for BBC Television, May 1968, in *Francis Bacon: Recent Paintings*, catalogue of an exhibition at the Marlborough New London Gallery, March-April 1967, p. 26.

2 Peter Selz and Jean Dubuffet, *The Work of Jean Dubuffet*, New York, The Museum of Modern Art, 1962, pp. 81–2.

3 Jean Dubuffet, *Prospectus et tous écrits suivants II*, Paris, Gallimard, 1967, p. 74.

Chapter Four

1 Barbara Rose, op. cit., p. 234.

2 Max Kozloff, 'The New American Painting' in Richard Kostelanetz ed., *The New American Arts*, New York, Collier Books, 1967, p. 102.

3 Clement Greenberg, 'Louis and Noland', *Art International*, vol. 4, No. 5, Zurich 1960.

4 Michael Fried, introduction to *Morris Louis 1912–1962*, Boston, Museum of Fine Arts, 1967, p. 21.

5 Michael Fried, catalogue of *Three American Artists*, an exhibition at the Fogg Art Museum, Harvard University, 1965, p. 27.

Chapter Five

1 William C. Seitz, *The Art of Assemblage*, New York, The Museum of Modern Art, 1961, p. 87.

2 John Cage, *Silence*, Middletown, Conn., Wesleyan University Press, 1961, p. 10.

3 Quoted by Pierre Descargues in *Yves Klein*, catalogue of an exhibition at the Jewish Museum, New York, 1967, p. 18.

4 Mario Amaya, *Pop as Art*, London, Studio Vista, 1965, p. 33.

5 Ibid., p. 33.

6 Harold Rosenberg, *The Anxious Object*, London, Thames and Hudson, 1964, pp. 27–8.

7 Quoted by Gene Baro in 'Claes Oldenburg, or the things of this world', *Art International*, New York, November 1966.

8 From replies to questions put by G. R. Swenson, *Art News*, New York, November 1963.

9 Quoted by Mario Amaya, op. cit., p. 95.

10 *Andy Warhol*, catalogue of an exhibition at the Institute of Contemporary Art, University of Pennsylvania, 8 October–21 November 1965.

11 Quoted by Adrian Henri, *Environments and Happenings*, London, Thames and Hudson, 1974, p. 168.

Chapter Six

1 Frank O'Hara, in *David Smith 1906–1965*, catalogue of an exhibition held at the Tate Gallery, London, 1966, pp. 9–10.

2 'Anthony Caro interviewed by Andrew Forge', *Studio International*, London, 1968.

3 Statement in *Tony Smith. Two Exhibitions of Sculpture*, catalogue of exhibitions held at Wadsworth Atheneum, Hartford, Conn., and The Institute of Contemporary Art, University of Pennsylvania, 1966–7.

4 Ibid., note on *Black Box*.

5 Donald Judd, 'Specific Objects', *Contemporary Sculptors*, New York, The Art Digest (Arts Yearbook 8), 1965, p. 79.

6 Robert Morris, 'Notes on Sculpture', *Artforum*, New York, February 1966, p. 44.

7 Dan Flavin '. . . In Daylight or Cool White', *Artforum*, December 1965, p. 24.

Chapter Seven

1 Marco Meneguzzo, in *Verso l'arte povera*, catalogue of an exhibition held at the Padiglione d'arte contemporanea, Milan, 1989, p. 17.

2   Meneguzzo, ibid., p. 19.

3   Germano Celant, *Arte Povera: storie e protagonisti*, Milan, 1985, p. 27.

4   Charles Hall in *Damien Hirst*, catalogue of an exhibition held at the Institute of Contemporary Arts, London, 1991, no pagination.

Chapter Eight

1   Christos M. Joachimides in *A New Spirit in Painting*, catalogue of an exhibition held at the Royal Academy of Arts, London, 1981, p. 14.

Chapter Nine

1   Quoted in Peter Schjeldahl, *Eric Fischl*, New York, 1988, p. 21.

2   Jeffrey Deitch in *Cultural Geometry*, catalogue of an exhibition held at the Deste Foundation for Contemporary Art, Athens, 1988, p. 39.

3   Peter Halley in ibid., p. 83.

4   Robert Rosenblum in *The Jeff Koons Handbook*, London, Thames and Hudson, 1992, p. 15.

5   Collective interview in Dan Cameron, *NY Art Now: The Saatchi Collection*, Milan, 1988, p. 27.

6   Article reproduced photographically on p. 242 of Henry Adams, *Thomas Hart Benton: An American Original*, New York, 1989.

7   This movement had been chronicled by Caroline E. Jones in an excellent book, *Bay Area Figurative Art*, Berkeley, 1990, which contains a detailed, year-by-year chronology of its development.

8   This impulse has been briefly but authoritatively discussed by Professor Whitney Chadwick in her essay 'Narrative Imagism and the Figurative Tradition in Northern California Painting', *Art Journal*, XLV, winter 1985, pp. 309–14.

9   Thomas Kellein in *Mike Kelley*, catalogue of an exhibition held at the Kunsthalle, Basel, 1992, p. 7.

10   Bill Berkson, 'Seattle Sites', *Art in America*, New York, June 1986, p. 72.

Chapter Ten

1   Jan Hoet in *Africa Now: The Jean Pigozzi Collection*, Groniger Museum, Groningen, 1991, p. 29.

2   Ibid., p. 30.

3   See, for example, *Peasant Paintings from Hu County, Shensi Province, China*, catalogue of an exhibition organized by the Arts Council of Great Britain, 1976, which illustrates a full range of these images.

Chapter Eleven

1   Edmund Barry Gaither, *Afro-American Artists*, New York and Boston (Boston, The National Center of Afro-American Artists), 1970, pp. 3–4.

2   Reprinted in Thomas Hess and Elizabeth Baker, eds., *Art and Sexual Politics*, New York and London, 1971; and in Linda Nochlin, *Women, Art, and Power and Other Essays*, New York, 1989, and London, 1991.

3   See Jack Fritscher, *Mapplethorpe: Assault with a Deadly Camera*, Marmaroneck, New York, 1994, p. 65 and passim.

4   Op. cit., p. 9.

5   See Melody D. Davis, *The Male Nude in Contemporary Photography*, Philadelphia, 1991, pp. 67 *et seq.*, directly comparing Mapplethorpe and Dureau.

6   Ross Bleckner, in *Ross Bleckner*, catalogue of an exhibition held at the Kunsthalle, Zurich, 1990, no pagination.

7   London and New York, 1994; first published 1986.

Select Bibliography

A New Spirit in Painting (exh. cat.), Royal Academy of Arts, London, 1981.

ADES, DAWN, et al. *Art in Latin America: The Modern Era, 1820–1980* (exh. cat.), Hayward Gallery, London, 1989.

Against Nature: Japanese Art in the Eighties (exh. cat.), Grey Art Gallery and Study Center, New York University, New York, 1989.

ALLBRIGHT, THOMAS, *Art in the San Francisco Bay Area, 1945–1980: An Illustrated History*, Berkeley, 1985.

ANDERSEN, WAYNE, *American Sculpture in Process: 1930–1970*, Boston and New York, 1975.

ARAEEN, RASHEED, *The Other Story: Afro-Asian Artists in Post-War Britain* (exh. cat.), Hayward Gallery, London, 1989.

ARCHER SHAW, PETRINE AND KIM ROBINSON, *Jamaican Art: An Overview*, Kingston, Jamaica, 1990.

ARMSTRONG, RICHARD, *Mind over Matter: Concept and Object* (exh. cat.), Whitney Museum of American Art, New York, 1990.

ARMSTRONG, RICHARD, *The New Sculpture, 1965–1975* (exh. cat.), Whitney Museum of American Art, New York, 1990.

Art of Our Time: The Saatchi Collection,

4 vols., London and New York, 1984.

ASHTON, DORE, *American Art Since 1945*, New York and London, 1982.

BATTCOCK, GREGORY AND ROBERT NICKAS, *The Art of Performance. A Critical Anthology*, New York, 1984.

BATTCOCK, GREGORY, ed., *Idea Art*, New York, 1973.

BATTCOCK, GREGORY, ed., *Minimal Art: A Critical Anthology*, New York, 1968.

BATTCOCK, GREGORY, ed., *New Artists Video, A Critical Anthology*. New York, 1978.

BATTCOCK, GREGORY, ed., *Super-*

Realism, New York, 1975.

BEARDSLEY, JOHN, *Earthworks and Beyond: Contemporary Art in the Landscape*, New York, 1984.

BECKETT, WENDY, *Contemporary Women Artists*, New York, 1988.

Black Art: Ancestral Legacy – the African Impulse in African American Art (exh. cat.), Dallas Museum of Art, 1989.

BONITO OLIVA, ACHILLE, *Europe-America: The Different Avant-gardes*, Milan, 1976.

BOWLT, JOHN E., *The Quest for Self-Expression: Painting in Moscow and Leningrad 1965–1990* (exh. cat.), Columbus Museum of Art, OH, 1990.

British Art in the 20th Century: The Modern Movement (exh. cat.), Royal Academy of Arts, London, 1987.

BROUDE, NORMA, AND MARY D. GARRARD, eds., *The Power of Feminist Art*, New York and London, 1994.

BUTTERFIELD, JAN, *The Art of Light and Space*, New York, 1993.

CARLOZZI, ANNETTE, *50 Texas Artists*, San Francisco, 1986.

CARUANA, WALLY, *Aboriginal Art*, London, 1993.

CELANT, GERMANO, *Unexpressionism: Art Beyond the Contemporary*, New York, 1988.

CHADWICK, WHITNEY, *Women, Art and Society*, London, 1990.

CHASE, LINDA, *Hyperrealism*, New York, 1975.

CHICAGO, JUDY, *The Dinner Party: A Symbol of our Heritage*, Garden City, 1979.

China Avant-Garde (exh. cat.), Haus der Kulturen der Welt, Berlin, and Museum of Modern Art, Oxford, 1993.

CHIPP, HERSCHEL B., *Theories of Modern Art*, Berkeley, Los Angeles and London, 1973.

COHEN, JEAN LEBOLD, *The New Chinese Painting 1949–1986*, New York, 1987.

COLPITT, FRANCIS, *Minimal Art: The Critical Perspective*, Ann Arbor, MI, 1990.

Contemporary Indian Art (exh. cat.), Royal Academy of Arts, London, 1982.

COOPER, EMMANUEL, *The Sexual Perspective: Homosexuality and Art in the Last 100 Years in the West*, 2nd revised ed., London, 1994.

DAY, HOLLIDAY T., AND HOLLISTER STURGES, *Art of the Fantastic: Latin America, 1920–1987* (exh. cat.), Indianapolis Museum of Art, 1987.

DEITCH, JEFFREY, AND DAN FRIEDMAN, eds., *Artificial Nature* (exh. cat.), Deste Foundation for Contemporary Art, Athens, Geneva, New York, 1990.

DEITCH, JEFFREY, AND PETER HALLEY, *Cultural Geometry* (exh. cat.), Deste Foundation for Contemporary Art, Athens, 1988.

DEITCH, JEFFREY, *Post Human* (exh. cat.), FAE Musée d'Art Contemporain, Pully/Lausanne, 1992.

DEITCH, JEFFREY, *Strange Abstraction* (exh. cat.), Touko Museum of Contemporary Art, Japan, 1991.

Difference: On Representation and Sexuality (exh. cat.), New Museum of Contemporary Art, New York, 1985.

Doubletake: Collective Memory and Current Art (exh. cat.), Hayward Gallery, London, 1992.

DUNN, MICHAEL, *A Concise History of New Zealand Painting*, Auckland, 1991.

English Art Today 1960–76 (exh. cat.), 2 vols., Palazzo Reale, Milan, 1976.

FINE, ELSA HONIG, *The Afro-American Artist: A Search for Identity*, New York, 1982.

FOX, HOWARD N., MIRANDA MCCLINTIC AND PHYLLIS ROSENZWEIG, *Content: A Contemporary Focus 1974–1984* (exh. cat.), Hirshhorn Museum and Sculpture Garden, Washington DC, 1984.

GABLIK, SUZI, *Has Modernism Failed?*, London and New York, 1985.

GELDZAHLER, HENRY, *New York Painting and Sculpture: 1940–1970* (exh. cat.), Metropolitan Museum of Art, New York, 1969.

German Art in the 20th Century: Painting and Sculpture, 1905–1985 (exh. cat.), Royal Academy of Arts, London, 1985.

GLUSBERG, JORGE, *Art in Argentina*, Milan, 1986.

GODFREY, TONY, *The New Image: Painting in the 1980s*, London, 1986.

GOLDBERG, ROSELEE, *Performance Art, from Futurism to the Present*, 2nd revised ed., New York, 1988.

Gutai – Japanische Avantgarde/Japanese Avant-Garde, 1954–1965 (exh. cat.), Mathildenhohe, Darmstadt, 1991.

HARRISON, CHARLES, *Essays on Art & Language*, Oxford, 1991.

HERTZ, RICHARD, ed., *Theories of Contemporary Art*, Englewood Cliffs, NJ, 1985.

HICKS, ALISTAIR, *New British Art in the Saatchi Collection*, London, 1989.

Hispanic Art in the United States: Thirty Contemporary Painters and Sculptors (exh. cat.), Museum of Fine Arts, Houston, 1987.

HUGHES, ROBERT, *Culture of Complaint*, New York and London, 1993.

India, Myth & Reality, Aspects of Modern Indian Art (exh. cat.), Museum of Modern Art, Oxford, 1982.

Italian Art in the 20th Century: Painting and Sculpture 1900–1988 (exh. cat.), Royal Academy of Arts, London, 1989.

JENCKS, CHARLES, *Post-Modernism: Neo-Classicism in Art and Architecture*, New York, 1987.

JOACHIMIDES, CHRISTOS M., AND NORMAN ROSENTHAL, eds., *American Art in the 20th Century* (exh. cat.), Royal Academy of Arts, London, 1993.

JOACHIMIDES, CHRISTOS M., AND NORMAN ROSENTHAL, eds., *Metropolis* (exh. cat.), Martin-Gropius-Bau, Berlin, 1991; English-language version of the catalogue, New York, 1991.

KARSHAN, DONALD, ed., *Conceptual Art and Conceptual Aspects*, New York, 1970.

KRAUSS, ROSALIND, *The Originality of the Avant-Garde and Other Modernist Myths*, Cambridge, MA, 1986.

LEVIN, KIM, *Beyond Modernism: Essays on Art from the '70s and '80s*, New York, 1988.

LEWIS, SAMELLA, *Art: African-American*, 2nd revised edition, Los Angeles, 1990.

LIPPARD, LUCY R., *Mixed Blessings: New Art in a Multi-Cultural America*, New York, 1990.

LIPPARD, LUCY R., *Six Years: The Dematerialization of the Art Object from 1966 to 1972*, New York, 1973.

LUCIE-SMITH, EDWARD, *American Art Now*, Oxford, 1985.

LUCIE-SMITH, EDWARD, *American Realism*, London and New York, 1994.

LUCIE-SMITH, EDWARD, *Art in the Eighties*, Oxford, 1990.

LUCIE-SMITH, EDWARD, *Art in the Seventies*, Oxford, 1980.

LUCIE-SMITH, EDWARD, *Latin American Art of the 20th Century*, London, 1993.

LUCIE-SMITH, EDWARD, CAROLYN COHEN AND JUDITH HIGGINS, *The New British*

Painting, Oxford, 1988.

LUCIE-SMITH, EDWARD, *Race, Sex and Gender in Contemporary Art*, London, 1994.

MAHSUN, CAROL ANNE RUNYON, ed., *Pop Art: The Critical Dialogue*, Ann Arbor, MI, 1989.

MAMIYA, CHRISTIN J., *Pop Art and Consumer Culture: American Super Market*, Austin, 1992.

MCSHINE, KYNASTON, ed., *Information*, New York, 1970.

MEISEL, LOUIS K., *Photo-Realism*, New York, 1980.

MEYER, URSULA., ed., *Conceptual Art*, New York, 1972.

MILLET, CATHERINE, *L'art contemporain en France*, Paris, 1987.

Modernidade: art brésilien du 20e siècle (exh. cat.), Musée d'Art Moderne de la Ville de Paris, 1987.

MORPHET, RICHARD, *The Hard-Won Image: Traditional Method and Subject in Recent British Art* (exh. cat.), Tate Gallery, London, 1984.

MOSZYNSKA, A., *Abstract Art*, London and New York, 1990.

MOUNT, MARSHALL W., *African Art – the Years since 1920*, 2nd revised edition, New York, 1989.

MULLER, GRÉGOIRE, *The New Avant-Garde: Issues for the Art of the Seventies*, London, 1972.

MUNROE, ALEXANDRA, *Japanese Art after 1945: Scream Against the Sky* (exh. cat.), Guggenheim Museum, New York, 1994.

MUSSA, ITALO, *La pittura colta*, Rome, 1983.

NOCHLIN, LINDA, *Women, Art and Power and Other Essays*, New York, 1989, and

London, 1991.

Nuevos Momentos del Arte Mexicano/New Moments in Mexican Art (exh. cat.), Parallel Project, New York, 1990.

Pacific Rim Diaspora (exh. cat.), Long Beach Museum of Art, CA, 1990.

PINCUS-WITTEN, ROBERT, *Postminimalism*, London, 1977.

PLAGENS, PETER, *Sunshine Muse: Contemporary Art on the West Coast*, New York, 1974.

RASMUSSEN, WALDO, *Artistas Latinoamericanos del siglo XX: Latin American Artists of the Twentieth Century* (exh. cat.), MOMA, New York, 1993.

RAVEN, ARLENE, ed., *Art in the Public Interest*, Ann Arbor, MI, 1989.

RAVEN, ARLENE,CASSANDRA LANGER AND JOANNA FRUEH, eds., *Feminist Art Criticism: An Anthology*, New York, 1988.

RISATTI, HOWARD, ed., *Postmodern Perspectives: Issues in Contemporary Art*, Englewood Cliffs, NJ, 1990.

ROSE, JACQUELINE, *Sexuality in the Field of Vision*, London, 1986.

ROSENBERG, HAROLD, *Art and Other Serious Matters*, Chicago, 1985.

ROSENBERG, HAROLD, *Art on the Edge*, New York, 1975.

ROSENBERG, HAROLD, *The De-Definition of Art. Action Art to Pop to Earthworks*, New York, 1992.

ROSS, DAVID A., *Between Spring and Summer: Soviet Conceptual Art in the Era of Late Communism*, Cambridge, MA, 1990.

RUSSELL, JOHN, *The Meanings of Modern Art*, New York, 1981.

SEYMOUR, ANNE, *The New Art* (exh. cat.), Hayward Gallery, London, 1972.

SHONE, RICHARD, *Some Went Mad, Some*

Ran Away . . . (exh. cat.), Serpentine Gallery, London, 1994.

SIEGEL, JEANNE, ed., *Art Talk: The Early 80s*, Ann Arbor, MI, 1988.

SUSSMAN, ELISABETH, WITH THELMA GOLDEN, JOHN G. HANHARDT AND LISA PHILLIPS, *1993 Biennial Exhibition* (exh. cat.), Whitney Museum of American Art, New York, 1993.

SZEEMAN, HARALD, ed., *Live in Your Head: When Attitudes Become Form*, Berne, 1969.

The New Culture: Women Artists of the Seventies (exh. cat.), Turman Gallery, Indiana State University, 1984.

The Spiritual in Art: Abstract Painting 1890–1985 (exh. cat.), Los Angeles County Museum of Art, 1986.

TOMKINS, CALVIN, *Post- to Neo-: The Art World of the 1980s*, New York, 1988.

Unbound: Possibilities in Painting (exh. cat.), Hayward Gallery, London, 1994.

VALLIER, DORA, *La peinture en France: début et fin d'un système visuel 1870–1970*, Milan, 1976.

VOGEL, SUSAN, *Africa Explores: 20th Century African Art* (exh. cat.), Center for African Arts, New York, 1991.

WALKER, JOHN A., *Art Since Pop*, London, 1975.

WALLIS, BRIAN, ed., *Art After Modernism: Rethinking Representation*, New York, 1984.

WHEELER, DANIEL, *Art Since Mid-Century: 1945 to the Present*, New York, 1991.

Who Chicago? (exh. cat.), Ceolfrith Gallery, Sunderland Arts Centre, Sunderland, 1981.

Working with Nature: Traditional Thought in Contemporary Art from Korea (exh. cat.), Tate Gallery, Liverpool, 1992.

Chronology

1940–49

1940

Mondrian leaves London and settles in New York.

1941

Pearl Harbor. German invasion of

Russia. Breton, Ernst and Chagall arrive in New York.

Adolph Gottlieb begins his *Pictograph* series.

1941–2

New York: Gottlieb, Motherwell,

Pollock and Rothko experiment with automatism.

1942

'First Papers of Surrealism', New York.

In Paris, Dubuffet resumes painting full time, after an interval. Fautrier paints the *Hostages* series.

1943

Gorky paints the *Garden of Sochi* series.

Clyfford Still has his first solo exhibition.

Pollock has first solo exhibition at the Art of This Century Gallery, New York.

1944

Breton meets Arshile Gorky. Dubuffet has his first solo exhibition.

1945

Atomic bombs dropped on Hiroshima and Nagasaki.

Germany surrenders.

Manifesto del Realismo issued by a group of leading Italian artists.

'Art Concret', Galerie René Drouin, Paris (first major show of abstract art in Europe since the war).

1946

Lucio Fontana issues his *White Manifesto*.

Madí manifesto published in Buenos Aires.

1947

India achieves independence and is partitioned into India and Pakistan. Pollock begins his 'drip' paintings.

Still exhibits his first colour-field abstractions.

In Britain Eduardo Paolozzi starts making collages using images from magazines and advertisements.

Abstraction-Création group revived in Paris.

1948

State of Israel proclaimed.

Gorky commits suicide.

Barnett Newman begins to make colour-field paintings.

The Cobra Group is formed in Paris.

Dau al Set group formed in Barcelona.

1949

Germany divided into the DDR (German Democratic Republic) and the Federal Republic.

Chinese People's Republic proclaimed under Mao Tse-tung.

Motherwell begins his *Elegies to the Spanish Republic*.

Francis Bacon starts using photographic source material.

Simone de Beauvoir publishes *The Second Sex*.

1950–59

1950

North Korea invades South Korea.

Le Corbusier commissioned to build a new capital for the Punjab, Chandigargh.

1951

'Abstract Painting and Sculpture in America', MOMA, New York.

1952

Publication of *Art Autre* by Michel Tapié.

American critic Harold Rosenberg coins the term 'Action Painting'.

1953

Beckett's play *Waiting for Godot*.

1954

Beginning of the Algerian War.

US Supreme Court rules against segregation in public schools.

Foundation of Gutai group, Japan.

Jasper Johns, first *Flag* paintings.

1955

'Man, Machine and Motion', Institute of Contemporary Arts, London.

1956

Suez seized by British and French troops.

'This is Tomorrow', Whitechapel Art Gallery, London.

1958

'New American Painting', MOMA, New York.

Group Zero formed in Düsseldorf.

1959

Castro takes over in Cuba.

Groupe de Recherche d'Art Visuel founded in Paris.

'New Images of Man' exhibition, New York.

Alan Kaprow's '18 Happenings in 6

Parts' at the Reuben Gallery, New York.

1960–69

1960

Claes Oldenburg's exhibition 'The Street' at the Judson Gallery, New York.

Andy Warhol makes his first comic strip painting, *Dick Tracy*.

'New Forms, New Media', Martha Jackson Gallery, New York.

César makes his first *Compressions*.

Pierre Restany publishes his New Realist Manifesto.

1961

Berlin Wall constructed.

'The Art of Assemblage', MOMA, New York.

Joseph Beuys begins teaching at Düsseldorf Kunstakademie.

Publication of Clement Greenberg's *Art and Culture*.

Independently of Warhol, Roy Lichtenstein paints his first works based on comic strips.

Claes Oldenburg opens his 'Store' on East 2nd Street.

David Hockney paints *We Two Boys Together Clinging*.

Nueva Prescencia group (opposed to Mexican Muralism) founded in Mexico.

Wesselmann exhibits his first *Great American Nudes* at the Tanager Gallery, New York.

1962

Warhol paints Marilyn Monroe and Campbell's soup cans, and has his first solo exhibition at the Ferus Gallery, Los Angeles.

Ed Ruscha produces his first book of photographs, *Twenty Six Gasoline Stations*.

'The New Painting of Common Objects', Pasadena Art Museum.

BBC television film 'Pop goes the Easel'.

Pop art covered by *Time, Life*, and *Newsweek*.

1963

Kennedy is assassinated. USA begins its involvement in Vietnam.

'Towards a New Abstraction', Jewish Museum, New York.

'Mixed Media and Pop Art', Albright-Knox Art Gallery, Buffalo.

1964

'Post-Painterly Abstraction', Los Angeles County Museum of Art.

'Amerikanste Pop-Konst', Moderna Museet, Stockholm.

First 'New Generation' exhibition, Whitechapel Art Gallery, London.

1965

Andy Warhol's first retrospective, Institute of Contemporary Arts, London, and University of Pennsylvania, Philadelphia.

Colombian critic Marta Traba publishes her book *Los cuatro monstruos cardinales* in Mexico City: a further attack on Muralism.

1966

'Primary Structures', Jewish Museum, New York.

'Systematic Abstraction', Guggenheim Museum, New York.

First 'Hairy Who' group show, Hyde Park Art Center, Chicago.

'Art of Latin America since Independence', Yale University Art Gallery.

1967

Six-Day War between Israel and Arab nations.

Che Guevara killed in Bolivia.

'Lumière et Mouvement' exhibition, Paris.

'Light-Motion-Space', Walker Art Center, Minneapolis.

'Arte Povera', Galleria la Bertesca, Genoa.

'Sculpture of the Sixties', Los Angeles County Museum of Art.

'Yves Klein', Jewish Museum, New York.

'Funk', University of California, Berkeley.

1968

Martin Luther King assassinated.

'Les évènements' – student rioting in Paris.

'Minimal Art', Gemeentemuseum, The Hague.

'Earthworks', Dwan Gallery, New York.

'Realism Now', Vassar College Art Museum, Poughkeepsie.

1969

'Anti-Illusion: Procedures/Materials', Whitney Museum of American Art, New York.

'When Attitudes Become Form', Kunsthalle, Berne, Museum Haus Lange, Krefeld, and Institute of Contemporary Arts, London.

'Conceptual Art', Städiches Museum, Leverkusen.

Joseph Kosuth publishes 'Art After Philosophy' in *Studio International*.

First issue of *Art & Language* is published.

1970–79

1970

'Conceptual Art and Conceptual Aspects', New York Cultural Center.

'Conceptual art, arte povera, land art', Galleri Civica de Arte Moderna, Turin.

'Information', MOMA, New York.

Judy Chicago organizes the first feminist art course at the California State College at Fresno.

1971

Fighting in Vietnam spreads to Laos and Cambodia.

'Art and Technology', Los Angeles County Museum of Art.

'Contemporary Black Artists in America', Whitney Museum of American Art, New York.

1972

'The New Art', Hayward Gallery, London.

'Sharp-Focus Realism', Sidney Janis Gallery, New York.

1973

Allende is overthrown in Chile.

'Photo-Realism', Serpentine Gallery, London.

Mary Kelly begins work on *Post Partum Document* (–1979)

1974

Nixon resigns in the aftermath of Watergate.

1975

Last Americans are evacuated from South Vietnam.

'Bodyworks', Museum of Contemporary Art, Chicago.

1976

'The Human Clay', selected by R. B. Kitaj, Hayward Gallery, London.

'Women Artists: 1550–1950', Los Angeles County Museum of Art.

1977

Opening of the Centre Pompidou, Paris.

'Europe in the Seventies: Aspects of Recent Art', Art Institute of Chicago.

'Unofficial Art from the Soviet Union', Institute of Contemporary Arts, London.

1978

'Bad Painting', New Museum of Contemporary Art, New York.

1979

'Moderne Kunst aus Afrika', Staatlichen Kunsthalle, Berlin.

'Joseph Beuys' (retrospective exhibition), Guggenheim Museum, New York.

'Un certain art anglais . . .: Sélection d'artistes britanniques 1970–1979', ARC/Musée d'Art Moderne de la Ville de Paris.

Judy Chicago, *The Dinner Party*.

1980–89

1980

'Women's Images of Men', Institute of Contemporary Arts, London.

Robert Mapplethorpe exhibits the series *Black Males* at the Galerie Jurka, Amsterdam.

1981

'A New Spirit in Painting', Royal Academy of Arts, London.

'Westkunst', Museen der Stadt, Cologne.

1982

'Transavantguardia', Galleria Civica, Modena.

'Zeitgeist', Martin-Gropius-Bau, Berlin.

'Englische Plastik Heute', Kunstmuseum, Lucerne.

'India, Myth & Reality, Aspects of Modern Indian Art', Museum of Modern Art, Oxford.

Postminimalism', Aldrich Museum of Contemporary Art, Ridgefield, CT.

1983

'The New Art', Tate Gallery, London.

Italo Mussa publishes *La pittura colta*.

Mary Kelly Publishes *Post Partum Document*.

1984

'An International Survey of Recent Painting and Sculpture', MOMA, New York.

'The Hard-Won Image', Tate Gallery, London.

'Content: A Contemporary Focus 1974–1984', Hirshhorn Museum and Sculpture Garden, Washington DC.

1985

Gorbachev comes to power in Russia – beginning of *perestroika*.

'Kunst in der Bundesrepublik Deutschland 1945–1985', Nationalgalerie, Berlin.

1986

'The Spiritual in Art: Abstract Painting 1890–1985', Los Angeles County Museum of Art.

1987

'New York Art Now', Saatchi Collection, London.

'Berlinart 1961–1987', MOMA, New York.

'Art of the Fantastic: Latin America, 1920–1987', Indianapolis Museum of Art.

'Hispanic Art in the United States: Thirty Contemporary Painters and Sculptors', Museum of Fine Arts, Houston.

'Modernidade: art brésilien du 20e siècle', Musée d'Art Moderne de la Ville de Paris.

'Similia/Dissimilia', Städisches Kunsthalle, Düsseldorf.

Charles Jencks publishes *Post-Modernism: Neo-Classicism in Art and Architecture*.

1988

'Cultural Geometry', Deste Foundation for Contemporary Art, Athens.

'Refigured Painting: The German Image 1960–88', Guggenheim Museum, New York.

1989

The wall comes down in Berlin.

'The Other Story: Afro-Asian Artists in Post-War Britain', Hayward Gallery, London.

'Black Art: Ancestral Legacy – the African Impulse in African American Art', Dallas Museum of Art.

'L'art conceptuel, un perspective', Musée de l'Art Moderne de la Ville de Paris.

'The New Italian Manner', Mayer Schwarz Gallery, Beverly Hills, CA.

Linda Nochlin publishes *Women, Art and Power and Other Essays*.

1990–

1990

Germany is reunited.

Collapse of the Soviet empire.

'The Quest for Self-Expression: painting in Moscow and Leningrad 1965–1990', Columbus Museum of Art, Columbus, OH.

'Contemporary Russian Artists: Artisti Russi Contemporanei', Centro per l'arte contemporanea Luigi Pecci, Prato.

'Artificial Nature', Deste Foundation for Contemporary Art, Athens, Geneva, New York.

'Ilya Kabakov, "He lost his mind, undressed, and ran away naked"', Ronald Feldman Fine Arts, New York.

'L'art en France, 1945–1990', Fondation Daniel Templon, Musée temporaire, Fréjus.

'Nuevos momentos del arte mexicano/New Moments in Mexican Art', Parallel Project, New York.

'Between Spring and Summer: Soviet Conceptual Art in the Era of Late Communism', Institute of Contemporary Arts, Boston, MA.

Lucy R. Lippard publishes *Mixed Blessings: New Art in a Multi-Cultural America*, New York.

1991

Civil war in Yugoslavia.

'CARA: Chicano Art, Resistance and Affirmation', Wight Art Gallery, University of California, Los Angeles.

'Strange Abstraction', Touko Museum of Contemporary Art, Japan.

'From Art to Archaeology', South Bank Centre, London.

'Arte & Arte', Museo d'Arte Contemporanea, Castello di Rivoli, Turin.

'Mana Tiriti: The Art of Protest and Partnership', Haeta Maori Women's Art Collective, Project Waitangi, Wellington City Art Gallery, Wellington, NZ.

'Headlands: Thinking Through New Zealand Art', Museum of Contemporary Art, Sydney.

'Metropolis', Martin-Gropius-Bau, Berlin.

1992

'Post Human', FAE Musée d'Art Contemporain, Pully/Lausanne.

'Young British Artists', Saatchi Collection.

'Quattro Artisti della Nuova Maniera Italiana', Museum of Modern and Contemporary Art, Città della Pieve.

'Working with Nature: Traditional Thought in Contemporary Art from Korea', Tate Gallery, Liverpool.

1993

'Aratjara: Art of the First Australians', Kunstsammlung Nordrhein-Westfalen, Düsseldorf.

'China Avant-Garde', Haus der Kulturen der Welt, Berlin, and Museum of Modern Art, Oxford.

'Artistas latinoamericanos del siglo XX: Latin American Artists of the Twentieth Century', MOMA, New York.

Biennial Exhibition (the 'politically correct Biennial'), Whitney Museum of American Art, New York.

1994

'Some Went Mad, Some Ran Away . . .', Serpentine Gallery, London.

'Unbound: Possibilities in Painting', Hayward Gallery, London.

'Japanese Art after 1945: Scream Against the Sky', Guggenheim Museum, New York.

List of Illustrations

1957. Oil on wood 50.5 × 63.8 (19⅞ × 25⅛). Tate Gallery, London.
49 JEAN BAZAINE *Shadows on the Hill* 1961. Oil on canvas. Galerie Maeght, Paris.
50 JEAN FAUTRIER *Hostage* 1945. Oil on canvas 27.3 × 21.6 (10¾ × 8½). Private collection, London.
51 WOLS *The Blue Pomegranate* 1946. Oil on canvas 46 × 33 (18⅛ × 13). Collection Michel Couturier, Paris.
52 HANS HARTUNG *Painting T 54–16* 1954. Oil on canvas 129.9 × 96.8 (51⅛ × 38⅛). Musée National d'Art Moderne, Centre Georges Pompidou, Paris.
53 HENRI MICHAUX *Painting in India Ink* 1960–7. 74.9 × 105.1 (29½ × 41⅜). Galerie Le Point Cardinal, Paris.
54 JEAN-PAUL RIOPELLE *Encounter* 1956. Oil on canvas 99.7 × 81.3 (39¼ × 32). Wallraf-Richartz Museum, Cologne.
55 MANOLO MILLARES *No. 165* 1961. Plastic paint on canvas 81.3 × 100.3 (32 × 39½). Courtesy Marlborough Fine Art Ltd, London.
56 ANTONI TÀPIES *Black with Two Lozenges* 1963. Oil on canvas 411.5 × 330.2 (162 × 130). Private collection, Buenos Aires.
57 ALBERTO BURRI *Sacco 4* 1954. Burlap, cotton, rinavil glue, silk and paint on cotton canvas 114.3 × 76.2 (45 × 30). Collection Anthony Denney, London.
58 PIERRE SOULAGES *Painting* 1956. Oil on canvas 150.5 × 194.9 (59¼ × 76¾). The Museum of Modern Art, New York. Gift of Mr and Mrs Samuel M. Kootz.
59 GEORGES MATHIEU *Battle of Bouvines* 1954. Oil on canvas 250.2 × 600.1 (98½ × 236¼). Collection the artist.
60 ASGER JORN *You Never Know* 1966. Oil on canvas 64.8 × 81.3 (25½ × 32). Arthur Tooth & Sons Ltd, London.
61 ALAN DAVIE *The Martyrdom of St Catherine* 1956. Oil on canvas 182.9 × 243.9 (72 × 96). Collection Mrs Alan Davie.
62 KAREL APPEL *Women and Birds* 1958. Oil on canvas 174.6 × 130.2 (63¾ × 51¼). Private collection.
63 PIERRE ALECHINSKY *The Green Being Born* 1960. Oil on canvas 184.1 × 205.1 (72½ × 80¾). Musée Royaux d'Art et d'histoire, Brussels.
64 CORNEILLE *Souvenir of Amsterdam* 1956. Oil on canvas 120 × 120 (47¼ × 47¼). Private collection.
65 HUNDERTWASSER *The Hokkaido Steamer* 1961. Watercolour on rice-paper with a chalk ground 47.9 × 66 (18⅞ × 26). Collection S. and G. Poppe, Hamburg.
66 JEAN DUBUFFET *Corps de Dame*

1950. Watercolour 31.1 × 23.5 (12¼ × 9¼). Collection Peter Cochrane, London.
67 BERNARD BUFFET *Self-portrait* 1954. Oil on canvas 146.4 × 114 (57⅝ × 44⅞). Tate Gallery, London.
68 NICOLAS DE STAËL *Agrigente* 1954. Oil on canvas 63.3 × 81 (25⅝ × 31⅞). Private collection, Paris.
69 MAX BILL *Concentration to Brightness* 1964. Oil on canvas 105.4 × 105.4 (41½ × 41½).
70 RICHARD LOHSE *Fifteen Systematic Colour Scales Merging Vertically* 1950–67. Oil on canvas 120.6 × 120.6 (47¼ × 47¼). Kunsthaus, Zurich.
71 JOSEF ALBERS *Homage to the Square 'Curious'* 1963. Oil on canvas 76.2 × 76.2 (30 × 30). Collection R. Alistair McAlpine, London.
72 ELLSWORTH KELLY *White – Dark Blue* 1962. Oil on canvas 147.9 × 83.8 (58¼ × 33). Arthur Tooth & Sons Ltd, London.
73 AL HELD *Echo* 1966. Acrylic on canvas 213.4 × 182.9 (84 × 72). André Emmerich Gallery, New York.
74 JACK YOUNGERMAN *Totem Black* 1967. Oil on canvas 312.4 × 205.7 (123 × 81). Betty Parsons Gallery, New York.
75 BARNETT NEWMAN *Tundra* 1950. Oil on canvas 182.9 × 226.1 (72 × 89). Collection Mr and Mrs Robert A. Rowan.
76 AD REINHARDT *Red Painting* 1952. Oil on canvas 365.8 × 193 (144 × 76). The Metropolitan Museum of Art, New York. Arthur H. Hearn Fund, 1968.
77 JACK TWORKOV *North American* 1966. Oil on canvas 203.2 × 162.6 (80 × 64). Collection the artist.
78 HELEN FRANKENTHALER *Mountains and Sea* 1952. Oil on canvas 219.4 × 297.8 (86⅜ × 117¼). Collection the artist.
79 MORRIS LOUIS *Untitled* 1959. Magna acrylic on canvas 264.2 × 193 (104 × 76). Photo Kasmin Gallery, London.
80 KENNETH NOLAND *Cantabile* 1962. Plastic paint on canvas 168.9 × 163.2 (66½ × 64¼). Collection Walker Art Center, Minneapolis.
81 MORRIS LOUIS *Omicron* 1961. Synthetic polymer paint on canvas 262.3 × 412 (103¼ × 162¼). Waddington Gallery, London.
82 KENNETH NOLAND *Grave Light* 1965. Plastic paint on canvas 259.1 × 228.6 (102 × 90). Collection Mr and Mrs Robert A. Rowan.
83 FRANK STELLA *New Madrid* 1961. Liquitex on canvas 193 × 193 (76 × 76). Kasmin Gallery, London.
84 EDWARD AVEDISIAN *At Seven Brothers* 1964. Liquitex on canvas 91.4 × 91.4 (36 × 36). Kasmin Gallery,

London.
85 FRANK STELLA *Untitled* 1968. Acrylic on cotton duck 243.8 × 487.7 (96 × 192). Collection Lord Dufferin. Photo Kasmin Gallery, London.
86 LARRY POONS *Night Journey* 1968. Acrylic on canvas 274.3 × 315 (108 × 124). Collection Carter Burden, New York.
87 JULES OLITSKI *Feast* 1965. Magna acrylic on canvas 236.2 × 66 (93 × 26). Collection Catherine Zimmerman, Brookline, Massachusetts.
88 JOHN HOYLAND *28.5.66* 1966. Acrylic on canvas 198.1 × 365.8 (78 × 144). Collection the artist.
89 JEREMY MOON *Blue Rose* 1967. Oil on canvas 218.4 × 251.5 (86 × 99). Tate Gallery, London.
90 JOHN WALKER *Touch – Yellow* 1967. Acrylic and chalk on canvas 266.7 × 518.2 (105 × 204). Collection the artist.
91 TESS JARAY *Garden of Allah* 1966. Oil on canvas 198.1 × 243.8 (72 × 96). Collection the artist.
92 ROBYN DENNY *Growing* 1967. Oil on canvas 243.8 × 198.1 (96 × 78). Collection the Peter Stuyvesant Foundation.
93 JOSEPH CORNELL *Eclipse Series* c.1962. Construction 304.8 × 487.7 × 152.4 (120 × 192 × 60). Collection of Allan Stone, New York.
94 ENRICO BAJ *Lady Fabricia Trolopp* 1964. Collage 100 × 81 (39⅜ × 31⅞). Galleria Schwarz, Milan.
95 JASPER JOHNS *Numbers in Colour* 1959. Encaustic and collage on canvas 168.9 × 125.7 (66½ × 49½). Albright-Knox Art Gallery, Buffalo, New York. Gift of Seymour H. Knox.
96 ROBERT RAUSCHENBERG *Barge* 1962. Oil on canvas 203.2 × 988.1 (80 × 389). Leo Castelli Gallery, New York.
97 ROBERT RAUSCHENBERG *Bed* 1955. Combine painting 188 × 79 (74 × 3). Collection Mr and Mrs Leo Castelli.
98 EDWARD KIENHOLZ *Roxy's* 1961. Mixed media 240 × 540.7 × 669.9 (94½ × 212⅝ × 263¾). Collection the artist. Photo Dwan Gallery, New York.
99 BRUCE CONNER *Couch* 1963. Assemblage 80 × 671 × 1,831 (31½ × 264 × 721). Pasadena Art Museum, California.
100 ARMAN *Clic-Clac Rate* 1960–6. Accumulation of photographic apparatus 60 × 100 (23⅝ × 39⅜). Galleria Schwarz, Milan.
101 PAUL THEK *Death of a Hippie* 1967. Pink painted hardboard, wax body 259.1 × 320 × 320 (102 × 126 × 126). Stable Gallery, New York.
102 CHRISTO *Packaged Public Building* 1961. Photomontage 33 × 91.1 (13 × 35⅝). Collection the artist.
103 YVES KLEIN *Feu F 45* 1961. Oil on

paper 79.4 × 102.9 (31¼ × 40½). Private collection, Paris.

104 Yves Klein's painting cermony (the creation of *Imprints*). Photo Shunk-Kender, Paris.

105 PIERO MANZONI *Line 20 Metres Long* 1959. Ink on paper. Collection Edward Lucie-Smith, London.

106 LUCIO FONTANA *Spatial Concept* 1960. Oil on canvas 97.1 × 59.7 (38¼ × 23½). McRoberts and Tunnard Gallery, London.

107 MICHELANGELO PISTOLETTO *Seated Figure* 1962. Collage on polished steel 125.1 × 125.1 (49½ × 49½). Kaiser-Wilhelm-Museum, Krefeld.

108 MARTIAL RAYSSE *Tableau simple et doux* 1965. Assemblage with neon light 194.9 × 130.2 (76¾ × 51¼). Collection André Mourgues, Paris.

109 TOMIO MIKI *Ears* (detail) 1968. Plated aluminium 17.1 × 15.9 × 7 (6¾ × 6¼ × 2¾). Tate Gallery, London.

110 RICHARD HAMILTON *Just What is it that Makes Today's Homes so Different, so Appealing?* 1956. Collage 26 × 24.8 (10¼ × 9¾). Collection E. Janss, Los Angeles.

111 RICHARD SMITH *Soft Pack* 1963. Oil on canvas 213.4 × 175.3 (84 × 69). Joseph H. Hirshhorn Collection, New York.

112 PETER BLAKE *Doktor K. Tortur* 1965. Cryla, collage on hardboard 61 × 25.4 (24 × 10). Robert Fraser Gallery, London.

113 PETER PHILLIPS *For Men Only Starring MM and BB* 1961. Oil on canvas 274.3 × 152.4 (108 × 60). The Calouste Gulbenkian Foundation, London.

114 DEREK BOSHIER *England's Glory* 1961. Oil on canvas 101.6 × 127.6 (40 × 50¼). Grabowski Gallery, London.

115 DAVID HOCKNEY *Picture Emphasizing Stillness* 1962–3. Oil on canvas 182.9 × 152.4 (72 × 60). Collection Mark Glazebrook, London.

116 DAVID HOCKNEY *A Neat Lawn* 1967. Acrylic on canvas 243.8 × 243.8 (96 × 96). Kasmin Gallery, London.

117 DAVID HOCKNEY *Rubber Ring Floating in a Swimming Pool* 1971. Acrylic on canvas 90.8 × 121.9 (35¾ × 48). Private collection, London.

118 RICHARD SMITH *Tailspan* 1965. Acrylic on wood 119.9 × 212.7 × 90.2 (47¼ × 83¾ × 35½). Tate Gallery, London.

119 PATRICK CAULFIELD *Still-life with Red and White Pot* 1966. Oil on board 160 × 213.4 (63 × 84). Harry N. Abrams Family Collection, New York.

120 ANTHONY DONALDSON *Take Away No. 2* 1963. Oil on canvas 152.4 × 152.4 (60 × 60). Collection Alistair R. McAlpine, London.

121 R. B. KITAJ *Synchromy with F.B. – General of Hot Desire* (diptych) 1968–9. Oil on canvas 152.4 × 91.4 (60 × 36) each panel. Courtesy Marlborough Fine Art Ltd, London.

122 ALLEN JONES *Hermaphrodite* 1963. Oil on canvas 182.9 × 61 (72 × 24). Board of Trustees of the National Museums and Galleries on Merseyside (Walker Art Gallery, Liverpool).

123 SIDNEY NOLAN *Glenrowan* 1956–7. Ripolin on hardboard 91.4 × 121.9 (36 × 48). Tate Gallery, London.

124 JIM DINE *Double Red Self-portrait (The Green Lines)* 1964. Oil and collage on canvas 304.8 × 213.4 (120 × 84). Courtesy Sidney Janis Gallery, New York.

125 ROY LICHTENSTEIN *Whaam!* 1963. Acrylic on canvas 172.7 × 40.6 (68 × 160). Tate Gallery, London.

126 CLAES OLDENBURG *Study for Giant Chocolate* 1966. Enamel and plaster 26.7 × 11.4 × 11.4 (10½ × 4¼ × 4¼). Robert Fraser Gallery, London.

127 ROY LICHTENSTEIN *Yellow and Red Brushstrokes* 1966. Oil on canvas 205.1 × 174 (80¾ × 68½). Collection Philippe Durand-Ruel.

128 ROY LICHTENSTEIN *Hopeless* 1963. Oil on canvas 111.8 × 111.8 (44 × 44). Collection Mrs and Mrs Michael Sonnabend, Paris-New York.

129 TOM WESSELMANN *Still-life No. 34* 1963. Oil on canvas 121.9 (48) tondo. Collection Mr and Mrs Jack Gelman, Kansas City.

130 TOM WESSELMANN *Great American Nude No. 44* 1963. Assemblage painting 265.7 × 243.8 × 25.4 (81 × 96 × 10). Collection Mr and Mrs Robert C. Scull.

131 LARRY RIVERS *Parts of the Face* 1961. Oil on canvas 74.9 × 74.9 (29½ × 29½). Tate Gallery, London.

132 JAMES ROSENQUIST *Silver Skies* 1962. Oil on canvas 198.1 × 41.9 (78 × 16½). Collection Mr and Mrs Robert C. Scull.

133 ANDY WARHOL *Green Coca-Cola Bottles* 1962. Oil on canvas 209.6 × 144.8 (82½ × 57). Collection Whitney Museum of American Art, New York. Gift of the Friends of the Whitney Museum.

134 ANDY WARHOL *Race Riot* 1964. Acrylic and silk-screen enamel on canvas 76.2 × 83.8 (30 × 33). Leo Castelli Gallery, New York.

135 JIM DINE *The Car Crash* 1960. Happening. Photo Robert McElroy, New York.

136 YAYOI KUSAMA *Endless Love Room* 1965–6. Environment.

137 CLAES OLDENBURG *Store Days* 1965. Action, New York.

138 STUART BRISLEY *And For Today –*

Nothing 1972. Action, Gallery House, London.

139 RUDOLF SCHWARZKOGLER, May 1965. Action, Vienna.

140 GILBERT AND GEORGE *Singing Sculpture* November 1970. Photo courtesy of Nigel Greenwood Inc.

141 JOHN MCCRACKEN *There's No Reason Not To* 1967. Wood, fibreglass 412.1 × 45.7 × 8.9 (120 × 18 × 3½). Nicholas Wilder Gallery, Los Angeles.

142 DAVID SMITH *Cubi XVII* 1964. Stainless steel 294 (115¾). Courtesy Marlborough-Gerson Gallery, New York.

143 ANTHONY CARO *Sun-feast* 1969–70. Painted steel 181.6 × 416.6 × 218.4 (71½ × 164 × 86). Private collection.

144 VICTOR VASARELY *Metagalaxy* 1959. Oil on canvas 159 × 147 (62⅝ × 57⅞). Galerie Enise René, Paris.

145 BRIDGET RILEY *Crest* 1964. Emulsion on board 166.4 × 166.4 (65½ × 65½). Rowan Gallery, London.

146 JESUS RAFAEL SOTO *Petite Double Face* 1967. Wood and metal 60 × 38.1 (23⅝ × 15). Collection Mr and Mrs Serge Sacknoff, Washington. Photo courtesy Marlborough-Gerson Gallery, New York.

147 CARLOS CRUZ-DIEZ *Physichromie No. 1* 1959. Plastic and wood 49.8 × 49.8 (9⅝ × 19⅝). Collection the artist.

148 TONY SMITH *Playground* 1962. Wood mock-up to be made in steel 162.6 × 162.6 (64 × 64). Fischbach Gallery, New York.

149 ROBERT MORRIS *Untitled (circular light piece)* 1966. Plexiglass 61 × 243.9 (24 × 96) diameter. Dwan Gallery, New York.

150 DONALD JUDD *Untitled* 1965. Galvanized iron and aluminium 88.8 × 358.1 × 76.2 (33 × 141 × 30). Leo Castelli Gallery, New York.

151 DANIEL BUREN *On Two Levels with Two Colours* 1976. Installation, Lisson Gallery, London.

152 DAN FLAVIN *Untitled (to the 'Innovator' Wheeling Beachblow)* 1968. Fluorescent light (pink, gold and 'day-light') 243.9 × 243.9 (96 × 96). Dwan Gallery, New York.

153 LARRY BELL *Untitled* 1971. Coated glass, nine units. Each unit 182.9 × 152.4 × 0.6 (72 × 60 × ¼). Tate Gallery, London.

154 ERIC ORR *Prime Matter* 1990. 2 bronze columns, water and fire 1219.2 (480). Xenon light ascends 1 mile into the sky. Downtown Los Angeles, California. Courtesy the artist.

155 JAMES TURRELL *Roden Crater* conceived 1974, work in progress.

156 ROBERT SMITHSON *Spiral Jetty* 1970. Great Salt Lake, Utah.

157 RICHARD LONG *A Line in Ireland* 1974. Courtesy of the artist.
158 ANDY GOLDSWORTHY *Tree Cairn* June 1994. Laumeier Sculpture Park, Missouri. Courtesy the artist.
159 JOSEPH KOSUTH *One and Three Chairs* 1965. Mixed media. The Museum of Modern Art, New York. Larry Aldrich Foundation Fund.
160 DENNIS OPPENHEIM *Reading Position for Second Degree Burn* 1970. Stage I and Stage II. Book, skin, solar energy. Exposure time: 5 hours. Jones Beach, New York. Photo courtesy of the artist.
161 JENNY HOLZER *The Survival Series: Protect Me From What I Want* 1985–6. Spectacolour board. Times Square, New York. Courtesy Barbara Gladstone Gallery, New York.
162 BARBARA KRUGER *Untitled (Your Gaze Hits the Side of my Face)* 1981. Photograph 139.7 × 104.1 (55 × 41). Mary Boone Gallery, New York.
163 BRUCE NAUMAN *Life Death/Knows Doesn't Know* 1983. Neon tubing with clear glass suspension frames. Lettering 8.3 (3¼), Life Death: 203.2 (80) diameter, Knows Doesn't Know: 273 × 271.8 (107½ × 107) diameter. Private collection.
164 ALIGHIERO E. BOETTI *Bringing the World into the World* 1973–9. Ball point pen on paper mounted on linen: 2 panels 134.6 × 179.7 (53 × 70¾), 133.9 × 200.7 (52¾ × 79). Courtesy Salvatore Ala Gallery, New York.
165 GIUSEPPE PENONE *Breath I* 1978. Terracotta H 160 Diameter 100 (63 × 39⅜). Courtesy Galerie Rudolf Zwirner, Cologne.
166 LUCIANO FABRO *Golden Italy* (Italia d'Oro) 1971. Gilded bronze 75 × 45 × 3 (29½ × 17¾ × 1¼). Collection the artist.
167 JANNIS KOUNELLIS *Work Incorporating Classical Fragments* (cast of 2nd century BC head of Athena). Collection of artist.
168 GIULIO PAOLINI *Apotheosis of Homer* 1970–1. Tape recorded sound and 32 photographs. Studio Marconi, Milan.
169 MARIO MERZ *610 Function of 15* 1971–89. Newspapers, glass, neon 50.8 × 86.4 × 692.8 (20 × 34 × 272¾). Courtesy of Margo Leavin Gallery, Los Angeles. Photo Douglas M. Parker Studio, Los Angeles.
170 TONY CRAGG *African Culture Myth* 1984. Plastics. 280 × 50, 255 × 47, 270 × 65 (110¼ × 19⅝, 100⅜ × 18½, 106¼ × 25⅝). Courtesy Galerie Crousel-Robelin-Bama, Paris.
171 RICHARD DEACON *Two Can Play* 1983. Galvanised steel 183 × 365.8 × 183 (72 × 144.1 × 72). Private collection.

172 RICHARD WENTWORTH *Jetsam* 1984. Steel, galvanised and enamelled, cable 196.9 × 80 × 80 (77½ × 31½ × 31½). Private collection.
173 BILL WOODROW *Self-Portrait in the Nuclear Age* 1986. Shelving unit, wall map, wooden box, coat, acrylic paint and globe 201.9 × 250.2 × 184.2 (79½ × 98½ × 72½). Saatchi Collection, London.
174 DAVID MACH *Thinking of England* 1983. 2160 HP sauce bottles with liquid dyes, area 183 × 246 (72 × 96). Tate Gallery, London.
175 ANISH KAPOOR *Passage* 1993. Sandstone and pigment 169 × 172 × 134 (66½ × 67¾ × 52¾). Lisson Gallery, London. Photo Stephen White, London.
176 ROBERT GOBER *Untitled* 1991. Wood, wax, leather, cotton, human hair, steel 90.2 × 69.8 (10 × 35½ × 27½). Courtesy Paula Cooper Gallery, New York. Photo Andrew Moore.
177 DAMIEN HIRST *Away from the Flock* 1994. Steel, glass, formaldehyde solution and lamb 96 × 149 × 51 (37¾ × 58⅝ × 20⅛). Courtesy Jay Jopling (London).
178 BILL VIOLA *The Sleep of Reason* 1988. Video installation: 3 video projectors, 1 monitor, ¾ in. videotape, 2 channels, sound, colour and black and white 429.2 × 584.2 × 670.5 (169 × 230 × 264). Collection of the artist. Assistance from Sony Corporation, JBL Professional Products Inc. and Dargate Galleries.
179 LUCIAN FREUD *Double Portrait* 1985–6. Oil on canvas 78.8 × 88.9 (31 × 35). Private collection.
180 JEAN RUSTIN *The Twins* 1987. Acrylic on canvas 162 × 130 (63¾ × 51⅛). Courtesy the Jean Rustin Foundation.
181 A. R. PENCK *T3 (R)* 1982. Acrylic on canvas 299.7 × 198.8 (118 × 78¼). Galerie Michael Werner, Cologne.
182 KEITH HARING *Ignorance = Fear* 1989. Sumi ink on paper 61 × 109.5 (24 × 43⅛). Collection The Estate of Keith Haring.
183 RAINER FETTING *Dancers III* 1982. Powder paint on cotton 224.8 × 280.7 (88½ × 110½). Anthony d'Offay Gallery, London.
184 PHILIP GUSTON *The Rug* 1979. Oil on canvas 193 × 162.9 (76 × 64⅛). The Museum of Modern Art, New York. Gift of Miss Bliss Parkinson.
185 LEON GOLUB *Mercenaries V* 1980–81. Acrylic on linen 305 × 437 (120 × 172). Private collection.
186 JULIAN SCHNABEL *Humanity Asleep* 1982. Painted ceramic relief on wood 275 × 365.8 (108¼ × 144). Tate

Gallery, London.
187 SUSAN ROTHENBERG *Beggar* 1982. Oil on canvas 100.3 × 128.3 (39½ × 50½). Willard Gallery, New York. Photo Roy M. Elkind.
188 GEORG BASELITZ *Die Mädchen von Olmo* 1981. Oil on canvas 250 × 248 (98½ × 97½). Private collection.
189 JÖRG IMMENDORFF *Eigenlob stinkt nicht* 1983. Oil on canvas 150 × 200 (59 × 78¾). Courtesy Michael Werner Gallery, New York and Cologne.
190 ANSELM KIEFER *Untitled* 1978. Oil, emulsion, woodcut, shellac, latex and straw in canvas 260.3 × 189.9 (102½ × 74¾). Anthony d'Offay Gallery, London. Photo Prudence Cuming Associates.
191 TERRY WINTERS *Caps, Sterns, Gills* 1982. Oil on linen 152.4 × 213.4 (60 × 84). Private collection.
192 SANDRO CHIA *Crocodile Tears* 1982. Oil on canvas 287 × 234 (113 × 92). Anthony d'Offay Gallery, London.
193 FRANCESCO CLEMENTE *Toothache* 1981. Pastel on paper 61 × 45.7 (24 × 18). Anthony d'Offay Gallery, London. Photo Prudence Cuming Associates.
194 MIMMO PALADINO *It's Always Evening* 1982. Mixed media on canvas (centre panel of triptych) 219.7 × 480.1 (86½ × 189). Private collection. Photo Prudence Cuming Associates.
195 ENZO CUCCHI *A Painting of Precious Fires* 1983. Oil on canvas with neon 298 × 390 (117½ × 153½). The Gerald S. Elliott Collection of Contemporary Art, Chicago.
196 ERIC FISCHL *Sleepwalker* 1979. Oil on canvas 176 × 267 (69¼ × 105). Coutesy Thomas Ammann, Zurich.
197 DAVID SALLE *His Brain* 1984. Oil and acrylic on canvas and fabric 297 × 274 (117 × 108). The Gerald S. Elliott Collection of Contemporary Art, Chicago.
198 PETER HALLEY *Yellow and Black Cells with Conduit* 1985. Day-glo acrylic and roll-a-tex on canvas 121.9 × 182.9 (48 × 72). Saatchi collection, London.
199 PHILIP TAAFFE *Four Quad Cinema* 1986. Acrylic, enamel and linoprint collage on canvas 220 × 221.9 (86⅝ × 87⅜). Private collection.
200 HAIM STEINBACH *Related and Different* 1985. Mixed media construction 91.4 × 52.1 × 50.8 (36 × 20½ × 20). Private collection.
201 ALLAN MCCOLLUM *25 Perfect Vehicles* 1986. Solid cast plaster, enamel, shellac 50.8 × 121.9 × 121.9 (20 × 48 × 48). Private collection.
202 JEFF KOONS *Michael Jackson and Bubbles* 1988. Porcelain, edition of 3, 106.7 × 179 × 81.3 (42 × 70½ × 32). Sonnabend Gallery, New York.
203 ELIZABETH MURRAY *Small Town*

1980. Oil on canvas 348 × 330.2 (137 × 130). Private collection.

204 JENNIFER BARTLETT *Yellow and Black Boats* 1985. Oil on 3 canvases 305 × 198 each (120 × 78), overall 305 × 594.5 (120 × 234). Yellow boat: wood, enamel paint 153.5 × 79 × 35.5 (60½ × 31 × 14). Black boat: wood, flat oil based paint 96.5 × 173 (38 × 68), mast 198 (78). Private collection.

205 THE STARN TWINS *Stretched Christ* 1985–6. Toned silver print with scotch tape 71.1 × 360.7 × 114.3 (28 × 142 × 45). Private collection.

206 TIM ROLLINS AND K.O.S. *Amerika II* 1985–6. Oil and china markers on book pages, *Amerika* by Franz Kafka on linen 198 × 426.7 (78 × 168). Private collection.

207 RIGOBERTO TORRES *Mermaid* 1993. Acrylic on cast plaster 88.9 × 114.3 × 22.9 (35 × 45 × 9). Courtesy Brooke Alexander, New York. Photo D. James Dee.

208 JOHN AHEARN *Audrey and Janelle* 1983. Acrylic on plaster 81.3 × 81.3 × 22.9 (32 × 32 × 9). Courtesy Brooke Alexander Gallery, New York. Photo © 1991 D. James Dee.

209 WILLIAM T. WILEY *Was It Ever Any Different From Now* 1987. Watercolour on canvas 57.2 × 77.5 (22½ × 30½). Photo courtesy L. A. Louver Gallery, Venice, California.

210 ROY DE FOREST *Untitled* 1990. Acrylic on canvas 185.4 × 215.9 (73 × 85). Courtesy John Natsoulas Gallery, California.

211 DAVID GILHOOLY *An Excessive Dragwood Sandwich* 1987. Clay 40.6 × 33 × 71.1 (16 × 13 × 28). Sherry Frumkin Gallery, Santa Monica.

212 ROBERT ARNESON *Californian Artist* 1982. Glazed ceramic 198 × 71 × 53 (78 × 28 × 21). Allan Frumkin Gallery, New York.

213 VIOLA FREY *Artist/Mind/Studio/World Series I* 1993. Ceramic 205.7 × 188 × 89 (81 × 74 × 35). Courtesy of Nancy Hoffman Gallery, New York, Photo Christopher Watson.

214 MIKE KELLEY *Center and Peripheries #5* 1990. Acrylic on panels 223.5 × 298.5 (88 × 117½). Courtesy the artist and Rosamund Felsen Gallery, Los Angeles. Photo Douglas M. Parker.

215 ED PASCHKE *Minnie* 1974. Oil on canvas 128.9 × 96.5 (50¾ × 38). The Art Institute of Chicago.

216 ROBERT WARRENS *When I Grow Up – the Fireman* 1993. Oil on canvas 214 × 153 (84¼ × 60¼). Courtesy Sylvia Schmidt Gallery, New Orleans.

217 PETER SAUL *Jeffrey Dahmer* 1993. Acrylic alkyd on canvas 182.9 × 167.6 (72 × 66). Frumkin/Adams Gallery, New York. Photo Ken Showell.

218 ROGER BROWN *Randie's Donuts with Hollywood Junipers and Ranchhouses* 1991. Oil on canvas 122 × 152.4 (48 × 60). Courtesy Phyllis Kind Gallery, New York.

219 DAVID BATES *Sheepshead* 1985. Oil on canvas 167.6 × 213.4 (66 × 84). Arthur Roger Gallery, New Orleans.

220 JACOBO BORGES *The Betrothed* 1975. Acrylic on canvas 120 × 120 (47¼ × 47¼). Photo courtesy of the CDS Gallery, New York.

221 ANTONIO BERNI *Juanito in La Laguna* 1974. Collage 160 × 105 (63 × 41⅜). Elena Berni Collection, Buenos Aires. Photo Ruth Benzacar Galeria de Arte, Buenos Aires.

222 FERNANDO BOTERO *The House of the Arias Sisters* 1973. Oil on canvas 227 × 187 (89⅜ × 73⅝). Photo courtesy of Marlborough Gallery Inc, New York.

223 FRIDA KAHLO *Self-portrait* 1940. Oil on canvas 62 × 47.5 (24½ × 18¾). Iconography Collection, Harry Ransom Humanities Research Center, The University of Texas at Austin.

224 VÍCTOR GRIPPO *Analogía I* 1971. Paper, electric circuits, measuring instruments, text, wood 48.5 × 155 × 11 (19 × 61 × 4⅜). Courtesy Ruth Benzacar Galeria de Arte, Buenos Aires.

225 GUILLERMO KUITCA *Triptych of Mattresses* 1989. Acrylic on 3 mattresses. Courtesy of Thomas Cohn, Arte Contemporanea, Rio de Janiero.

226 TUNGA *Lizart 5* 1989. Installation. Copper, steel, iron and magnets. Museum of Contemporary Art, Chicago.

227 LYGIA CLARK *Rubber Grub* 1964 (remade by artist 1986). Rubber 142 × 43 (55⅞ × 16⅞). Museu de Arte Moderna do Rio de Janeiro. Donated by the artist.

228 GONZALO DÍAZ *The Founding Father* 1994. Installation 4000 × 800 × 400 (1574⅞ × 315 × 157½). Courtesy the artist and Luz Maria Williamson, Cuerpos Puntados, Chile.

229 JUAN DÁVILA *The Liberator Simon Bolivar* 1994. Oil on canvas on metal 126 × 107 (49⅝ × 42⅛). Courtesy artist and Luz Maria Williamson, Cuerpos Puntados, Chile.

230 EUGENIO DITTBORN *The Car of the Dead Spy* 1994. Offset on couche paper 22 × 16.5 (8⅝ × 6½). Courtesy the artist and Luz Maria Williamson, Cuerpos Puntados, Chile.

231 ARTURO DUCLOS *Black Mirror* 1993. Acrylic, oil and enamel on canvas 141.5 × 135 (55¾ × 53⅛). Courtesy the artist and Luz Maria Williamson, Cuerpos Puntados, Chile.

232 ERIC BULATOV *Perestroika* 1989. Oil on canvas 274.3 × 269.2 (108 ×

106). Courtesy Phyllis Kind Gallery, New York.

233 ILYA KABAKOV *My Mother's Life II* detail from the installation *He Lost His Mind, Undressed, Ran Away Naked* 1989. 70 framed pages of black and white photos with texts mounted on decorative paper 78.7 × 58.4 (31 × 23). Courtesy Ronald Feldman Fine Arts, New York. Photo D. James Dee.

234 JIRO YOSHIHARA *Untitled* 1971. Oil on canvas 162 × 131 (63¾ × 51⅝). Tokyo Gallery, Tokyo.

235 YASMASU MORIMURA *Playing with the Gods, No. 1 Twilight* 1991. Colour photograph 360 × 250.2 (141¾ × 98½). Courtesy Luhring Augustine Gallery, New York.

236 YUKINORI YANAGI *Union Jack Ant Farm* 1994. Coloured sand, plexiglass, plastic, tubes 206 × 381 (81 × 150). Anthony d'Offay Gallery, London.

237 JOHN MUAFANGEJO *Lonely Man, Man of Man* 1974. Linocut print 47.9 × 45.4 (18⅞ × 17⅞).

238 CHÉRI SAMBA *Pourquoi un Contrat?* Courtesy Annina Nosei Gallery, New York.

239 PETER BLACKSMITH JAPANANGKA *Snake Dreaming* 1986. Acrylic and house paint on composition board 110.5 × 210.4 (43½ × 82⅞). National Gallery of Victoria, Melbourne. Purchased through the Art Foundation of Victoria from funds provided by CRA Limited, 1989.

240 HA, CHONG-HYUN *Conjunction 94–07* 1994. Oil and pushed from back of hemp cloth 100 × 45 (39⅜ × 17¾). Courtesy the artist.

241 YU YOUHAN *Mao Voting* 1993. Acrylic on canvas 118 × 166 (46½ × 65⅜). Courtesy Hanart TZ Gallery, Hong Kong.

242 RALPH HOTERE *The Black over the Gold* 1993. Wood, glass, paint, gold leaf. Photo Edward Lucie-Smith.

243 JOHN SCOTT *Women's House* 1993. Painted metal 73.7 × 48.3 × 111.8 (29 × 19 × 44). Courtesy Galerie Simonne Stern, New Orleans.

244 ROMARE BEARDEN *The Family* 1948. Watercolour and gouache on paper 64.8 × 49.5 (25½ × 19½). Evans-Tibbs Collection, Washington D.C.

245 JACOB LAWRENCE *One of the Largest Race Riots Occured in East St. Louis* from the series *The Migration of the Negro* 1940–1. Tempera on gesso on composition board 30.5 × 45.7 (12 × 18). The Museum of Modern Art, New York. Gift of Mr and Mrs David Levy.

246 MARTIN PURYEAR *Noblesse O.* 1987. Red cedar and aluminium paint 246.4 × 147.3 × 116.8 (97 × 58 × 46). Dallas Museum of Art, Central

Acquisitions Fund and a gift of The 500, Inc.

247 SAM GILLIAM *Horizontal Extension* 1969. Acrylic on canvas 304.8 × 2286 (120 × 900). Installed at the Corcoran Gallery of Art, Washington D.C. Photo courtesy Annie Gawlak.

248 JEAN-MICHEL BASQUIAT and ANDY WARHOL *Collaboration* 1984. Acrylic on canvas 193 × 249 (76 × 98). Courtesy Mayor/Mayor Rowan Gallery, London.

249 BETYE SAAR *The Liberation of Aunt Jemima* 1972. Mixed media 29.8 × 20.2 × 6.8 (11¾ × 8 × 2¾). University Art Museum, University of California, Berkeley. Purchased with the aid of funds from the National Endowment for the arts (selected by The Committee for the Acquisition of Afro-American art).

250 HEW LOCKE *Ark* 1992–4. Mixed media 457.2 × 335.2 × 1573 (180 × 132 × 619⅜). Courtesy the artist.

251 KEITH PIPER *The Nanny of the Nation Gathers her Flock* 1987. Acryl unstretched canvas. Courtesy the artist.

252 FAITH RINGGOLD *The Wedding: Lover's Quilt No. 1* 1986. Acrylic on canvas, tie-dyed, painted, pieced fabric 196.5 × 147.5 (77½ × 58). Collection Marilyn Lanfear. Photo Bernice Steinbaum Gallery, New York.

253 MARY KELLY *Post-Partum Document, Documentation VI* 1978–9. Slate and resin 18 units 35.6 × 27.9 (14 × 11). Arts Council Collection, London.

254 JUDY CHICAGO *The Dinner Party* 1979. Mixed media, length of each side 119.4 (47). Photo Michael Alexander, courtesy Through the Flower Corporation.

255 ROSS BLECKNER *8,122+ as of January 1986* 1986. Oil on linen 122 × 101.6 (48 × 40). Private collection.

256 CINDY SHERMAN from *Untitled Film Stills* 1979. Black and white photograph 20.3 × 25.4 (8 × 10). Courtesy of Metro Pictures, New York.

257 DELMAS HOWE *Theseus and Pirithoüs at the Chutes* 1981–2. Oil on canvas 111.8 × 172.7 (44 × 68). Tate Gallery, London.

258 ROBERT MAPPLETHORPE *Thomas* 1986. Photograph. Copyright 1986 The Estate of Robert Mapplethorpe.

259 GEORGE DUREAU *Wilbert Hines* 1972. Photograph. Courtesy the artist.

260 DAVID WOJNAROWICZ *Bad Moon Rising* 1989. Acrylic, photo and collage on wood 94 × 92.7 (37 × 36½). Courtesy of P.P.O.W, New York.

261 DEREK JARMAN *Blood* 1992. Oil on photocopy on canvas 251.5 × 179 (99 × 70½). Courtesy Richard Salmon Ltd, London.

262 NANCY FRIED *The Hand Mirror* 1987. Terracotta 25.4 × 24.1 × 20.3 (10 × 9½ × 8). Courtesy the artist.

263 KAREN FINLEY *The Vacant Chair* 1993. Chair, flowers, moss and foliage 165.1 × 91.4 × 106.7 (65 × 36 × 42). Courtesy the artist.

Index

Illustration numbers are given in italics